AGENT
EXTRAORDINAIRE

AGENT
EXTRAORDINAIRE

THE STORY OF
MICHEL HOLLARD
D.S.O., CROIX DE GUERRE

by

GEORGE MARTELLI

© George Martelli and Michel Hollard, 1960, first published by Collins. Reprinted in the Mount series by Little Hills Press in 1989.

Tavistock House
34 Bromham Road
Bedford MK40 2QD
United Kingdom

Regent House
37—43 Alexander Street
Crows Nest NSW 2065
Australia

ISBN 0 949773 97 2

Martelli, George, 1903— .
   Agent extraordinaire : the story of Michel Hollard,
   D.S.O., Croix de Guerre.

   ISBN 0 949773 97 2.

   1. Hollard, Michel. 2. Spies — France —
   Biography. 3. World War, 1939—1945 —
   Underground movements — France — Biography.
   I. Title. II. Title : Agent extraordinaire.

940.54'86'440924

Capitaine de Réserve Michel Hollard

DISTINGUISHED SERVICE
ORDER

CITATION

This officer in January 1942 organised and conducted, with the greatest skill and devotion for two years, a highly successful information service in favour of the Allied Cause in Northern France.

He, at great personal risk, reconnoitred a number of heavily guarded "V.1." sites and reported thereon with such clarity that models thereof were constructed in this country which enabled effective bombing to be carried out.

His courage, devotion to duty and unsparing efforts were a constant inspiration to his team.

Finally arrested in February 1944 by treachery, he was deported to Germany, from where, after severe privations and despite torture under which he revealed nothing, he succeeded recently in escaping.

FOREWORD

BY

LT.-GENERAL SIR BRIAN HORROCKS

K.C.B., K.B.E., D.S.O., M.C.

During the preparation of my recent "Men of Action" television programmes I have been privileged to read many stories of incredible courage. This, however, is the most remarkable story of them all, for Michel Hollard was the man who literally saved London.

When France capitulated in 1940, he determined to continue the struggle against the Germans by acting as an Allied agent, and he built up a network of spies, called the *réseau "Agir"* which soon became familiar in British intelligence circles for the accuracy of its reports. The success of the organisation was due entirely to his own outstanding capacity for leadership. He chose the agents himself, collected their information and nearly always handed it over personally to our intelligence officers in Switzerland. It sounds quite incredible but he succeeded in crossing this heavily defended frontier on ninety-eight separate occasions.

The *réseau "Agir"* was completely self-contained; no wireless was used and it did not rely on parachute drops for supplies. It was entirely dependent on the initiative of one quick-witted, cool-headed and extremely brave Frenchman.

It was typical of Michel that hearing about some new curious buildings which the Germans were constructing he obtained employment as a labourer there. And in spite of the strict screen of secrecy maintained by the Germans his agents subsequently uncovered one hundred similar sites. One day, even, while a German engineer was in the lavatory, an *"Agir"* agent succeeded in stealing the drawing of a site from his coat and making a quick tracing. From this the first blueprint

9

of a V.1. launching platform was made, and despatched via Switzerland to England.

With this information available, in December, 1943, the R.A.F. struck with such devastating effect that the Germans were forced to abandon their original plan of despatching 5,000 flying bombs a month to London and to adopt a much more modest programme.

It has since been estimated that had it not been for Michel's information the V.1. attacks on this country would have been six times more severe and would have lasted six months longer. Not only would London have suffered terribly but our invasion of Europe would unquestionably have been made much more difficult. This was the climax of his success as a master spy. But the charmed life he had been leading could not continue for ever and shortly afterwards he was betrayed to the Germans. Michel was subjected to every sort of barbarity: the bath torture, flogging, a ghastly train journey which lasted for three days and three nights when the prisoners were packed so tight—100 to a wagon—that they all had to stand wedged against each other, and ultimately incarceration in the Neuengamme extermination camp.

This sort of treatment was calculated either to kill the prisoners or at any rate reduce them to the state of animals. In ninety-five per cent of cases it succeeded. Michel belonged to that rare five per cent of remarkable men who had the courage to resist to the end.

Finally, when the victorious Allied armies were approaching, the prisoners were forced into the holds of merchant ships (which the Germans intended to scuttle) and taken out to sea where they were bombed by the Allies; the majority perished. Michel's escape from death was almost a miracle.

No one reading this book could have any doubt that Michel Hollard was entitled to the highest decoration for bravery which we can give to a foreigner under these circumstances, namely, the D.S.O. But it seems to me that many statues have been erected in London—the city he saved—to less deserving people.

CONTENTS

MAPS

ACKNOWLEDGMENTS

The main source of material for this book is Michel Hollard himself, to whom I am principally indebted for his breaking down, after ten years' resistance, and allowing me to tell his story. I have also been assisted by many others and wish particularly to express my gratitude to Mme. Hollard, M. Maurice Guchuy, M. Joseph Brocard, Captain V. C. Farrell and Mr. E. J. Kruger for much essential information; to Captain B. H. Liddell Hart for lending me the papers of the late Chester Wilmot; and to Count F. G. von Saurma, formerly technical director of the flying bomb sites, not only for expert advice, but for allowing me a glimpse of the "other side of the hill."

I would like to acknowledge thanks for permission to reproduce certain illustrations: the Imperial War Museum, for the model of a V.I. site and a V.I. in flight; Mme. E. Mignon, for the photograph of Auffay Station.

G.A.M.

PROLOGUE

If you arrive at the Gare du Nord and leave by the side exit, you come out into a long straight narrow street which ascends steadily in the direction of Montmartre.

This is the Faubourg St. Denis.

The street is ugly and depressing: a street of tall and forbidding tenements, blackened by smoke from the railway; of small and untidy shops and shabby office buildings.

At the lower end, opposite the station, are five or six cafés of nondescript character. None of them is the kind one would choose in which to spend a pleasant hour over a *demi* or a *pernod*. They are patronised chiefly by travellers in a hurry and station employees going to and from work.

Perhaps the least distinguished of them all is a little bar called *Aux Chasseurs*. It was probably given this name in some distant past to attract sportsmen on their way to catch a train for *la chasse*.

Wedged between two larger and more opulent establishments, the *Aux Chasseurs* has a diffident, self-effacing aspect.

Its entrance is so narrow that there is barely room, between the zinc counter on one side and the bench and tables on the other, for the patrons to pass between. At the end is a little space partly screened from the front, with a door on the left marked LAVABO.

One could pass by such a place a hundred times without giving it a glance or remembering its existence—if it weren't for one thing that caught one's attention.

This is a small marble plaque displayed on the outside wall with the following inscription engraved on it:

ICI
ONT ÉTÉ ARRÊTÉS
LE 5 FEVRIER 1944
PAR LA GESTAPO
LE CHEF DE RÉSEAU "AGIR"
MICHEL HOLLARD
LES CHARGÉS DE MISSION
JOSEPH LEGENDRE
HENRI DUJARIER
et
JULES MAILLY
Mort pour la France
le 1ᵉʳ Juin 1944
A Mauthausen

"Here were arrested, on the 5th February, 1944, by the Gestapo, the Chief of the network "Agir," Michel Hollard; the agents Joseph Legendre, Henri Dujarier and Jules Mailly (who died for France, on the 1st June, 1944, at Mauthausen)."

The event which the plaque commemorates was both an end and a beginning: the end of a great adventure, in which great risks were taken and great results achieved in a great cause, with almost a certainty ever in mind that the reward would be death, or worse than death; and the beginning of a calvary which it seemed could have only one conclusion.

This book is the story of both the adventure and the calvary, and the justification for telling it now, so long after the event, is the ever-present need to remind ourselves of the heights, as well as the depths, which human beings can attain—and of the sacrifices necessary to keep freedom alive.

*   *   *

This is a true story and every incident in it is vouched for, either by the principal character or by other eyewitnesses, most of whom are still living.

Since, however, it is impossible for anyone to remember the exact words of every conversation—and even if it were possible the record would be unreadable—the author has devised dialogue where necessary to carry the narrative forward, but always and only in the sense of what was actually said.

Part One

1

FLIGHT FROM PARIS

On that hot summer's day the people of Paris seemed less shocked than apathetic; not so much appalled by the catastrophe as resigned to it.

It was the reaction of a nation already beaten even before the battle started. There was almost a sense of relief that the inevitable end had come so quickly: better be knocked out in the first round than cruelly battered through ten.

And now that it was over they could get on with their business...or so they thought.

There was no real panic, not even when columns of white smoke, curling from the gardens of the Quai d'Orsay, indicated that that last futile rite of a doomed capital, the burning of the national archives, was being solemnly enacted by the tail-coated janitors of the Foreign Ministry.

It was already known that the Government had left Paris, and the Parisians—or those who could—prepared to do like-wise, carefully packing or hiding away their most treasured possessions as though about to set out on an extended holiday.

Throughout most of the city there was a strange sort of

quiet—like a Sunday afternoon before the cinemas open. All the shops and many of the cafés were closed, but people were still strolling about the boulevards as though they had nothing better to do.

In the smarter residential quarters cars were being loaded with as much as they could carry. Not only luggage, but also silver, valuable rugs and *objets d'art* were carefully stowed away.

At the Gare de Lyon and the Gare d'Austerlitz long queues of humbler fugitives waited hopefully for a train which might or might not start, sitting on their suitcases and munching the food they had brought with them. The only ominous phenomenon was the thick pall of smoke, relic of some bombed refinery, drifting slowly eastward in the light summer breeze.

At the *Centre d'Etudes de Mécanique, Balistique et Armement*—a government institution for the testing of proto-types—where Michel had a war-time job, the personnel had been given their evacuation orders several days before. They were to find their own way south and report for duty at an armaments factory owned by the Brandt Company at Tulle, in the Corèze Department. If necessary they could break their journey at La Fierté St. Aubain, where Brandt had another factory.

Michel had already sent his family to the country and was in no hurry to leave. Unlike the majority of Frenchmen, his whole heart was in the war and he could not bring himself to believe that it was lost so soon.

He had fought the Germans in the first war—volunteering at the age of seventeen and winning a Croix de Guerre—knew the qualities of the French soldier and could not understand how the natural defences of France could have been abandoned one after the other almost without a fight.

It was only when he heard that the Germans had crossed the Oise and were at Persant-Beaumont, twenty-five miles from Paris, that he realized the battle was over.

He lingered a little longer, reluctant to leave as a man is to abandon a sinking ship; but when the first lorry loads of retreating soldiers appeared on the boulevards, most of them with no sign of an officer, he decided it was time to get out.

He owned neither car nor bicycle, there was no public transport, and every available vehicle had been requisitioned. In consequence he had to face a journey on foot.

Since he was to travel light, taking only a satchel and a brief-case, there was not much to pack: a change of clothes, his engineering tools, and a handful of family photos which he threw in as an afterthought. The last, as it later proved, was an unfortunate choice.

At about seven p.m. on 13th June, 1940, he locked the door of his flat and set out on his journey.

Throughout the day police cars mounting loud-speakers had been touring the streets exhorting the population to stay at home. This, of course, was a signal to the Parisians to leave the city *en masse*. Michel had not gone far on his way before he found himself taking part in one of the greatest exoduses in history. It has been estimated that a million people quitted the capital that week.

Avoiding main thoroughfares, Michel made his way to the Poterne des Peupliers, from which he gained the main road which leads to Orléans. Every street was filled with people going in the same direction. Outside a factory the workers were clambering on to the company's lorries.

Beyond the *Porte* the crush was greater than ever and seemed to increase every moment, as the main flood of fugitives was swollen by tributaries flowing in from side roads. Pedestrians, bicycles, cars and hand-carts jostled together in a procession that proceeded at walking pace. Occasionally an aeroplane droned overhead, but as yet there was no bombing.

After walking for two hours, Michel reached the Croix de Berny, a cross-roads just outside Paris, where *Route Nationale* 20 is intersected by another strategic road. To-day it is the hub of a fast-growing suburb, with new blocks of municipal flats going up on every side; but twenty years ago the area was only partly built over, with detached rows of small houses and gardens, terminating in what the French call *terrains vagues*.

About fifty yards beyond the cross-roads there were some houses and shops and here many refugees had stopped to spend the night. People with cars slept inside them or on the roof; others lay on the ground. The only two cafés in sight were closed and it was very evident that there was "no room at the inn."

Walking on a little farther, Michel found a plot between two houses, which was protected from the road by a fence. He decided it was as good a resting-place as he was likely to find.

He had eaten nothing since midday and only had with him the remains of a loaf. This he now proceeded to eat for his supper.

Music from Paris Radio could be heard through an open window and a number of people had gathered to hear the news. Just before midnight it was announced that M. Paul Reynaud, *Président du Conseil,* was to address the nation.

The speech was quite short and consisted largely of the negative reply given by President Roosevelt to France's appeal for help, which the Premier read out in full. He concluded by expressing his faith that France would be "resurrected."

As it is only the dead that are resurrected, this sentence struck Michel as sinister.

Except for the announcement that Paris had been declared an "open city," no news of the battle was given. It wasn't necessary. Everyone knew that this was the end, although what that meant exactly for France's future nobody yet could envisage.

Michel returned to his plot and, although somewhat cold about the feet, managed to sleep for a few hours.

When he awoke, at five in the morning, it was to the sound of firing. The road, which the previous evening had been filled with refugees, was now completely deserted. The houses were still shuttered and there was not a soul in sight. He had an uncomfortable feeling of utter isolation, as if he were the last man alive.

Then, looking back along the way he had come, he saw that he was not alone. Stopped at the cross-roads, with its guns pointed towards him, was an enormous tank: on its side a large swastika, painted in black and white.

As Michel watched, more fascinated than fearful, two French soldiers appeared, carrying their rifles and bent double, running alongside a wall. The tank opened fire again. Clearly it was time to move on.

Keeping out of sight, Michel climbed a fence, crossed several gardens and reached a small river. He followed this for some time until eventually it brought him back to the main road, which was still entirely filled with one-way traffic.

A company of infantry were marching along, looking tired and demoralised. Michel approached the officer and walked beside him.

"Tell me," he said, "what's happening?"

The officer shrugged. "I haven't an idea. We've come from Lille—eight days on the move. The men are just about finished."

"Where are you making for?"

"I don't know. We're trying to find the rest of the battalion. They may be anywhere."

"Yes, France is a big place."

"I should get off the road. It's already been bombed and they are sure to be coming back—with this lot as target."

Michel took the advice and for the rest of the day travelled by side roads, or across country. In the fields, where the corn was already ripening, men and women were working normally, as though quite unconscious of what was happening to their country. They glanced at Michel without interest. He lived "off the land," chiefly on strawberries and cherries, and by nightfall was so exhausted that he lay down in a ditch and slept.

The next morning he reviewed the situation. He had come thirty miles out of the three hundred he had to cover and was already feeling tired and footsore. He had seen there was no hope of getting a lift, and in any case, apart from the danger of being bombed, travelling by car was scarcely quicker than walking. He decided to make for the nearest railway station, which was at a small town called Etampes.

The ticket office when he arrived was closed, but the platform was crowded, mostly with soldiers.

As Michel walked on to it a woman took one look at him, pointed and screamed hysterically: "There he is! The parachutist!"

Thinking she was pointing at somebody behind him, Michel turned around. Simultaneously there was a shot and a soldier standing near him shrieked and fell on the ground. Looking to see who had fired, Michel noticed another soldier in the act of lowering his rifle. Then pandemonium broke out.

The woman had collapsed on a seat and the wounded man was sitting up clasping his thigh, while everyone crowded round him. Michel moved quickly and in a moment was outside the station and walking rapidly away, still pursued by the hubbub. He took the first turn and did not slow down until he felt safe.

Stations were obviously something to be avoided.

Soon after, the road he was following arrived at a level-crossing. The gates were closed and a halted goods train blocked the way. Ahead of it men were working to clear the track, which was covered with the debris of electric cables. In a nearby field groups of onlookers were watching the proceedings.

The train was heading in the right direction and it occurred to Michel that if he could climb on to one of the wagons it might take him for some of his way.

While he was considering this the drone of an engine was heard and a small white aeroplane appeared, flying low; an Italian. Michel saw three black objects drop from it. A few moments later there were two explosions, close beside him.

A woman who had been standing only a few feet away, and who had flung herself on the ground at the approach of the bomber, was still in the same position. Michel could see without approaching that she was dead: her lungs had been blown out of her.

A little farther away a man was lying still. Michel went over and saw that he was badly wounded in the leg. He bound up the wound with a handkerchief and applied a tour-niquet. Then with the help of two others he carried the wounded man to the road.

Nobody was stopping even for a casualty and it took some time before Michel succeeded in halting a military vehicle and persuading the driver to accept the extra passenger, who was still unconscious, and drop him at the nearest hospital.

He then remembered that only two of the three bombs had exploded. Returning to the field where they had fallen, and where the same group of people were still standing about, he picked up a twig, tied a rag to the end of it, and approached the third bomb, with the intention of placing his warning signal beside it.

At this the bystanders started shouting at him to keep away. Ignoring them, Michel went up to the spot, fixed his marker, and started walking away.

This was too much for the honest citizens. They could imagine only one explanation for Michel's action: an enemy agent.

Who started it he never knew, but the next instant he was the centre of a howling, milling mob. Punched, buffeted, scratched, his clothes torn off him, he was thrown on the ground.

When he had been stripped of every garment, while some held him down, others emptied the contents of his brief-case. As the family photos fell out, a man seized on one of them— taken of his grandfather in the First World War—and, brandishing it triumphantly aloft, screamed: "There you are, his beloved Führer!"

At this one of Michel's assailants, a big man wearing a leather jacket and a beret, produced a Colt and pressed the muzzle against Michel's temple. Michel till then had been protesting his innocence; now he thought it better to keep quiet.

At that moment he observed some Senegalese soldiers marching along the road about fifty yards away.

Making an effort to speak calmly, he said: "Don't you think you'd better to hand me over to that troop?"

There was a second's hesitation, then the man holding the revolver, who seemed to be the ringleader, dropped his hand.

"Good idea. They'll know how to deal with him."

Michel was then dragged across the field and handed over, stark naked, to the troop, which in response to shouts had been halted.

Fortunately the warrant-officer in command sized up the situation immediately.

"All right," he said, "we'll take care of him."

However, the crowd, by now quite numerous, were not to be cheated of their fun. They assumed that their victim would be executed immediately and were determined not to miss the spectacle.

The ringleader evidently thought that shooting was too good for him. Looking meaningly at the Senegalese, he drew his finger across his throat.

It took the warrant-officer some time to convince them that things were not done in that way, that it would be necessary to conduct the prisoner to the nearest command post. In the end he ordered the troop to disperse the crowd, which gradually and reluctantly drifted away.

A soldier was sent to recover Michel's possessions. His suit was still intact, but vest, pants and shirt had been torn to shreds. Fortunately the resources of the troop were able to supply these deficiencies.

He was then escorted out of sight and advised to *"filer vite"* — which he did. When he saw it last, his danger signal — cause of the trouble — was still flying, but he never heard what happened to the unexploded bomb.

Having thus for the second time in one day narrowly escaped death at the hands of his own compatriots, Michel was coming to the conclusion that they were more to be feared than the Germans. He resolved in future to behave with greater circumspection. However, the day's adventures were not yet over.

Arriving towards nightfall on the outskirts of Orléans, he saw that a heavy raid was in progress. Flames were going up from the cathedral and half a dozen big fires raged in the city.

It would have been better to avoid the place, but as this meant making a wide detour, he decided to go on; and his road taking him close to the cathedral he turned off to inspect the damage.

There the scene which met him was alarming. A number of people, mostly women and children, who had been trapped when the flames spread to neighbouring houses, were trying to fight their way through a dense cloud of smoke.

Seeing that they would be choked, Michel approached a group of women and started urging them to escape through the narrow gap in the circle of fire by which he himself had come. One or two followed his advice, but others were reluctant and he was obliged to conduct them to safety one by one.

He had been engaged on this work of rescue for about half an hour when he noticed two men, who were standing nearby, conversing confidentially and occasionally looking towards him.

Something in their attitude struck him as sinister and instinctively he began to move away. Glancing over his shoulder he saw they were following, started to run and did not stop till he reached the bridge across the Loire. He continued walking until he was well into the country, where he found a friendly haystack and bedded down for the night.

There was no doubt in his mind that had he hesitated another second he would have found himself faced by a second lynching mob, as firmly convinced as the first that he was an enemy agent.

At the time it was a mystery to him why his appearance among a group of Frenchmen should invariably have had the effect of touching off hysteria. But later he realised that there was a simple reason: when there is an atmosphere of panic and *sauve qui peut* the man who keeps his head and tries to be helpful makes himself conspicuous and therefore suspect.

It was a useful lesson from which he profited during the next four years, when he always strove to make himself one with the crowd.

By comparison with the first forty-eight hours the rest of Michel's journey was uneventful. He duly arrived at the half-way stop at La Fierté St. Aubain, enjoyed a good meal for the first time since leaving Paris, and left the Brandt factory just before it was completely destroyed by bombs.

After another two days of cross-country walking and sleeping in the open, he found a bed at Angoulême: and the next day was given a lift in a car carrying gold from the Bank of France. This was lucky, as the car was allowed to pass the barrier, which police had erected to stop the southward flood of refugees.

The car dropped him at Brive and he completed the last stage of his journey by bus. He sat beside the driver, a simple country type, and as they discussed the situation the man remarked, *"Moi, vous savez, je crois à la victoire."*

This was the first time Michel had heard such a sentiment

expressed. Coming from so humble and honest an individual, it filled him with emotion. From that moment he too started to believe in the same victory.

On reporting to the new headquarters of the *Centre d'Etudes* at Tulle, Michel saw at once that nothing was happening. The war was over and the *Centre* had no justification. He could have continued, like the others, to kick his heels and draw his salary, but that was not his idea.

He asked for indefinite leave—unpaid—borrowed a bicycle and left immediately to join his family.

After two days bicycling he arrived at the place where they were staying: near Ganges in the Hérault Department. He had not seen them since September and there was a happy but brief reunion.

Brief, because it was necessary for Michel to find a new means of livelihood. After a few days' rest, he set out again, first for Bézier and then on to Lyons. At Lyons he found a job, but it was not well paid and soon he had to look for something else.

Meanwhile on 25th June the armistice had been signed, Pétain was in the saddle, and life in France, as much as it might under the Germans, was rapidly returning to normal. Many of the refugees were returning to Paris and Government Departments, which had been evacuated, including the *Centre d'Estudes*, were reopening their offices in the capital.

Michel decided to return. In the middle of July, with his whole family, he arrived back in Paris and resumed possession of the flat in the Rue des Arènes.

The next day he reported at the *Centre d'Estudes*. The Director received him cordially. His job was still open for him, but with higher responsibilities and an increased salary.

"Whom are you working for?" Michel asked.

"Naturally for the Occupying Authority."

"Then you are doing exactly the opposite of what we were doing before. I thank you, but I am not a weathercock. I regret I must decline your offer."

He then got up, bowed formally, and walked out.

It was his first contact with the new régime and he didn't like it.

No, he didn't like it at all.

2

FIRST VENTURE

Michel was forty-one when the war started. Five foot seven, of spare but athletic build, with dark hair brushed back, lively eyes and a quick-changing expression, dressed usually in a neat dark blue suit only distinguished by the ribbon of the Croix de Guerre, he appeared no different at first glance from any other French business man of medium prosperity However, there was something about him—a sort of inner intensity—which, to a student of character, would have announced that here was no ordinary man.

At sixteen he had run away from home to join up in the First World War, working for a year as an orderly in a military hospital until he was of age to be accepted as a combatant. Even then, being physically undeveloped, he had been obliged to fake his chest measurement and adorn his body with false pubic hairs in order to pass the medical!

At nineteen he was already a veteran, decorated for valour, and a year later was leading his platoon in pursuit of the retreating Germans when the armistice put an end to his military career. By then he had already gained more experience of men than many people acquire in a lifetime.

By comparison the years between the wars were an anti-climax: he did not find the return to civilian life easy. His schooling had been erratic. Now he had to complete his own education and at the same time earn a living, since his father, a distinguished scientist but with five daughters to provide for, was not in a position to assist.

To complicate matters still further, he had fallen in love and become engaged, against the opposition of both families, to a girl who, like himself, was a Protestant and descendant of a Huguenot family, but better educated than Michel. To separate her from her fiancé, she was sent abroad for three years, and he employed the interval making himself worthy of her. Finally the parents gave their consent to the marriage. Three children followed, and to provide for the growing family absorbed all Michel's energy, leaving little time for the other interests—political, musical and literary—to which he was really drawn.

To qualify for his chosen profession of engineering, while keeping himself alive, he had attended night classes at the *Conservatoire National des Arts et Métiers* (corresponding to the London Polytechnic), gaining a diploma in mechanics, machinery and metallurgy.

Armed with this and by dint of industry and strict economy, he made his way in the fiercely competitive world of the inter-war years, holding a variety of posts including—for a short time—that of a proprietor of a small taxicab business.

At the date when the war broke out he had abandoned this and was employed as technical representative by an important French firm specialising in the manufacture of brake linings.

As an officer on the reserve with the rank of Captain of Infantry, Michel hoped to rejoin the army. But his class was not called up, and in spite of his efforts to be accepted for active service he found himself mobilised in a civilian job under the auspices of the Ministry of War.

Now he had thrown up this on discovering that the *Centre d'Estudes*, with all the resources of the French armaments industry at its disposal, was working for the enemy with the full approval of the Vichy Government.

The question was what to do next.

The most urgent task, of course, was to find a new job. The

war might be lost, France prostrate, the Germans masters of Paris, but one still has to eat, with a wife and three children to support.

Once, however, one decided to do nothing to help the enemy, obtaining a job became extremely difficult. In agreement with the authorities and with the acquiescence, more or less willing, of the majority of the nation, the French economy was being rapidly harnessed to serve the Occupying Power. In the engineering industries especially, for which Michel was qualified, almost every big firm was working directly or indirectly for the German war machine.

It was probably from the shock of this discovery that Michel's own rebellion dated. For one had to take a line: either adjust oneself to the situation or reject it—utterly.

It did not take him long, after his return to Paris, to decide which course to adopt. In fact, it scarcely required a conscious decision: it was rather a reflex action, an instinctive attitude, deriving less from any intellectual process than from some fundamental element in his make-up.

Having rejected the idea of defeat, the only logical consequence was to go on fighting; and this is what Michel now resolved to do, even if it meant fighting single-handed, and although at the moment he could not see how such a thing was possible.

Meanwhile the search for a job continued. Michel answered advertisements, attended interviews, received offers—but invariably turned them down on discovering that acceptance would mean violating his principle.

Early in August, when he was getting very short of money, he saw an advertisement in a Dijon paper which appeared to fulfil his conditions. An engineering firm, producing gas engines for motor cars, required a Paris representative. These engines, which ran on charcoal, were in great demand owing to the shortage of petrol.

Although applicants were requested to reply by letter, Michel decided to do so in person. Tearing up the letter he had started, he took the first train to Dijon and presented himself without warning at the firm, which was called the *Maison Gazogène Autobloc*.

The next day he returned to Paris with the job "in the

bag." He had obtained the agency for half Paris, and a promise that no one else would be appointed for a fortnight.

Thanks to his pre-war employment he had excellent contacts in the motor industry and by the end of the two weeks was back in Dijon with a first batch of orders.

He now demanded the agency for the whole of Paris and another fortnight during which no other agent should be accepted. This was willingly conceded.

Finally, after much running about and a couple more journeys to Dijon, he was appointed by the firm as their sole concessionaire for the Seine Department, with the title of Agent-General and powers to sign contracts and appoint his own representatives.

This position, besides making him financially independent, was for the next four years to provide the perfect "cover" for Michel's clandestine activities. Although he obtained it by pure chance and at a moment when he was desperate to find work to keep himself and his family, it would have been difficult to find another, as it turned out, which could have served his purpose as a *résistant* so effectively.

Worrying as his time of unemployment had been, Michel had not allowed it to oust his main preoccupation: how to carry on the war against Germany; and as soon as he was installed in the new job, and the financial problem solved, he applied himself to ways and means.

This was not easy. Although the B.B.C. were already talking of the French Resistance movement, in fact at this date it hardly existed. Michel made inquiries, followed clues, but they all led him nowhere. Finally he decided that the only solution was a direct contact with the Allies; and during the winter of 1940—41 he gave his mind constantly to this project.

Meanwhile the gas engine business flourished. Orders flowed in and the difficulty was to meet them. There would have been many more but for his refusal to supply the Germans.

This could have got him into trouble—in fact, it eventually did so—since the Germans themselves were short of petrol and made increasing use of gas. But for the time being he managed, by skilful avoiding tactics, to keep the enemy at bay, while satisfying his genuine French customers. At first he used his flat to work in, but soon was rich enough to rent offices in the Avenue Parmentier.

The more the business prospered the freer he felt to devote himself to his plan. He considered the various alternatives. A Channel crossing was out of the question: every inch of the coast was guarded. The frontier of Spain was remote from Paris and he knew nothing of its conditions.

That left Switzerland. The frontier was relatively near, he knew the region, above all it possessed the priceless advantage of affording an excuse for his journey. For it was rich in forests, forests produced charcoal, and as a salesman of gas engines Michel had a special and legitimate interest in charcoal.

Indeed, it was so much in demand and so difficult to find, that he had been obliged to undertake the additional business of procuring and supplying it to his customers. Otherwise the gas engines enterprise would have collapsed for lack of fuel.

So there, without his seeking it, was a ready-made "cover story." What more natural than that the Agent-General of *Gazogène Autobloc*, which also supplied charcoal to its customers, should himself go prospecting for that increasingly rare commodity? Or that he should choose for his searches that region of France which produced the kind of timber from which charcoal is made? And if his quest happened to take him rather close to the Swiss frontier, who could blame him for that?

There was only one snag. In order to reach the frontier it was necessary to cross the *Ligne d'Arrêt Nord-Est* and enter the *Zone Rouge.* This was a corridor varying in width from fifty to sixty miles and running the whole length of France's eastern frontiers.

For anyone living outside the zone special permission was required to enter it, which Michel knew there was no chance of his obtaining. Merely to ask would have invited suspicion.

But nothing venture, nothing gain. He decided he must take this hurdle when he met it.

Early in the spring of 1941 he started to make his preparations. Each week he saved some money to finance his expedition, and by casual remarks accustomed his staff to the idea that he would be going on a journey to look for charcoal.

At last all was ready: his secretary briefed to answer questions in his absence, enough money in his wallet to last a fortnight, and a return ticket bought. On the evening of the 15th May he boarded the night train for Dijon. With him he took a bicycle, a brief-case and a haversack.

Arriving at Dijon early next morning, he went straight to the *Gazogène* factory. There he spent the morning attending conferences and discussing his charcoal project.

Having thus established his alibi, he left the factory, and taking the Langres road set out on his great adventure.

He had chosen the Langres road, which runs north-eastwards from Dijon, after careful consideration of the main obstacle in his path. This was the *Canal de la Marne et Saône*, which form the western boundary of the *Zone Rouge*.

The canal ran north and south to the east of Dijon and for much of its way through built-up areas.

To avoid these, Michel had decided to make for a place called Cusey, twenty-five miles north of Dijon, which appeared to lie in fairly open country, and where there was a lock as well as bridges.

His road ran straight through level country and he cycled along easily, enjoying the fresh air, the summer afternoon and the pleasant country sights. It was hay-making time and the air was filled with the sweet scent of sun-dried grass. He planned to reach the canal at dusk, and it was about seven p.m. when it came in sight.

As he rode along beside it he saw that crossing was not going to be easy. Every bridge was guarded by sentries, while access to the lock was barred by a fence of spiked railings reinforced with barbed wire. In addition a large notice warned anyone approaching that the fence was connected to a mine, which would detonate on being touched.

It began to look as though he would have to swim. As the canal was quite narrow and probably fairly shallow, that was not impossible, even with a bicycle; but it was inconvenient, to say the least, and, what was more serious, liable to attract attention. There seemed, however, to be no alternative. He did not mind the barbed wire, but the mine was another thing.

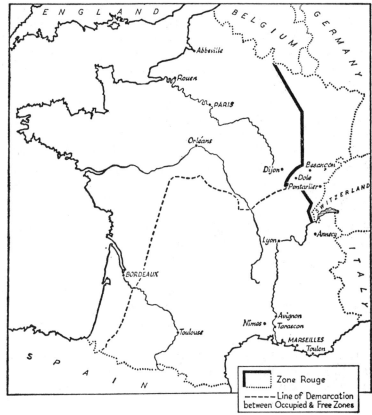

France, showing the Occupied Area and the *Zone Rouge*

While he was considering the problem, concealed behind a hedge, three cyclists appeared in the distance. As they approached he saw that it was a German patrol, consisting of a corporal and two privates.

Passing within a few yards of his hiding place they stopped at the lock. Then the corporal got off, handed his bicycle to one of the others, and went up to the barrier.

Michel, who was close enough to observe every move, saw him hesitate, then seize a section of the railing and push.

Like the secret door in a panelled room, the section swung inwards, leaving a gap wide enough for a man to pass.

When the patrol had passed through, the corporal replaced

the section, carefully dusted the railings, glanced round the horizon to see if he had been observed, and finally followed his companions across the lock gates.

The whole scene was so improbable, occurring at that moment, just as he had made up his mind to swim, that Michel could hardly believe in it. But there was the lock with its apparently impassable barrier, he could see the Germans moving away on the other side of the canal, and the mine had not gone off.

Still not wholly convinced the trick would work for him, he waited five minutes before leaving his hiding place. He had kept his eyes glued on the innocent-looking section and had also counted the number of railings on either side of it.

Repeating the motions he had observed, he was soon through the gap with the barrier closed behind him. First obstacle passed.

Just inside the barrier was a small square house, presumably occupied by the lock-keeper. There had as yet been no sign of him, but as Michel was passing, the door was opened by an elderly man. In his shirt-sleeves and slippers, rather lean, with reddish hair and a fair moustache, he looked at any rate like a Frenchman.

Michel was unprepared. He had his story ready for the Germans, but had not considered what he would do if caught behaving suspiciously by one of his own compatriots. Should he run for it or put his cards on the table?

He stopped and placed his finger over his lips.

"Listen," he said, "I'm trying to reach the frontier. And I'm not particularly anxious to run into Germans."

The lock-keeper looked him up and down, then jerked his head towards the house. Michel followed him indoors. In the small living-room there were the remains of a supper and a bottle of wine.

The lock-keeper filled a glass and handed it to Michel. Then he replenished his own, raised it and said: "*Salut.*" No further explanation was asked or needed.

The lock-keeper, whose name was Vrignon, would have pressed supper on his visitor, but it was now getting late and Michel was anxious to be under cover before curfew. So after thanking his host and promising to return, he bade him *au revoir* and set off again.

This encounter raised his spirits amazingly. The discovery both of a safe place to enter the zone, and also of a reliable accomplice, was the first encouragement he had received, and it seemed to him to augur well for his plan.

M. Vrignon had advised him to keep to side roads. Since however, it was now nearly dark and he still had fifty miles to go to reach the place where he had planned to spend the night, he decided to risk the main road and take the shortest route.

He had covered about forty miles when just outside a village he saw two German soldiers walking in the same direction. Pedalling madly he dashed past, ignoring their challenge, and kept going till he was out of range.

An hour later he arrived at Dole without further incident and booked in at the only hotel.

It was about six o'clock the next evening when Michel rode into the small hamlet of Le Cernois, a few miles this side of the Swiss frontier. He had been bicycling since early morning, it had been raining all day and he was tired and soaked through.

The choice of Le Cernois as the springboard of his attempt was the result of a chance conversation in Paris. One of his customers had happened to mention that he knew the local *douanier*[1] and had found him a friendly person.

The customs house, which also served as a residence for the *douanier*, was the largest of the three or four buildings in sight, the others being farms. As Michel waited outside, after knocking at the door, he could see through a passage into a courtyard at the back, where several bicycles were propped against the wall.

When the *douanier* came to the door, Michel said: "I'm a friend of Monsieur X. I'd like to talk to you."

The *douanier* looked him over.

"All right. You'd better come inside."

He led the way into his office.

"I suppose you know I've got Germans here."

"No, I didn't, but I saw some bicycles at the back."

"That's them. It doesn't matter but you'd better be quick."

---

[1] Customs guard.

Michel then made a clean breast of it. He was trying to cross the frontier and he'd be coming back. He'd chosen Le Cernois because his friend had told him the *douanier* might be helpful. Could the latter show him a good way? If he met any Germans he would say he was looking at forests.

The *douanier* nodded understandingly. Then he went over to the wall, where a large-scale map of the district was displayed, and traced with his finger the route for Michel to follow.

While they were talking a German officer entered the room. Without turning, and slightly raising his voice, the *douanier* remarked: "But you know nearly all the best wood has been cut down."

The officer crossed the floor, opened the door to an inner room, and disappeared.

"When is the best time to try?" Michel asked.

The *douanier* looked at his watch.

"Now. Everybody is at supper. You'll make it before dark if you hurry."

"What about my bike?"

"I'll look after that. You can call for it on your return. Go fifty yards down the road and turn right. You'll find the path straight ahead.

A quick handshake, "good luck," and Michel was on his way.

But not for long. He had gone half a mile and not yet reached the woods, when there, straight ahead of him, was another German patrol: two soldiers, rifles slung over shoulders, sauntering down the path towards him.

He stopped and searched desperately for cover. There was none in sight: besides they had already seen him. There was nothing for it but a bold face.

When he was five yards away from the Germans they stopped. In his town suit, carrying his brief-case, wet and bedraggled, Michel was conscious of the effect his appearance must produce on a lonely country path at that hour.

One of the soldiers started questioning him in German.

Where was he going? What was he doing? What papers was he carrying?

Michel, who could speak it a little, answered in German.

He repeated the story he had so often rehearsed: he was on his way to look at forests. At this time of night? Well, it had been raining all day, and as it was now clearing up, he thought he would save some time.

The Germans were not convinced. He must accompany them, please, to the *Feldgendarmerie*.[1]

Back at the customs house there was no sign either of the *douanier* or the officer. But there was a military truck waiting outside. Michel and his escort climbed into it and the truck was driven off.

Michel now began to feel some alarm. The soldiers had scarcely glanced at his identity card but it seemed certain that the *Feldgendarmerie*, when they saw he lived in Paris, would ask him how he had entered the *Zone Rouge*.

After a short drive the truck stopped in a small town called Mouthe, where the *Feldgendarmerie* had its local head-quarters. Michel was taken to a small room and locked in for the night. There was neither bed nor couch, so he lay on the wooden floor, and, tired and dispirited, was soon fast asleep.

The next morning, he was removed to the Hotel du Grand Poste, at Pintarlier, for questioning. The interrogating officer, a youngish man in German army uniform, looked stern. He was obviously not disposed to credit Michel's story.

The only document the latter carried, apart from his identity card, was a statistical report he had obtained from some Ministry in Paris. It showed the monthly production in French factories of military vehicles for the Germans. This he now produced with a flourish, explaining that he had been given the information in connection with his gas engine business.

Since the document carried the official stamp of the Ministry, it made some impression on the German, but it was clear that he was still not happy about the affair.

For some reason he had not put the one question Michel feared: how he had crossed the *Ligne d'Arrêt* without a permit. But at any moment it might be asked, which would be fatal. It was essential to get away before that happened.

The interrogation had been proceeding for half an hour,

[1] Military Police

without any sign of its concluding, when Michel had a happy inspiration. Why, he suggested, not hand him over to the French authorities? He would then be able to explain himself in his own language and the French magistrate would be able to judge whether he was telling the truth.

The officer hesitated. Clearly he was tempted, it was the easy way out. At the same time he was pretty sure there was something fishy. He studied the prisoner's face and Michel returned the stare blandly. Finally he stood up.

"All right. We'll send you across to the French."

3

BEHIND THE MOUNTAIN

The action of the *Feldgendarmerie* in handing over Michel to the French was consistent with Hitler's policy at the time. The Germans were trying to rule with the velvet glove, using the French authorities to enforce their rule. To show themselves worthy of this confidence the Vichy Government applied the new laws with zeal. At the same time they could exercise a certain discretion.

In consequence the examining magistrate at Pontarlier, when Michel was brought before him the next day, having spent the night in the police station, was less anxious to find fault with the prisoner than to make sure he did not release a dangerous malefactor whose crimes would later recoil on his own head.

Michel, of course, was all innocence: had no idea that his search for charcoal would take him so close to the frontier. Admittedly he should have looked at a map, but it had never occurred to him that he was doing anything wrong, etc., etc.

Nobody could look more honest than Michel and his story was plausible enough. There was only one flaw in it: his

45

illegal entry into the *Zone Rouge*. It seemed inevitable that sooner or later he must be questioned on this, and the truth then discovered.

In fact, the point was never raised. It was so elementary that doubtless the magistrate supposed that the *Feldgendarmerie* had already raised it and received a satisfactory explanation. Otherwise there was no charge which could be laid against Michel and after half an hour's interrogation he was allowed to go free.

One condition, however, was imposed. He must take the first train back to Paris; and to make sure he complied with it two policemen were detailed to escort him to the station and put him on the Paris express.

At this point, and after so narrow an escape, Michel might well have decided to abandon the attempt, and return to Paris to recuperate before trying again. As it was, the only result of the incident was to make him more determined than ever.

Trustingly the two policemen did not wait to see him off. Having seen him comfortably settled in an empty compartment, they bade him *bon voyage* and took their departure.

Michel gave then a few minutes, then opened the door away from the platform, jumped down the track, crossed the line, and, after circling the station, arrived back at the entrance, where he had previously noticed that a bus was waiting.

The bus was still there. It was the bus for Morteau, a smaller town fifteen miles from Pontarlier and somewhat closer to the frontier.

Michel hung about, keeping out of sight, until the Paris express had pulled out. Then he boarded the bus and sat down behind a newspaper. Soon it started off.

So ended his first encounter with the enemy. He had pitted his wits against the Germans and their French accomplices and come off best. It was an encouraging start and gave him a new confidence in his plan.

Morteau, where he arrived about noon, was a quiet little place in the foothills of the Jura, washed by River Doubs. Michel liked the look of it: there were no Germans and no police.

He bought a map of the district and studied it while eating a snack at a café. Morteau was only four miles from the Swiss frontier by the main road, but this was obviously to be avoided.

As he was searching the map for an alternative route his fancy was caught by two curious names, not very far apart: Au-Dessus-de-la-Fin (Above-the-End) and Derrière-le-Mont (Behind-the-Mountain).

He liked the sound of these places: it smacked of small and lonely outposts, remote from the beaten track. Furthermore, the road that led to them seemed to end at Derrière-le-Mont. He therefore decided to make this his first objective. Leaving Morteau on foot he found a side road, which soon began to climb as it entered the forest. Here the only sign of life was the occasional woodsman's cabin, or primitive farmstead standing on the edge of a clearing.

He had been walking for about an hour when there appeared ahead the first of the scattered buildings which constituted the tiny hamlet. As he approached closer he observed that it was a sawmill.

Michel entered the yard, asked for the boss, and was shown into a rudimentary office. Soon a middle-aged man appeared and introduced himself as the owner, M. César Gaiffe. Michel gave his own name and explained that he was looking for charcoal.

M. Gaiffe, large and prosperous-looking, but with the hands of a worker, was disposed to be helpful. Yes, there was some suitable timber which could be purchased, but it was a good way higher up the mountain and he would need someone to show him the path. No doubt but that the carter, who was frequently in that direction, would be willing to act as guide.

M. Gaiffe then sent for the carter and introduced him to Michel.

Paul Cuenot was a typical Jura peasant. Lean and wiry, with thinning hair and a wizened, weather-beaten face, he could have been any age between thirty and sixty. At this, their first meeting, he examined Michel closely but spoke very little. Michel had the impression that he was curious, but not unsympathetic.

After some more discussion it was arranged that Cuenot

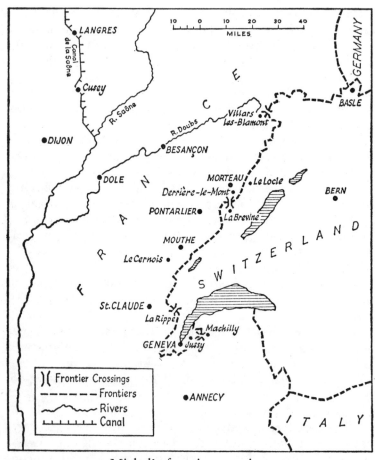

Michel's frontier crossings

should conduct him to a place called Mont Chateleu, one of
the highest points in the region, where trees of the right type
were to be found. As it was now growing late they would
start early next morning. For the night he could get a room
chez Jacquot, a primitive sort of guest house open for occasional summer visitors. Apart from the dwellings of M.
Gaiffe and Paul Cuenot, this was the only residence in the
place.

So far so good, thought Michel, as he lay in the Jacquots' only spare bed that night. He still had no idea how he would proceed the next day; but he could see from his map that Mont Chateleu straddled the frontier, and felt sure that once he was there some plan would suggest itself.

Punctually at seven Cuenot was outside. The carter was leading a small horse and cart—the latter a home-made affair on rubber tyres. It was used for carrying timber and was the only kind of transport practicable on the narrow forest paths.

Michel was ready, having breakfasted, and set off at once with his guide. The morning was fine and cool and there was a scent of pines which Michel, accustomed to the urban smells of Paris, sniffed with appreciation. The narrow path wound through the trees. All around was silence and solitude, only disturbed by the occasional flapping of wings, or the gurgle of a mountain stream.

As they proceeded, climbing steadily through the forest, he considered alternative plans of action. Should he take the carter into his confidence, or wait till they were near the frontier and then give him the slip? He was pretty certain that Cuenot would not betray him deliberately, but there must always be a danger in sharing his secret.

While he was still debating the pros and cons with himself, they arrived at a point where the path divided. Cuenot stopped and turned to him.

"That's the quickest way," he said, pointing to his left, "but I think we'll take the other. Less chance of running into the *boches*. After all, there's no point in having to explain oneself to them."

This was enough to make up Michel's mind.

"You are quite right," he replied, "especially as I'm planning to cross the frontier."

Cuenot nodded understandingly.

"I suspected as much—as soon as I saw you. You might as well have told me. And all that story about charcoal?"

"Just a blind."

"I guessed it was. Well, now I know, I can take you to the right place."

"Good. That's just what I was hoping."

After they had climbed for another hour the trees began to thin and they came on another track which led gently downwards. They followed this a little way, then Cuenot stopped. They had come to the edge of the forest.

Concealed from below by bushes, Michel found himself looking down on a little valley. Covered with lush grass and partly shaded, it looked pleasantly cool and refreshing. Immediately ahead of him the ground fell steeply. At the bottom was a stream and beyond that another grass slope, rising to where the forest began again. From there onwards the ground, densely covered with brush and pine trees, ascended steeply to the sky-line, half a mile away.

Cuenot pointed to the summit. "At the top you'll find a wall," he said. "That's the frontier."

As Michel gazed he felt he was seeing the promised land. After all the vicissitudes of the last four days, he could scarcely believe that he was actually in sight of his goal. For six months past he had been living for this, and the odds had always seemed against him. Now success was almost in his grasp.

Below and a little to the right of where they were standing a large chalet-like building stood in the fold of the valley. This, Cuenot explained, was an abandoned farm-house now used by himself for storing wood and hay.

Cuenot was examining the valley intently, looking first to the right and then to the left.

"This is the moment," he whispered. "The Germans patrol the valley incessantly. Look——" he pointed to another farm-house built on some high ground farther down the valley and on the opposite side of the stream, "that's one of their observation posts, and they use my place too. But it's all clear now and you should have time to get across. When do you expect to return?"

"To-morrow with any luck. At about the same time."

"Good. If it's safe I'll leave the door of the barn open. You can see it easily from the other side. If it's closed don't try."

"Agreed. And thanks—for everything."

"Don't rush it. Just walk steadily as though you knew the way. And good luck."

As Michel emerged into the open, he experienced for the

first time since the start of his expedition a sensation of fear. After the protective shelter of the forest, to appear in full view of anyone in the valley was like entering a public place stark naked.

The Germans, Cuenot told him, didn't hesitate to shoot; and as they were usually accompanied by their police dogs, the chances of escape if he ran into a patrol were negligible. Nor was it conceivable, if he was caught now, that any explanation would be accepted.

Without glancing to right or left he began the descent to the stream. Except for some cows gazing on the pasture there was no sign of life.

Not hurrying, and trying to look unconcerned, he reached the stream, crossed it and started to ascend the far side. A hundred yards brought him to the cover of the wood, but there was still a long steep climb, picking his way through fallen branches, waist-high scrub and rocks, before he came in sight of the boundary—a low wall loosely built of flat stones laid on top of the other. A hundred metres...fifty...twenty-five...five... With a bound he was over the obstacle and standing on the free soil of Switzerland. As he paused to collect himself his heart was beating wildly.

It was a moment to remember but not to prolong. Without even glancing round, he hurried on; not until he was safely out of sight from the wall did he turn to look back in the direction of his beloved France.

The date was the 21st May, 1941.

He soon struck a path, and on the principle that all paths lead somewhere, followed it and eventually came out on a road.

In the distance was a house. As Michel approached he spelled out the name painted large on its side: LA BREVINE.

By its look it was the customs post and, sure enough, as Michel drew level, the customs guard came out on his porch. Michel went straight up to him and showed his identity card.

"I've just crossed the frontier. I've urgent business in Switzerland and I had no time to get a passport."

The customs guard took the card and examined it.

"What sort of business?"

"Family business."

In fact, Michel did have a sister living in Switzerland, who was married to a nephew of General Guisan, commander-in-chief of the Swiss Army. But except as a last resort he preferred not to drag her into it.

"How long are you staying?"

"Twenty-four hours."

"Returning the same way?"

Michel nodded.

"All right. You can carry on. But I'll keep this. You can pick it up on your way back."

"Supposing I'm stopped and asked for it?"

"Just say I'm holding it and have let you pass."

"Thanks a lot. I'll be here to-morrow."

"I'll be waiting," said the customs guard and returned to his house. Michel continued his journey.

It was a three hour walk to Le Locle, where he hoped to find a train for Berne. But the sun was shining and he marched along jauntily, revelling in the sense of freedom.

In the villages through which he passed the people were dressed in their Sunday best. The sight of them going peacefully about their business, without the shadow of fear and want which hung over his compatriots, filled Michel with happiness. It was a foretaste of what they too would one day enjoy again; and the thought that by his action he might bring the day closer gave a new zest to his mission.

At Col des Roches, the last village before Le Locle, the congregation were just emerging from church. They looked so placid and contented in their solid Swiss way, standing about in their neat clothes and exchanging greetings, that he felt himself drawn towards them. He turned off the road and entered the cemetery, where various family groups were inspecting the graves.

While he mingled with them a Swiss gendarme approached and asked to see his papers. Michel explained his situation. The Swiss was polite but unconvinced. Michel then suggested they should go together to the police station and telephone the customs guard. This was agreed to.

Michel's story duly confirmed, the friendly Swiss invited

him to lunch and afterwards arranged for a colleague to conduct him by bicycle to Le Locle.

The colleague, a sergeant, was full of enthusiasm for Michel's exploit. He was sure his lieutenant, who was always anxious to meet visitors from France, would like to hear of it first-hand. Would Michel do him the favour of stopping at the office and allowing himself to be presented to the lieutenant?

All this was a great bore as he had already lost valuable time. However, it seemed advisable to keep in with the Swiss, so he reluctantly gave his consent.

The sergeant had not exaggerated the lieutenant's interest in Michel. As local Intelligence Officer, one of his duties was to collect information brought across the frontier. Michel, coming from Paris, represented a windfall. Placing a large sheet of paper on his desk, he waited, with fountain pen poised, for the pearls about to drop from his visitor's mouth.

Michel was somewhat embarrassed. He had come to offer his services to the British, not to supply information to the Swiss. Anyhow, he was quite incapable of answering detailed questions on German military dispositions. He had never done any spying and had as yet no idea of the sort of things that spies are expected to discover. All he could do was to describe his journey, while mentioning such Germans as he had met on the way.

Fortunately this appeared of the highest interest to the lieutenant, who scribbled away happily as Michel told his story. The lieutenant, of course, knew much more than he did of what was going on along the frontier; but the fact, for example, that the 2nd Company of the 3rd Regiment of *Feldgendarmerie* was now stationed at Morteau—which Michel was able to confirm—evidently afforded him the liveliest satisfaction.

Getting up from his chair he went to the large-scale map which covered the whole of one wall, carefully selected one of the innumerable little flags with which it was dotted, and moved it to its new position a few centimetres away. Those who have worked in Intelligence will understand the pleasure this gave the lieutenant and the gratitude he felt towards Michel.

Conscious that he had hardly earned it, Michel next produced the only document he was carrying. It was the report on French production of military vehicles which he had already used to prove his bona fides to the Germans. This also was highly appreciated by the Swiss.

At last the interview ended. Michel had lost two hours. But he had made a friend, and one who might be useful in future.

As for the lieutenant, he was so pleased with the day's work that he escorted Michel to the station himself, and, since it was Sunday and impossible to change French money, insisted on buying his ticket to Berne.

Sunday afternoon was not the best time to call at a British Embassy, especially for a complete stranger. Nor did Michel's appearance help him. He had been travelling four days and nights, mostly on foot or on bicycle, and had spent two of the nights in custody. Since leaving his last resting place early that morning, he had walked twenty miles, partly across country. He was dusty and dishevelled and had lost the sole off one of his shoes. In short, he looked, and felt, like a tramp.

This was doubtless also the impression he made on the Embassy porter when he asked to see the Ambassador. The porter looked at him dubiously, then coldly directed him to an annexe, where he was shown by a clerk into a waiting-room.

Michel will always remember that waiting-room: not because of the furniture, which was what one might expect; or the ancient and dog-eared numbers of *Picture Post*; but for the solitary picture which adorned the walls.

It was not strictly a picture, but rather a framed strip of parchment inscribed with the following lines:

IN WAR: RESOLUTION
IN DEFEAT: DEFIANCE
IN VICTORY: MAGNANIMITY
IN PEACE: GOODWILL

Michel knew scarcely any English but during his two hours' wait, before anybody came to see him, he had ample time first to translate (with the help of a dictionary conveniently left in the waiting-room), then to copy out, and finally and laboriously to commit to memory these characteristically Churchillian sentences.

He has never forgotten them and until this day they have remained almost the only English phrases he can repeat without prompting. During the next four years they were to be a constant inspiration—especially the second line.

At last the door opened and there appeared a tall, fair Englishman dressed in a grey tweed suit. He looked Michel over quickly, then without sitting down or inviting his visitor to be seated, coldly inquired his business. He did not introduce himself and it was only later Michel learnt that he was Major B——, assistant military attaché.

Aloof in expression and glacial in manner, he listened to Michel's story and the offer of his services to the Allies with the air of one receiving, much against his will, a most distasteful confidence.

His response to the offer was entirely negative. He regretted it was quite impossible to take advantage of it. Michel should know that since the fall of France all direct communication with the United Kingdom had ceased. In any case, Switzerland was a neutral country and it would be quite improper for the British Embassy to engage in espionage against a power with whom the Swiss were in friendly relation.

That he should not be welcomed exactly with open arms was, of course, to some extent understandable. Michel's appearance, as we have seen, was against him, and he carried no credentials. There was no means of proving his bona fides; he could have been a double agent employed by the Germans or an *agent provocateur* sent by the Swiss. Secret agents are not thus recruited and B—— was justified in proceeding cautiously, although he might, perhaps, have used more tact.

Anyhow, Michel was furious. Barely able to control his anger, he wrote on a piece of paper and handed it to B——.

"Here are the names and addresses of two Englishmen. My brother-in-law, Mr. Robert Best, has an important business in Birmingham. The other, Mr. Sturge Moore, the poet and critic, is probably known to you by name. If you will be good enough to refer to them they will answer any questions about myself."

B—— glanced at the paper without any sign of interest, then laid it on the table as though he feared that the mere possession of such a document might compromise him.

"I shall return in a month," Michel continued. "Meanwhile, as I wouldn't like to have wasted my journey entirely, I will leave you this. You can rely on the accuracy of the information."

He then produced for the third and last time the famous document about the French factories. It had come in useful twice and, who knows, might be of some service to the British. Anyhow, he knew the contents off by heart by now and was tired of carrying the thing about with him.

Actually, the information proved quite useful to the British Government, and after being forwarded by B—— to London was broadcast by the B.B.C. as part of its anti-Vichy propaganda.

This was heard by Michel's informant in the Ministry, who was greatly annoyed, since it placed him in danger and might easily have compromised Michel himself. Its publication was, in fact, a first class blunder on the part of the British.

At the moment, however, B—— scarcely deigned to glance at it.

Seeing no point in prolonging the interview any further, Michel bowed out formally, snapped "*Au revoir*, Monsieur," and showed himself out, slamming the door behind him.

It wasn't till he reached the station that his temper started to cool.

Ah, mon dieu, ces Anglais!

Looking across the valley from his hiding-place in the trees, Michel saw that the barn door was open. So Cuenot had kept his promise.

He observed the prospect carefully. The same cows were munching on the same patch of grass. Otherwise the landscape was deserted. This, of course, did not prove that nobody was watching.

However, there was Cuenot's signal, giving him the "all clear." Nothing was to be gained by waiting; he must take the plunge.

This time, instead of going straight across the valley, he

decided to steer a diagonal course. Though it would take a little longer, he would avoid going close to Cuenot's place. Thus, if by any chance the Germans *were* watching, at least he would not incriminate his accomplice.

To emerge from his hiding-place, descend the grassy slope, and cross the stream was the matter of a few minutes; another four at his ordinary pace brought him to the shelter of the French forest. . .and he had done it; crossed the frontier in both directions without being caught.

After proceeding a little farther to make his concealment more certain, he stopped. . .not to rest, but, in silent prayer, to offer up thanks to God.

He was not, of course, yet out of danger; his presence so near the frontier would still be a matter of suspicion if he encountered a German patrol. Veering to the left he soon found the path, which he had climbed with Cuenot the previous day, and followed it down till it brought him back at Derrière-le-Mont.

He had arranged to call at Cuenot's house on his return and found the carter and his family waiting to welcome him with a meal.

Although the worst was over, there was no safety while he remained in the forbidden zone. So as soon as he had eaten he said good-bye to the hospitable Cuenots and set off once more on foot.

His next destination was Le Cernois, some thirty or forty miles away, and he hoped to reach it that day. But before he had gone half-way exhaustion overcame him and he decided to spend the night at Pontarlier.

For once he slept late and it was noon when he came in sight of Le Cernois. This was the hamlet, it will be remembered, where he had left his bicycle shortly before meeting the German patrol; and although he risked meeting Germans again, since they occupied the customs house where the bicycle was held, he was determined not to return to Paris without it. For one thing, he needed it to cross the *Zone Rouge*; for another, bicycles were extremely precious.

By this time Michel was in poor shape. During the last thirty hours he had walked over sixty miles, and in spite of a night spent in a hotel in Pontarlier, where he had bathed and rested his blistered and bleeding feet, he was weary, footsore and nervously exhausted.

It was the hour of the midday meal and the dusty road was deserted. As he approached the customs house, however, a German soldier came into sight. Michel was prepared for this, but he was not prepared for what happened next, which was a mutual and simultaneous recognition by them both that they had met somewhere before. The soldier was, in fact, the same one that had arrested him a few days previously.

Michel stopped and said politely: "Good morning. You see, the French have released me. I have come to ask your Commandant for permission to take my bicycle."

The German eyed him sceptically and without much friendliness, then jerked his head in the direction of the customs house.

"You'll find him there," he said surlily and walked on.

It was now too late for Michel to turn back; he could only continue on his way and trust to bluff to see him through.

On arrival at the customs house he found it deserted. In the courtyard where he had left it there was no sign of his bicycle, but after opening several out-houses he found it stowed away.

It seemed rather rude to remove his property stealthily — also, perhaps, suspicious. So he returned to the empty building, borrowed a sheet of paper and wrote a note to the German officer thanking him for keeping the bicycle and for leaving the shed unlocked. Then he mounted and rode away.

There was no way out of the hamlet except by the road by which he had come, so it seemed very likely he would meet his old friend again. And there, in fact, when he turned the corner was the German soldier coming towards him once more. As they passed Michel waved gaily and the soldier nodded back.

The remainder of his return journey was uneventful. After leaving Le Cernois he followed his previous route in reverse; sleeping again at Dole, drinking another glass of wine with his friend the lock-keeper, and duly reporting to the firm in Dijon on the charcoal resources of the Jura. Seventy-two hours after recrossing the frontier he was back in his flat in Paris.

He had not achieved his object, he was not yet accepted as an ally by the British. But he had done something perhaps more important. He had proved to his own satisfaction that his long-matured plan was a practical possibility. He had discovered a means of leaving and re-entering France with a reasonable chance of escaping detection, and he had made initial contact with France's friends abroad.

And this, in spite of his reception by B——, and a certain irritation with the English manner, filled him with a secret exultation and an iron determination to persevere in his project.

4

SECOND ATTEMPT

Michel had promised to return to Berne in a month's time, and on the morning of the fifth of June he boarded the train once more for Dijon.

His previous journey had been started in a mood of light-heartedness. This time he was both impatient and apprehensive. He knew now the dangers of the enterprise—not the least of which was another rebuff from the British. In that case all the trouble and the risk he was taking would be for nothing.

For three weeks he had been carrying his secret inside him. His escapade had taken him away for a week, and so long an absence needed some explaining to his wife and secretary. In the end they accepted his story about the difficulty of finding charcoal, bad transport, etc.

Meanwhile his normal life was resumed. Dividing his time between his flat in the Rue des Arènes and his office in the Avenue Parmentier, he appeared entirely concerned with his family and his business. But always uppermost in his thoughts was the PLAN.

To go between his flat and the office he had to cross the

Seine four times a day. Each time as he reached the bridge his eye was caught by the gaunt silhouette of a gigantic crane rising above the roofs of the city. Far away on the south-eastern horizon, it was a landmark visible for miles around.

This object became a symbol, at once inviting and menacing, which he found more disturbing with every day that passed. South-east was the direction of Berne, and to Michel it was as if a hand were pointing and a voice saying: "That is the road you have to take." Like some fateful decision from which there is no escape, and which is both a challenge and a temptation, the crane came to exert on Michel an almost hypnotic power and he could never see it without a sort of tightening inside.

It was therefore a relief to be sitting in the Dijon train, knowing that now there could be no turning back. Satisfactory also that out of the profits of his business he had succeeded once again in putting by sufficient money to finance the expedition without denuding his family; and this while continuing to refuse orders from the Germans, who could have been his best customers.

He had already informed the proprietor of the *Gazogène* factory that he was taking another trip to look for charcoal, so his arrival at the works occasioned no surprise. The afternoon was spent discussing various business matters. This suited Michel, as he did not want to leave Dijon too early.

When all was settled he took his bicycle and set out on the familiar Langres road. Three hours' pedalling brought him to the vicinity of Cusey. As it was still daylight, he turned down a side road, found a small inn and stopped to eat and await the dusk.

When it was nearly dark he left the inn and set a course across fields to approach the canal. He had noticed before that all its bridges were guarded and had he approached along the road he could have been seen by a sentry.

The lock, when he came in sight of it, looked just as forbidding as ever, with its barricade of spiked railings and the warning of mines. But it no longer held any secrets for Michel. Going straight to the right spot, he pushed the hinged section, opened the passage and went through with his bicycle. Then he carefully replaced the barrier.

A light was still burning in the lock-keeper's house, and a discreet knock brought him to the door. The good M. Vrignon at once recognized his visitor.

"Ah, it's you," he said. "I wondered who could be calling at this hour."

"I said I would be coming back."

"I remember. We'd better go inside."

In the modest living-room glasses and a bottle were produced, as before, and mutual healths drunk.

"You had no difficulty?" M. Vrignon inquired.

"None at all. I came across the fields."

"Just as well. They change the sentries at dusk and you would have met the relief on the road."

"That's why I avoided it."

"You're playing a risky game. They've tightened up since you were here before."

"We have to take risks in my business."

The lock-keeper eyed him shrewdly.

"I don't know what your business is, but we have a notion, my wife and I, that you're not working for yourself."

"No," said Michel, "I'm working for France."

"I suspected it," said M. Vrignon, "and I wish you success. *Salut.*"

It was Michel's intention to continue his journey without pause, but the lock-keeper strongly advised against it. Both he and his wife were so pressing, that Michel finally agreed to spend the night with them. A bed was made up and he was soon asleep.

Waking at dawn he dressed quickly and stole downstairs, meaning to leave without disturbing his hosts. But Mme. Vrignon was already in her kitchen preparing coffee, and insisted on his breakfasting first.

Once again no questions were asked. All the Vrignons ever knew about Michel was that the he had his own good reasons for avoiding the Germans. To these simple people that appeared sufficient justification for risking punishment themselves by offering him shelter.

It was raining heavily when Michel left Cusey and the prospect of a hundred mile ride to the frontier was unattractive. By good luck, after cycling for two hours, he found a bus bound for Besançon. Putting his bicycle on the roof he got a seat inside and travelled the next forty miles in relative comfort.

The bus was full of country people, most of them carrying baskets of provisions, and there was the usual animated chatter as it slowly progressed, with frequent stops to put down and pick up passengers. The talk was of local matters: crops, markets, prices, families. Nobody mentioned the war or the German occupation. Compared with the Parisians, his fellow travellers struck Michel as well fed and contented. They had not yet felt the Nazi boot, they were minding their own business and would have been rather shocked, he suspected, if he had taken it into his head to confide in them.

At Besançon, where it was still raining, he remounted his bicycle and took to the road again. Following the valley of the River Doubs he rode through green and wooded country, climbing most of the way until he reached Avoudrey. Here he left the main road and headed south, passing Col du Tounet and La Grande Combe, and eventually arrived at Derrière-le-Mont.

The tiny hamlet was as deserted as ever. As he knocked at Cuenot's door he looked at his watch. It was six o'clock. He had been travelling for exactly twelve hours without a stop, was drenched to the skin and extremely hungry.

Although he had warned the carter that he might be returning, he had given no date and his arrival was a complete surprise. However, he was welcomed like an old friend and immediately invited to join the family meal which was just beginning.

The Cuenots had nine children, ranging from ten to twenty years old. As Michel entered they were all seated at a long table, in front of steaming bowls of soup and an enormous loaf of black bread. After his long, exhausting and illegal journey, it was a cheerful and reassuring sight and he needed no pressing to take the place prepared for him. As for the simple, peasant fare, he thought he had never tasted anything more delicious.

The long low room, which served both as kitchen and living-room, was almost bare of furniture. Apart from a Madonna, its only decoration was a framed photograph of the head of the household as a soldier in the first war.

But what was lacking in comfort was made up for by the

friendliness of the whole family. Like the Vrignons the Cuenots knew nothing about Michel except that he was defying German regulations, but this was enough to make him an ally who should be afforded all help.

With his usual impatience at any delay, and although he had travelled nearly a hundred miles since morning, Michel was anxious to push on and cross the frontier that night. From this he was dissuaded by Cuenot on the grounds that it was too dangerous—in the dark anything could happen. A bed was vacated and, tired as he was, he gladly accepted.

Rising again at dawn he found breakfast already prepared for him. After swallowing it quickly he thanked his hosts warmly, promised to return soon, and started off on foot up the mountain.

An hour's march brought him to the highest point of the forest. A little to the right was the deserted farm, and there stretched below him lay the valley he had to cross before reaching the frontier.

As on the previous occasions, it appeared completely deserted. But this, as Cuenot warned him, could be deceptive, since all along the frontier the Germans had observation posts from which they could watch without being seen. One could only pray and hope that the prayer would be answered.

Michel started the descent. As before, he walked slowly, pretending to look for mushrooms. Thus he reached and crossed the stream, climbed the further slope, and ten minutes later scaled the wall and was standing on Swiss soil. It was seven-thirty a.m.

This time he did not stop to look back, but hurried on through the woods until he struck the road and soon arrived at the customs house of La Brevine.

Here he met with his first check. The customs guard remembered him well, but was far from friendly. He must return immediately by the way he had come.

Suspecting what had happened, namely that the guard had been reproved for letting him through before, Michel played for time. It would be a pity, he suggested, to send him back, for then the Swiss would lose the benefit of the important military intelligence that he was bringing especially for them.

He then told the story of his interview a month earlier with the Intelligence Officer at Le Locle.

This impressed the guard sufficiently for him to go inside and telephone his superior. On returning he informed Michel that he had instructions to detain him until an officer arrived to investigate.

Two hours later the officer appeared. Michel repeated his story, giving the name of the lieutenant who had interviewed him and suggesting he be asked to confirm it. A telephone call was put through to Le Locle, when it was discovered that the lieutenant was no longer serving.

Michel now remembered the latter telling him that in civilian life he was an architect with a practice at Colombier. The exchange was requested to try and trace him; and with admirable efficiency, after a few minutes, produced the former Intelligence Officer at the other end of the line. He then not only confirmed Michel's story, but urged that he should be received as an informant of proved value.

The end of it all was that, instead of being turned back, Michel was treated like a V.I.P. An appointment was made with the Intelligence Officer at La Chaux de Fonds, arrangements were made for his transport, and Swiss francs provided for his expenses.

It would mean, as before, a tiresome delay, but that was a price worth paying for free entry into Switzerland.

It was about nine the next morning when Michel's train reached Berne. He had lost a day, but in compensation had spent the night at the best hotel in La Chaux de Fonds as a guest of the Swiss Army. Furthermore, in return for the information he had given them, he was authorised to circulate freely for twenty-four hours.

As it was still rather early and a lovely day, he decided to walk from the station to the Embassy. The latter was situated on the outskirts of the city, in a luxurious residential quarter lavishly laid out with trees and gardens. As Michel strolled along he contrasted its air of well-being with the desperate and lawless business in which he was engaged. How could

people living in such a respectable neighbourhood have anything to do with a man like himself? Would he not be shown
the door again?

He glanced down at his suit. He had brushed it carefully
that morning and his shoes were clean and in good repair. At
least he no longer looked a bandit.

On arrival at the Chancellery he was shown into the
same waiting-room and a few minutes later Major B——
appeared. The Assistant Military Attaché was still reserved
in his manner, but his expression was not quite so forbidding.

He held out his hand, said, "I'm glad to see you," and
then took Michel into another room, where they sat down
facing each other across a table.

"I would first like to ask a few questions," B—— began.
"What was your mother's maiden name and where and when
was she born?"

Other questions followed of an equally personal nature.
At what university had his father graduated? How many
sisters did he have and to whom were they married?

Whilst Michel answered B—— would glance at a sheet of
typescript lying on the table in front of him. When at last he
was satisfied he smiled for the first time and pushed the sheet
across to Michel.

"If the gentleman you are inquiring about," Michel read
in French, "is called Michel Louis Hollard, born at Epinay-
sur-Seine on the 10th July, 1898, son of Madame Hollard, née
Monod, and of Monsieur Auguste Hollard, Doctor of Science,
Professor of Chemistry, etc., then he is a genuine patriot who
in 1916 at the age of seventeen engaged to fight against the
Germans."

"You see," said B——, "we have to take our precautions.
When you first came to see me I knew nothing about you and
it could easily have been a trap. Now that I know you are
speaking the truth, I should be glad to accept your offer—that
is, if you are still in the same mind."

"If I wasn't I wouldn't be here," replied Michel.

"Good. Then let's get down to business. First of all, how
often do you think you can make the journey to Berne?"

Michel reflected. It wasn't going to be easy to find pre-
texts in future. The charcoal story was wearing rather thin.

But he never took his fences till he met them, so after hesitating a moment he answered: "Every three weeks."

"Splendid," said B——. "That would be ideal. Next question: do you think you can obtain the information we need?"

"Well, I don't yet what it is."

"First and foremost the exact position and description of all enemy units in the Occupied Zone."

Michel looked surprised. He wasn't expecting anything quite so simple.

"Is that all?" he said. "What about the aerodromes, and the petrol and munition dumps? And the defences, which the Germans are building everywhere? Doesn't that interest you too?"

"Of course," replied B——, "everything interests us, but your most important task is to locate and identify all German military formations, particularly armoured divisions."

"Don't you have that information already?"

B—— smiled. "Naturally we have a great deal of information, but another check is always useful."

Michel said nothing. He had a feeling of anti-climax. As an army officer he knew the rudiments of military intelligence; realised that it was not a matter of individual prowess, producing dramatic coups, but a painstaking labour, the result of team work piecing together an infinite number of small facts.

And yet the streak of naïvety in his make-up had led him to expect something...well, less hum-drum than merely providing "another check."

However he was a soldier. He had offered to serve, he had been accepted, and he was there to take orders.

"All right," he said, "I understand. I'll do my best."

With that the interview concluded.

As B—— was showing him out Michel made some reference to the charm of the Embassy's surroundings. B—— agreed and proceeded to expatiate on the beauties of Berne generally. It was then that Michel discovered that his coldly reserved Englishman was an enthusiast for the arts with a quick sense of humour. In addition, his French was impeccable.

After chatting in a friendly way for several minutes B—— held out his hand.

"Well, *au revoir*. And good luck to you."

As he walked away Michel's heart was light. He had attained his first objective, and if the assignment given him was not terribly inspiring, at any rate it should be easy. He had merely to keep his eyes open.

So little did he foresee what exactly he was undertaking, or where it would lead him in the end.

By midday Michel was back at the station. After a quick bite he caught a train to Le Locle, and from there set out on foot for La Brevine.

Three hours' walking brought him to the little village. Stopping only to buy some tins of French sardines—unobtainable in Paris—he plunged into the forest and soon reached the wall which marked the Swiss boundary.

It had been raining all afternoon and he scarcely met a soul; but as he stepped on to French territory, there, not ten yards away, was the one person in the world he had hoped to avoid.

Half hidden by a bush a German sentry was examining the valley through thick glasses. At the moment he had his back turned to Michel, but was swinging round slowly as he swept the horizon.

Michel dropped to the ground and lay still, scarcely breathing. Now he could see the glasses pointing in his direction. Should he make a dash for the wall—only a few yards away? Even if he reached Swiss soil it would not stop the soldier from shooting. And then there was Cuenot to consider—he would surely come under suspicion as the owner of the nearest farm.

As he watched, still undecided, he saw the soldier lower his glasses, sling them round his neck, shoulder his rifle, and stroll away.

He waited for another half-hour; then, feeling fairly certain that he would not meet another patrol, descended the slope, crossed the stream and rapidly climbed the other side. An hour later he was knocking at Cuenot's door.

When he joined the family at the evening meal, all were delighted at his safe return. Although the children were not in the secret, they sensed in the mysterious visitor an exciting character and had already adopted him as "Uncle Michel." It was taken as a matter of course that he should stop for the night.

The next morning he was up at five, before anyone was awake. Leaving a message of thanks on the table, he slipped out, found his bicycle, and started off.

All day he rode, with two short stops to eat, and at six o'clock was back at the Cusey lock. This time he did not stop even for the ritual glass of wine. M. Vrignon opened the secret passage himself and waved gaily as Michel started on the last lap of his marathon.

At nine he arrived at Dijon station. The Paris express was already at the platform. Michel just had time to put his bicycle in the cloak-room and climb into the train before it started. He was completely done in and aching in every limb. But he was also filled with an intense feeling of satisfaction— not least with the physical feat he had just performed of cycling a hundred and twenty miles between dawn and dusk.

Altogether during his five days' absence, he had travelled two hundred and thirty miles by his own means; and when he awoke in Paris at five the next morning, after sleeping sitting up in the train, he was ready if necessary to repeat the performance.

This exceptional physical endurance was no accident. All his life Michel had made a fetish of physical fitness—he was also extremely abstemious—and as a factor in his survival from great danger this came only second to his moral courage.

5

ORGANISATION OF A RÉSEAU

The task set by B—— had sounded simple enough
to Michel, sitting in the Embassy in Berne, but
back in Paris he realised, as soon as he began to think about
it, that it was not going to be easy at all.

Paris, for example, was full of German soldiers, but many
of them were on leave from other parts of France, or other
occupied countries, or even from Germany. In a single street
one could meet men from a hundred different units, and even
if one succeeded in interpreting their insignia—which was not
by any means easy for a foreigner—one was not much further
advanced.

There were known to be several divisions stationed in the
Paris region, but which they were and where exactly they
were located was another matter. How did you set about
looking for them? Whom could you ask—knowing that merely
to show curiosity on such a subject might well lead to your
arrest?

Moreover, Paris was only one centre. B—— had given him
a list of "strategic points," but it was simply a list of the

principal towns in the Occupied Zone. Anyhow, the Germans seldom set up their headquarters in the town; they were usually in some remote and closely guarded château, which it was sufficient to approach to arouse suspicion.

After a week spent tramping the streets of Paris, travelling to the suburbs and frequenting the cafés where German troops were most often to be seen, Michel was not much wiser than before.

He soon reached the conclusion that he could do nothing alone. He needed helpers, plenty of them and quickly. But where to find them? Whom could he turn to without risk of being betrayed? It was June, 1941, and if there already existed a French Resistance movement Michel had not yet been able to discover it.

The problem was still unsolved when one day there came to his office a little man dressed in worker's clothes, who asked if he could be supplied with a gas engine. Interviewed by Michel he gave his name as Louis Margot, ex-prisoner-of-war recently repatriated owing to wounds. He had acquired an old lorry and planned to equip it with a gas engine, with a view to starting a one-man haulage business.

Michel took the order, promised to expedite it, and made an appointment for Margot to return a few days later, when the engine would have arrived from the factory at Dijon.

It took several days to adapt the lorry and fit the engine, during which Michel had opportunities to talk to his new customer. Aged thirty-five, with a working-class background, Margot impressed him by his common sense, receptive mind, and firm character. He was also apparently a fervent patriot.

On the last day, when their business was finished, Michel invited him into his private office.

"I have been thinking that perhaps you could help me," he said.

Margot looked blank.

"You see," Michel went on, "I've gathered from our conversations that you don't like our new masters any more than I do."

"Surely I don't like them. How could any Frenchman like them?"

"I agree. And do you believe in an Allied victory?"

Margot looked dubious. "That depends. If the English can hold out and the Americans come to their help..."

"The English *will* hold out. And the Americans *will* come in—not this year, perhaps, but sooner or later, as they did before. But we musn't leave it all to our Allies. The French must help themselves. Otherwise we're finished—whoever wins."

Margot gave a shrug. "I think you're right. But what can we do?"

Michel hesitated. By now he was pretty sure of this man, but it was the first time he had gone as far with another Frenchman and he realised that the next step would be fateful. If he had made a mistake his whole plan might be ruined.

"I'll tell you," he said quickly. "But first are you sure you would like to help?"

Now it was Margot's turn to hesitate. He was beginning to perceive what Michel was driving at. He was being asked to make a serious decision, but under Michel's calm gaze, as he confessed to him later, he felt he had no choice.

"Yes, I would like to."

"You realize it could be dangerous?"

"I don't mind that."

"Good, then this is what I want you to do. You have your lorry and you will be plying between Paris and the suburbs. There are German troops stationed in various sectors of the perimeter. Without going out of your way, find out all about them: exactly where they are and what they consist of."

Margot showed no surprise: he had evidently guessed what was coming.

"That shouldn't be difficult," he said. "I saw a great deal of the German Army when I was a prisoner."

"You won't find it so easy, but it's not impossible. As you know, each division has its own symbol, which is painted on its vehicles and embroidered on the flag displayed outside its headquarters. By noticing where vehicles with the same markings converge, you will discover their point of concentration. Inquiries in the neighbourhood should then reveal the location of the command post. If you can discover the name of the commander so much the better."

"Is that all?"

"That's the most important. But of course anything else you can find out will be useful. For instance, petrol and ammunition dumps, defence works, air strips, A.A. installations, et cetera."

Margot nodded.

"Write down the least possible," Michel continued. "And if you have to make notes, don't carry them with you. Practice memorising. And be accurate. One precise detail is worth a dozen vague rumours. Do you understand?"

"I understand. You can count on me."

"Good. You can come and see me at the garage when you have anything to tell me. We can always find a pretext."

A few days later Margot reappeared with his lorry, ostensibly to have some small defect repaired. He brought with him his first report. It was all and more than Michel had hoped for. Disregarding the latter's injunction he had gone out of his way to obtain the required information. After supplying some additional details, he left with a promise to return with more in a few days' time.

Michel was delighted. At last something was happening. Further, the success of this first experiment gave him confidence in approaching others.

During the next few weeks he engaged several more accomplices, all in the Paris region, and set them to work in the same way. They came from all walks of life—one was a railway employee, another owned a café, a third drove a taxi—and they gathered the information Michel wanted in the course of their ordinary duties.

Later, others were recruited in the Seine Department, at Dijon and various other centres. By the end of the year he was getting reports from a dozen different sources, in addition to the information he gathered himself, and passing them on regularly to B—— in Berne.

Some of his best workers were those, like Margot, whom he had met in connection with his business. Margot himself was perhaps the best of all. Devoted and conscientious he would go to endless trouble in following up a clue, or confirming some detail.

In choosing likely people Michel relied largely on intuition. Usually they were complete strangers and he had to form an opinion on the strength of a chance meeting, often brief. He would first observe a person closely, looking for something experience had taught him to seek in a man's bearing or expression; and then if possible engage him in conversation. Sometimes even this preliminary was impracticable and he had to take the plunge relying on his *flair*.

There was Louis Jouanen, for example. Station-master at Porte-les-Valence, the most important marshalling yard on the P.L.M. railway, Jouanen was in the act of inspecting some points when Michel first set eyes on him. As he had only a few minutes to catch his train, and could not afford to miss it, this was a case where there was no time for preliminary soundings.

After watching the man for a moment, he approached and asked if he could speak to him privately. They walked a few yards down the line, then Michel said: "I'm a French officer. I'm engaged in important work which will assist the Allies and help rid us of the *boches*. I need someone here to collect certain information, and I believe you're the man I'm looking for. I therefore appeal to your patriotism to help me, but I warn you it's not without danger."

Since the station-master made no reply, they walked a little farther in silence. Then he stopped and faced Michel.

"I don't know who you are, Monsieur," he said, "but I think you are telling the truth and if you are, then you've knocked at the right door. Tell me what you want me to do."

"Keep a note of all movements of German troops and material and look out for me again in a week's time."

There was no time for more—Michel's train was already in. Without another word he quitted Jouanen and hastened back to the platform.

His judgment of Jouanen, based on a single impression, was fully vindicated by the outcome. When he returned a week later the station-master produced, in a neatly compiled report, all the information he needed. Thereafter Jouanen proved himself the most reliable of agents, as well as the most enthusiastic.

Another outstanding success was Louis Villette. Michel had known him before the war, when he had a garage in the Rue de la Gaieté, near the station of Montparnasse.

They did not meet again until the summer of 1941 and then purely by accident. It was at the Ministry of *Ponts et Chaussées*,[1] which Michel was visiting to renew his permit to install gas engines. While he was waiting Villette appeared, bound on the same errand. Afterwards they had a drink together and exchanged news.

From this Michel learnt that Villette was employed as a driver by a large transport company serving the Channel ports. One of his runs was between Abbeville and Boulogne, and this took him regularly into the forbidden coastal zone.

The zone extended for the whole length of the French seaboard, from Calais to the Spanish frontier, and was much more closely guarded than the other frontier areas. Michel himself had found the greatest difficulty in entering it. Obviously, therefore, Villette, who had a permanent pass into the zone, could be very useful to him.

Villette was delighted and set to work at once. Since he frequently came to Paris, where his company had their offices, there was no difficulty in contacting Michel and delivering his reports every week. Among his discoveries were the exact position of German coastal batteries, the plan of a new submarine base at Boulogne, and details of the elaborate system of camouflage, which included a dummy village complete with church, masking the important airfield at Abbeville.

This airfield was used chiefly by night fighters stationed for the interception of British bombers. When off duty the German pilots often foregathered at a place called Nouvion-en-Ponthieu, about five miles away on the Abbeville-Montreuil road, where there was an excellent restaurant. Here Villette would call after hours and collect from the *patron*, who understood German, a full report of the evening's conversation. After a glass or so of wine the young airmen lost almost all sense of security, and their own comments, which were usually very critical of their own command, were found most interesting by the R.A.F. when they received them via Berne a few days later.

Foreseeing that sooner or later the British would bomb the aerodome, Villette asked Michel to arrange for him to be

---

[1] Responsible for the upkeep of roads and bridges.

warned and suggested a message in code to be broadcast by the B.B.C. Some weeks later he was delighted, after listening to the news bulletin, to hear the announcer add, following a short pause: "Here is a special message. 'The beer is good.' I repeat, 'the beer is good.'" This was the pre-arranged signal.

A few nights later Abbeville airfield was attacked with great effect. Surprise was complete, many enemy aircraft being destroyed on the ground.

Michel's success in enlisting help resulted partly from his ability to assess character, and partly from his personality. A natural leader, his own faith was infectious and he rarely had to use his powers of persuasion.

Only once was he rebuffed by a stranger and the incident is worth recording as an example of the other mentality.

He had received information that an important troop movement, involving forty train loads of men and material, would shortly be taking place via Toulouse. As it happened, the station-master at Toulouse was known to one of his agents, another railwayman called Turcan. He therefore did not hesitate but took the first train to Toulouse and knocked on the station-master's door.

Aged forty-five, tending to corpulence, the station-master received his preliminary overtures without enthusiasm. Seeing that he was going to have difficulty, Michel decided to mention the name of Turcan.

"Yes, I know him," said the station-master coldly.

"I'm glad to hear it," Michel replied, "as he is one of my friends and that should help in the matter I wish to discuss with you."

"Perhaps you would tell me what it is."

"I will. You are a Frenchman. Like us all, you must detest the occupation of our country by a foreign power. Thanks to our British and American Allies, who are continuing the fight against the invader, France will eventually be freed. Meanwhile, I am here to offer you the opportunity of assisting in her liberation."

"I'm afraid, Monsieur, that I don't understand you," said the station-master with dignity.

"It's quite simple," Michel continued. "I am asking you to furnish me with certain information, of which you are in possession by reason of your official position, and which is of strategic importance to our Allies. I refer to the big troop movement you are expecting. I want to know what it consists of, where it comes from and where it is going, and I hope you won't refuse me, as the consequences would be serious."

"If that's what you came for," replied the station-master shortly, "I can tell you that you've wasted your time."

"Really?"

"Absolutely."

"May I ask what prevents you? Several of your colleagues in other localities are helping me and they are happy to do so."

"Well, I'm having nothing to do with that nonsense."

"It's far from that. This is important work and not without danger. Wouldn't you like to give us a hand?"

"I don't mix in politics and I don't intend to."

"But you do. By carrying out your official instructions you assist the policy of Hitler, instead of helping our Allies to get the better of him. Is that the nonsense you prefer?"

The station-master stood up, flushed with anger.

"Monsieur, I don't have to justify my conduct to you. I am judge of what is my duty. Now get out. What's more, I advise you to leave the station immediately, for if you are not gone in ten minutes the German police will remove you."

He pushed his visitor towards the door. There was no alternative for Michel but to beat a retreat. However, he did not leave the station. He had already made the acquaintance of one of the traffic controllers, whose office was farther down the platform, and from him he was able to obtain a certain amount of information.

He continued his inquiries all that night, visiting Sête and Narbonne, and finally arriving at Nîmes. Here the dispatching clerk, a certain Rozier, who was already working for him, completed the information. From this it transpired that an entire German Army Corps was moving to Italy via Ventimiglia. Ten hours after Michel had learnt all the details, they were in the hands of his British contact in Switzerland.

A few days later the Gestapo descended in force on Nîmes station, and placing guards at every exit proceeded to search for the informer. Rozier just had time to leave his office, run down a staircase and reach the goods yard, where a locomotive was standing, with steam up, and neither engine driver nor fireman in sight.

This presented no problem to the dispatch clerk. Mounting the cab he put the engine in motion, gave three strident blasts of the whistle and drove off gaily down the line.

Ignoring signals and punctuating its progress with warning shrieks, the stolen locomotive proceeded at a cracking pace in the direction of the Mediterranean. After a scarifying journey of fifteen mile it drew up safely in the station of Lunel and its temporary driver then made himself scarce. He remained in hiding until the hunt was over. No disciplinary action was taken against him by the company, but for his own safety he was removed to another post.

As for the station-master at Toulouse, he too was removed, but only to be promoted.

One lesson Michel learned was not to look for recruits among former acquaintances. Apart from two comrades of his regimental days, both of whom responded to his appeal, only one other old friend was approached by him. This was a man whom he had known intimately in peace time and who since the war had become Head of Passive Defence in an important town on the Atlantic coast. As such he could move freely in the forbidden zone and was thus exceptionally well placed for assisting Michel.

His response was immediate and negative. Reason: concern for his family. Michel accepted the refusal and respected the reason; but he resolved never again to look to his pre-war circle. And for every old friend he lost as a result, he made a hundred new ones.

The system of voluntary helpers, who gathered information in the course of their ordinary duties, functioned reasonably well as far as it went, but Michel soon realised it was not enough. The results, though often valuable, were too erratic. A person would start with enthusiasm and then become discouraged or distracted, or perhaps move to another job where he could no longer be useful. Since their services were given free, Michel could not be too exacting.

He was, therefore, forced to the conclusion that the only solution was to employ full-time agents, paid by himself and working under his orders.

It was soon after he had taken this decision—towards the end of 1941—that Olivier Giran first came to see him.

Olivier, son of a friend of Michel's father, was just twenty at the time, but seemed several years older. Of medium height, with broad shoulders and a deep voice, brimming over with confidence, he looked and acted as one capable of enjoying life to the full and ready for any adventure.

His one ambition, he told Michel, was to fight the Germans. He had already made an abortive attempt to reach England, had been arrested at Marseilles and imprisoned. Could Michel suggest anything?

As it happened the boy had passed his childhood in Switzerland, in a village near the frontier poetically named La Côte aux Fées, not very far from Pontarlier. He therefore knew the region well through which Michel travelled on his way to Berne. Who better to act as courier?

It was not what Olivier had hoped for; but after Michel had explained that the job he was offering was possibly no less dangerous than soldiering, and probably a lot more useful, he agreed to take it on. An additional incentive was the hope that once known to the British he might eventually be accepted as a combatant.

It was thus that Olivier Giran became the first and youngest of the permanent agents of the future *réseau* "*Agir*".[1]

Their pact concluded, Michel lost no time in initiating the new recruit in his duties. The first need was to provide him with a safe passage across the frontier. Since Michel was reluctant to compromise his own route, it was necessary to find a new one.

In this he was helped by the Swiss. The Swiss Intelligence Officer at La Chaux de Fonds who had interviewed him on his second visit had given him an introduction to his father, a Monsieur Grandi.

Monsieur Grandi, although a Swiss, lived in France, being the manager of a factory at Les Verrières de Joux, a small

---

[1] The name Michel eventually gave to his network.

village in the region of Pontarlier. The factory was only five hundred yards from the frontier, and was therefore an excellent starting point for a clandestine crossing.

It was here that Olivier, thanks to M. Grandi, successfully made his first entry into Switzerland. Thanks also to the same connection he had no trouble with the Swiss guards, arrived safely in Berne and delivered his parcel to B——. He then returned by the same route without incident.

Thereafter he made the journey regularly in place of Michel. In addition he was given the area round Dijon in which to collect information. He soon showed himself brave, resourceful and energetic, and if he had a fault it was excess of enthusiasm and over-readiness to accept risks.

This arrangement brought great relief to Michel. By saving him the journey to Berne, which took up several days every three weeks, it enabled him to devote more time both to the running of the *réseau* and to the conduct of his business. Since the latter was not only his sole means of livelihood, but also provided both the "cover" and the finance for his other activities, he could not afford to neglect it.

In his next choice Michel was equally fortunate. Joseph Brocard was a very different type from Olivier. Of the same age but small and slightly built, with pinched features and a voice which was little more than a whisper, he looked anything but robust, but had something in his expression which suggested unusual determination.

Michel first met him in Switzerland, where he had tried unsuccessfully to enlist with the Allies and was about to return in disgust to France. This was the spirit that Michel always looked for. He made an appointment to meet Brocard again in Paris and there and then engaged him as his second full-time agent.

A few day later, equipped with a false identity card and a labour certificate in the name of Joseph Bart, the new agent set off on his first mission. Its object was to identify German units in Brittany.

Bart, as he was henceforth known, was so successful that his area was soon extended to a large part of northern France, including the forbidden coastal zone. He was quite fearless, indefatigable, and meticulously accurate.

Only once did Michel have occasion to find fault with him. It was of the utmost importance that all rendezvous should be kept to the minute. Failure of either party to arrive at the appointed time was a sign to the other that something had gone wrong, and if he waited he might be risking arrest himself. Therefore precise punctuality was an absolute rule.

One day Bart, who was usually most punctual, arrived at the meeting place two minutes late. Michel made no comment, but simply handed over his watch and begged the other to keep it. Blushing like a girl Bart pocketed the watch. He was never late again.

By the beginning of 1942 Michel had recruited four more permanent agents, bringing the total to six, who were distributed throughout the Occupied Zone. All of them gave their full time and were paid their living and other expenses out of his own pocket. Their main task was keeping track of the occupying forces, which the British still insisted on as priority.

Meanwhile he did not dispense with his voluntary informants, but these had the easier and less important job of reporting on the enemy's static installations, such as aerodromes, arms factories, stores, etc.

In addition there was a special category of volunteers, used exclusively to report *movements* of German troops and material. These were all railway employees and they played an essential part in disclosing changes in the enemy's dispositions.

For example, a station-master at X would report the departure of a certain German division for destination Y. This would set in train further inquiries by Michel's team, as a result of which it would be discovered, in addition to the original information: (a) which division had replaced the former one at X; (b) by whom *it* had been replaced; (c) where the division previously at Y had gone to; (d) which division it had replaced there; and (e) where the latter had gone to.

One could, in fact, extend inquiries in both directions indefinitely, and the further they went the more complete the picture which emerged.

This, then, was the organisation which, starting from scratch, Michel created in the second half of '41. With minor adjustments it remained unchanged until November, 1942, when the German occupation of the whole of France called for a great increase in its activities.

He built it piece by piece with no preconceived plan and nothing to aid him but common sense. Each move was an experiment and he learnt, as he went, by experience.

This, perhaps, was a blessing in disguise. With no advice from outside, no rules to observe—except those he made himself—he approached each problem unbiased and solved it by light of his intelligence. In all his decisions the only influence was his own judgment.

Equally important as a factor in its success, the *réseau* was entirely self-sufficient. It drew its strength from its own resources and no extraneous aid was ever offered or made use of. There were no parachute drops, no wireless transmitters, no system of internal couriers or "post-boxes." All the impedimenta of the cloak and dagger business, which so often proved fatal to other networks—especially those controlled directly from London—were dispensed with. In fact, Michel never knew of their existence.

It might be argued that through not using wireless there was a loss of time in communicating with London. In fact, however, very few intelligence reports are urgent, unless they are concerned with some immediate operation. And what was gained in time by using wireless was more than outweighed by the disadvantages.

Radio messages which could be intercepted and their source detected were the most effective means at the disposal of the Gestapo for tracking down Allied agents. Moreover, having captured an agent with his transmitter, the Germans would send messages to London purporting to come from him and in this way laid traps for many of their victims.

Then again only the shortest messages could be sent by wireless, whereas Michel's reports, forwarded in code through the Swiss post office, could be sent in full; while documents, plans, photographs, etc., which it would have been impossible to transmit by wireless, could be safely dispatched to London through neutral countries.

Finally, Michel's was a "one-man show," and this was its greatest safeguard. In the whole of the *réseau*—and by the end it numbered over a hundred persons—the sole connecting link was Michel himself, and he was the only member of whose existence any of the others knew. Thus he alone risked being betrayed if one of them was caught and questioned. It was only much later, and in case something should happen to himself, that he appointed three deputies and took them partly into his confidence.

All reports were delivered to him personally; either the agent came to Paris or he visited him in the provinces. These direct contacts, made at regular intervals, were invaluable. They enabled him to control the work at first-hand, without any danger of misunderstanding. They were also essential for maintaining the morale of his team.

The only drawback of the system was that it involved a lot of travelling. Fortunately his business was a perfect excuse for this, while it also provided cover for most of the permanent agents, whose labour certificates showed them as salesmen for the *Société Gazogène Autobloc de Dijon*.

6

ARREST OF OLIVIER

Olivier Giran, having been engaged by Michel as his courier, made his first journey into Switzerland in January, 1942; and for the next six months he made the journey to and from Berne every three weeks.

This arrangement worked admirably. Olivier knew the country, he got on well with B—— and there was no difficulty with the Swiss, who had agreed, in exchange for the information they brought, to allow Michel or his courier free passage whenever they wished.

But in June a disaster occurred.

Olivier had a friend, a young Dutchman, whom he had met at the Netherlands Chamber of Commerce in Paris. Early in the spring this friend asked if he could arrange for a group of Dutchmen, recently escaped from Holland, to be smuggled out of France into Switzerland.

Olivier, always looking for some new adventure, jumped at the proposal, and it was agreed that he should leave Paris with the party the same night.

By good luck there was no control at Auxonne, where

the railway entered the *Zone Rouge*, and the train reached Pontarlier without incident. From there the party proceeded on foot across country, crossed the frontier undetected in spite of one alarm, and arrived safely at La Côte aux Fées.

Delighted with his success, Olivier returned to Paris, to receive an ovation from his friends at the Netherlands Chamber of Commerce.

It was only some weeks later that Michel heard of the escapade. Realising the risk he asked Olivier not to repeat it. Unfortunately in the meantime the latter had already promised to escort another party of nine; and on the understanding that this should be the last Michel reluctantly gave his consent.

At eleven a.m. on the 30th June, having arrived in Dijon the previous evening, Olivier went to the station to meet the train bringing the Dutchmen from Paris. He was accompanied by a youthful friend of his schooldays, Jean Bouhey.

They waited outside the exit as the passengers came off the train, but there was no sign of the party. Olivier then decided to look for them on the platform, leaving Jean to keep watch outside.

Five or ten minutes passed while Jean waited anxiously. Then he saw an armed German soldier emerge. Others followed escorting a group of civilians, handcuffed two by two. In the middle of them, handcuffed to a guard, was Olivier. As he passed he glanced at Jean and made a sign of discouragement. Jean was about to reply when he saw that the guard was looking at him. Turning away he discreetly made his escape.

Michel heard the news three days later, on his return from a journey. It came from Olivier's parents, whom he knew, and who had been informed by Jean Bouhey.

He was shocked. Not only was it the first serious setback, but he was closely attached to Olivier—the earliest and the youngest of his full-time agents. While the young man had brought it on himself, he felt personally responsible for the disaster.[1]

Although for all he knew he was now in danger himself, his first thought was for Olivier. It was essential to discover

[1] In fact, Olivier was betrayed by a German agent called Engbert, posing as a Dutchman. The latter was eventually detected by the Dutch and executed.

where he was imprisoned, so that arrangements might be made for sending food parcels and messages and, if possible, organising an escape.

He decided to investigate himself, and after informing the Girans took the first train to Dijon.

The Departmental Prison, which the Germans had taken over, was a massive grey building standing at the end of a wide boulevard. Its grim facade, only broken by the rows of iron bars guarding windows of frosted glass that were never opened, formed a sinister contrast to the gaily flowering chestnuts which lined each side of the boulevard.

Some of the windows, Michel noticed, were covered with sheet iron. They were those of the punishment cells.

Michel had no plan, but he thought it unlikely that Olivier would already have been removed from Dijon. It was a question of making certain he was still in the prison.

As he approached the building he saw that the main entrance, flanked by a massive iron gate, was open; and decided on the spot to beard the lion in his den.

Just inside the entrance was a small lodge, where a German N.C.O. was seated at a table. At a smaller table next to it sat a young woman: blonde, pretty, but with an insolent expression, and speaking French perfectly.

Michel approached the lodge, knocked on the open door, and as the German looked up said in French: "Excuse me, Monsieur, but I am inquiring after a certain Olivier Giran. Can you tell me, please, if he is here?"

While the girl translated into German, the N.C.O. looked Michel over. Then, turning to the interpreter and speaking in German, he told her to ask the gentleman why he was interested in Giran.

Michel, who had learnt German as a child, knew enough to understand. He had his answer—and his warning—and did not wait for the translation. As a precaution he had already started edging away. Mumbling some excuse he moved swiftly towards the gate and a second later was outside in the street, where he was soon lost in the crowd.

Back in Paris Michel informed the Girans. Olivier's mother immediately left for Dijon and the next day, accompanied by a friend, visited the prison. Thanks to a humane guard, an

Austrian, she was able to send not only food but a message to her son. A few days later a reply was smuggled out to her, and thereafter communication was regularly maintained.

By this means Michel learned that in spite of repeated interrogations Olivier had kept his mouth shut. All he had confessed to was smuggling for money. This was not regarded by the Germans as a very serious offence and there thus seemed some hope of his eventual release.

But in October a new blow fell. M. and Mme. Giran were both arrested in Paris and taken to Fresnes prison. Soon after, Olivier himself was transferred to Fresnes. Thanks to the charity of the German chaplain, a Lutheran pastor, Mme. Giran was able to communicate with her son; and when she and her husband were released for lack of evidence against them, they continued to exchange messages through the same intermediary.

Early in 1943 Olivier was again removed, this time to Angers. There he was subjected to a new series of interrogations. Once again and thanks to another German chaplain, who showed the same compassion as the one at Fresnes, Mme. Giran succeeded in keeping in touch with her son; and it was through this clergyman that she learnt of his death and the manner of it.

On the morning of the 16th April, 1943, Olivier and two other young men were taken from their cells to the place of execution and shot by a German firing squad. Here is the account of their last moments which the German chaplain wrote for Mme. Giran.

About twenty minutes before the execution he was taken from the prison with the other two condemned men. A truck was waiting to take them to the place. Each was handcuffed to a soldier of the *Feldgendarmerie*. I got into the truck and sat beside him. He asked me if I could persuade the guards to leave it open, saying, "the morning is beautiful and the world looks so lovely, I want to gaze at it for as long as possible. I give you my word of honour that we won't give you any trouble."

During the drive he asked me if I knew France well. I replied that I did. "Then," he said, "you must understand

how wonderful it is to die for such a country. It is so
beautiful...and the people are so fine. It is a pity that as a
German you can never meet them."

One of the others showed me the photograph of his
child, whom he would never see again. He had tears in his
eyes. Olivier tried to comfort him. "Don't cry," he said.
"Try to be brave."

The third asked, "How much longer?" I looked at my
watch and told him. "About twelve minutes."

After that we didn't talk any more. On arrival at the
place their eyes were bandaged. Then the sentence was read
in German and French ...

It was all over in a second. As the order was given I heard
Olivier shout, "*Vive la France!*" All three died instantly.

In the same letter the chaplain enclosed another, written by
Olivier to his parents. It was started a few days before his
death and finished on the morning of the execution: between
seven a.m. when he was informed it was taking place, and
nine a.m. when they came for him.

This profoundly moving document is too long to quote in
full, but the following extracts will give an idea of its tone.

Monday, 12th April, 1943

I am condemned to death. And then? An appeal for
mercy? I have already explained why I had no illusions
about that. So the hope is too slim to cling to. I am at the
bottom of a pit and I can still see the light, but it is only the
size of a pinhead and I have no means of reaching it. I can
only wait. Wait till the light goes out completely. It is
better to wait calmly.

I feel confused, my head is full of disconnected ideas, but
I want you to know what they are and it seems to me I
have a duty to tell you. Besides it gives me great happiness
to write to you—it is as if we were all together, chatting.

In all I write there are only two things I want you to
remember: my eternal gratitude for a life of such great and
constant happiness as, thanks to you two, I have had; and
the strength of my love for you.

I won't say any more on that. There are things so great,

so beautiful, so sacred, that one would only spoil them by trying to express them in words.

Friday, 16th, April

I didn't write anything on Tuesday or Wednesday, the atmosphere wasn't congenial. Yesterday I was given back my suitcase. And this morning, at seven, they came to tell me that it was fixed for *nine o'clock*.

My beloved parents, forgive me; I'm afraid this will be the hardest of all for you to bear—and I must confess I was still hoping—until one minute to seven.

I'm quite calm, but death is already pressing, and I've so much to tell you. First of all certain things must be said once and for all.

I shall stand before God conscious and confident. I believe in Him. I believe in the life of the soul...where it seems—in fact, I'm sure, because my heart tells me—that I shall still commune with you, and with all that's fine, noble, just ... just ...

Among men I did what I thought was my duty—but I did it with joy in my heart. It was war, and I fell, as others did, and as many more must do...I saw them on the Marne, buried in long rows. Now it's my turn—that's all.

I must admit it's not easy to keep calm... these last minutes on earth are going so quickly.

Oh, my adored parents, how I feel for you at this moment. You've had so much grief, so much misery already. And now this! But remember, the world goes on, all is life, movement...and I see, as if I was *there*, on this last morning, the red sun rising behind Franquevaux, free and glorious and for ever the symbol of *light*.

I love you, I love you, I love you. Cross out everything I have done to hurt you. Remember me only as the child, who, thanks to our love, died happy...

You can rest assured that I have betrayed no one. I have never been a coward or accused others to save myself. As the curtain falls at the end of this last act, I can make my bow with clean hands.

After farewell messages to his friends and relations, and a

request to be buried in the cemetery at Vauvert—"against the wall where the cypresses grow"—Olivier only had time for a few more words.

I have just seen the chaplain and said the "Our Father" with him. I said it as never before, and it seemed to me of a sublimity not to be expressed.

Now I have only a few minutes more.

My cell is in disorder...I didn't get the letter you sent me; it must be still at the Tribunal.

Yes, France will live. Men are cowards, traitors, rotters. But France is pure, clean, vital.

I am happy. I'm not dying for any faction or man. I'm dying for my own idea of serving *her*, my country...and for you too whom I adore.

I'm happy I love you.

The door is opening.

Adieu

I hug you both

Olivier

Through the Girans Michel had followed Olivier's fate to the end; but it was only some time later that he learnt the full story and not till after the war that the last act was played. This is what had happened.

During the spring of 1942, when he was acting as courier for Michel, Olivier had made the acquaintance of a young man called Carnet, who lived at Morteau, close to the Swiss frontier. Thinking that Carnet might be useful to him, he had taken him partly into his confidence and introduced him to his parents.

Shortly after Olivier's arrest at Dijon station, Carnet himself was caught trying to cross the frontier. He was then offered his freedom if he agreed to work for the Germans. At the same time they threatened that, if he refused, his mother would be arrested too.

Under this double incentive Carnet accepted the offer and began his new career by bringing fresh charges against Olivier. It was as a result of this that Olivier was removed, first from Dijon to Fresnes, and then from Fresnes to Angers; and that his interrogation by the Gestapo started all over again.

For the Germans, who had accepted his story that he was simply a smuggler operating for money, now knew a good deal more, including the fact, which he had rashly revealed to Carnet, that Olivier was in touch with the Allies.

How much more, if any, was extracted from him by torture will never be known; one is entitled to suppose very little. The only member of the *réseau* known to him was Michel, and the fact that the latter was not arrested himself confirms the truth of Olivier's assertion that he betrayed no one. Like others before and after him, he was faithful unto death.

There was nothing exceptional about Olivier Giran. He was just an ordinary young man with a young man's love of life and adventure; and only one of the thousands of his country-men who died in the same way and for the same cause. They may not have contributed much to the Allied victory, but for France they did something more important. By their heroism and their sacrifice they saved her honour and restored her proud place among the nations. For this all free men should be grateful.

Not content with sending Olivier to his death, Carnet next denounced his father; as a result of which the latter, who had already been arrested once and released, was re-arrested.

M. Giran, a distinguished Protestant theologian and historian, had written an open letter to Marshal Pétain protesting against his gesture in shaking hands with Hitler—"in the name of the French people"—on the occasion of their meetimg at Montoire in 1940. Combined with the pro-Allied activities of his son, this was enough to condemn him. He was deported and died at Buchenwald in 1944.

It often happens, once a man has turned traitor, that he works harder for the enemy than he did for his own side. Perhaps he feels that having lost his honour, he has nothing more to lose; and might just as well, therefore, make a success of his treachery.

This was the case of Carnet. After winning the confidence of the Germans he extended his activities to Switzerland. Posing as a *résistant* he sought out other Frenchmen, who had clandestinely crossed the frontier, lured them back to France and then handed them over.

Eventually the suspicions of the Swiss were aroused. Carnet

was arrested, mercilessly grilled and ended by making a full confession, including his betrayal of Olivier.

Condemned to death in 1945, he was actually standing blindfolded in front of the firing squad when a motor cyclist arrived with an order staying the execution. The German Army had capitulated that morning and with the cessation of hostilities, under Swiss law, the death penalty was not permissible. Carnet's sentence was commuted to life imprisonment and he is still serving it in a Swiss jail.

When Olivier's fate hung in the balance Michel himself had been in trouble for a different reason. As we have seen, in his business capacity he always refused to have any truck with the enemy; and although he could have sold many gas engines to the Germans, he invariably declined their orders or made some excuse.

Finally, in the spring of 1942, two officers called at his office and made a requisitioning order. By virtue of this all gas engines received thereafter from the Dijon factory were to be delivered to the Occupying Authority.

Michel accepted the order but made no attempt to comply with it. Instead he arranged for the engines, which were normally delivered to his own workshop in Paris, to be sent direct to the customer.

This went on for some weeks, and then one day he received a summons to appear before the German magistrate in Paris. He did not attend the hearing and in his absence was sentenced to six weeks' imprisonment at Fort d'Hauteville, Dijon. He was given fourteen days to comply with the judgment.

Michel was now in a quandary. If he refused to obey he would put himself outside the law, and might be forced to go into hiding. This would make it impossible to carry on his business and might seriously interfere with his secret activities.

If on the other hand he served the sentence, the Germans might leave him alone afterwards. Several of his friends, whom he consulted, advised this course. Michel himself was undecided and to help make up his mind resolved to inspect the prison. After all, six weeeks was quite a long time and it was just as well to see the place first.

Fort d'Hauteville was an ancient fortress which had been

converted into a prison. Surrounded by an empty moat and a wall, it appeared as a gigantic earthwork, in the sides of which tunnels had been cut to allow some light to penetrate to the cells within. It did not seem to be very well guarded and Michel had no difficulty in approaching. In fact, the only living thing he could see was a goat grazing in the moat.

All the same, he thought, it might not be easy to escape if he decided to serve his sentence and then changed his mind. He measured the height of the wall with his eye, calculating the chances of scaling it unassisted. In doing so he noticed that there was an electric cable running right round the perimeter and serving a number of searchlights.

The cable passed not far from where he was standing—on a grassy slope overlooking the moat. The opportunity seemed too good to miss. In any case it would be something to justify his journey. Dropping on his stomach he wriggled forward until by leaning down he could reach the cable. Then he took out his knife and using the saw blade neatly severed the copper wire. After that he felt less inclined than ever to march up to the gate and request admission.

Still undecided he returned to Paris and the same evening called on the Girans to hear the latest news of Olivier. They had just come back from Dijon, where they had tried to see him in prison, and had themselves been detained and questioned by the Gestapo. Among other things, M. Giran had been asked why his son was carrying a document showing him to be a traveller in *gazogènes;* to which he had replied that it had no doubt been obtained for him by his employer, M. Hollard, a highly reputable business man. At the mention of Michel's name the policeman had made a face, as though he knew all about him and nothing good.

This was quite sufficient to make up Michel's mind. He now knew that if he gave himself up he would certainly be questioned on his connection with Olivier, which, taken in conjunction with his conviction for "non-collaboration," would be still more suspect. There was only one thing to do: disappear.

A few more days had still to run before the fortnight's grace expired, but already he was conscious of being under supervision. Several times he discovered that inquiries had been made for him at some café or other rendezvous which he had just left.

He avoided sleeping at home and only visited his flat or office at safe times. The German police had very regular habits and rarely arrested a man at meal time, or after office hours, unless it were the early morning.

Two or three days after his return from Dijon, two Germans officers called at the flat. It was about twelve in the morning and Mme. Hollard was alone. She was not surprised, since although she knew nothing about it, and they never discussed the matter, she had realised for some time past that Michel was engaged in secret work.

Assuming an air of indifference, she explained that she and her husband were more or less estranged, that she seldom saw him and had no idea where he was. However, he occasionally sent her a postcard and when he did so again she would let the gentleman know.

This appeared to satisfy the visitors, who thanked her for her "co-operation" and took their departure. As soon as they had gone Mme. Hollard hurried out, and from the nearest café telephoned a message to Michel's office, asking him to ring her back "at the usual place." This was another café which they always used for telephoning. Michel then telephoned from *outside* his office, when she told him what had happened.

It was decided he should leave Paris at once after putting it about that he was retiring from business; and the same night he took the train to Toulouse. From there he sent a card to Mme. Hollard, informing her that he intended to settle in that region. This she duly showed to the Gestapo, who again expressed their gratitude for her "helpful" attitude.

At the same time Michel wrote his secretary a letter, which he intended to be intercepted, instructing her to close the office after settling all accounts. What the letter did not say— and he had already arranged with her—was that she was immediately to look for new offices and reopen the business under a different name.

After a week's absence Michel returned to Paris and by the

beginning of August was installed in new premises—at 43 Rue Beaubourg—and trading under a new name: the *Office Téchnique du Gazogène de France*. In fact, however, he scarcely ever went there, leaving the direction of the business entirely to the secretary.

It seemed he had shaken off the scent, but he was still concerned about his family. In September he moved them to a *pension*, and a few months later found a more permanent home in the suburbs, where, thanks to an understanding with the Mayor of the *commune*, they were reasonably safe from being discovered.

From now on, however, he himself was on the run.

7

ILLEGAL PASSAGE

After the arrest of Olivier Giran, Michel resumed his rôle of courier himself.

He was not entirely sorry to do so. He had missed the periodical contact with B——, with the chance, once in a while, to breathe free air and to hear news of the world outside the prison that France was rapidly becoming.

During the summer and autumn his arrangements for leaving and returning to France worked without a serious hitch. The two critical obstacles were the line of demarcation of the *Zone Rouge* and the immediate vicinity of the frontier, and for both he had evolved an improved technique.

When he arrived from Dijon at the Cusey lock, always at a pre-arranged time, M. Vrignon would be waiting and if Germans were about would make a warning signal. On the return journey he cycled straight to the lock-keeper's house, which, being inside the zone, could be approached openly.

From the windows of the house the German sentries could be seen. If one of them came too close, a diversionary operation might be necessary. In this case, Mme. Vrignon would stroll out, engage the soldier in conversation and manoeuvre until his back was turned to the lock. Michel would then slip out of the house, pass through the barrier and disappear in the dusk.

For the frontier he always telephoned Cuenot the day before, to inform him at what time he would be arriving "to collect the load of charcoal." Cuenot then arranged to go on ahead, and if the valley was clear of Germans he opened a window of the farm-house. On the return journey the "green light" was the open barn door.

Thus all went well until the coming of winter. Then one day Michel arrived at Derrière-le-Mont to find snow covering the ground. Since this was a new hazard he decided to wait for nightfall when his tracks were less likely to be seen.

Setting out after dark he climbed the familiar path until it brought him to the edge of the forest. Below him the valley gleamed white in the starlight, making every dark object more conspicuous. Worse, the snow had stopped falling, so that his footsteps remained visible should a German patrol pass. In that case he would be in danger from an ambush on his return.

While he was considering what to do, he noticed that there was a barbed wire fence extending right across the valley. It ran from a point near where he was standing, down to the stream, and up the slope on the farther side, to end where the forest began again. This gave him an idea.

Placing his feet on the bottom wire and holding on to the top one, he began to walk sideways along the fence. As anyone knows who has tried, this is a tedious process at the best of times; in Michel's circumstances it was excruciating. While the stillness of the night was shattered by the twanging of the wire, he was horribly conscious of his black form vividly silhouetted by its white background.

Half a dozen times, as he hooked himself on a barb, or struggled to keep his balance when the wire sagged, he was almost in a mind to give up; but telling himself this would be illogical, he continued his crab-like progress and eventually arrived safely at the edge of the wood.

Determined never to repeat this experience, the next time he tried attaching his boots back to front. He also made the same experiment with the snow shoes. But apart from their discomfort these ruses were dangerous; they might mislead the enemy as to the direction he had taken, but could not conceal his passage of the frontier.

Reluctantly he decided he must find another route, below the snow line; and after careful investigation of various localities selected two alternatives.

The first was a good way farther north, at a place called Villars-les-Blamont. This was a small village on the main road between Pont-de-Ronde, in France, and Porrentruy, in Switzerland. Here Michel discovered two valuable accomplices, Emile Mathiot and his wife Geneviève.

Emile was about thirty-five, short, sturdy and extremely talkative. He had served during the war in a regiment of Zouaves and was now employed in a tool factory ten miles away.

Geneviève, ten years younger, was a blonde with blue eyes, always very neatly dressed. She kept chickens and a goat and grew vegetables in a small garden.

Their home was a two-room bungalow, built on a steep bank overlooking the main road. Behind it the ground rose gently to a plateau, beyond which was a wood. The edge of the wood marked the frontier. It was about four hundred yards away.

As soon as Michel arrived at the bungalow, Geneviève would leave, driving her goat, and let it graze along the fringe of the wood. On reaching the highest point she took a good look round, then turned and faced the bungalow. This was the signal for Michel to start.

Half-way to the wood was a patch of bushes. Here he remained in hiding to await a further signal. This was a red handkerchief which Geneviève dropped if the coast was still clear. He then made a dash and gained the shelter of the wood, where he was safe on Swiss soil. For the return journey, always at a pre-arranged time, the process was reversed, except that he avoided the bungalow. This was so as not to compromise the Mathiots should he be seen by a German.

Apart from the assistance of the Mathiots, this route had the advantage of being close to the village of Glay, where Michel had a son at school. In consequence there was always a good excuse for his presence.

The second alternative route, and the one he eventually

came to use most often, crossed the frontier at a point south of the Lake of Geneva, and about ten miles from Geneva itself, between Machilly (France) and Jussy (Switzerland). A side road, little used, connected the two villages and the whole district was thickly wooded.

This made the approach to the frontier relatively safe, but the actual crossing was not so easy, as it was obstructed by a barbed wire entanglement three feet high and six feet across. Beyond this obstacle was a stream, which marked the boundary.

On all his expeditions Michel dressed like a peasant, in blue canvas jacket, brown corduroys and beret. In his hands he carried a spade, a hoe, or an axe, and on his back a sack partly filled with potatoes under which were hidden any compromising documents. Thus if he ran into a patrol they would suppose he was a farmer or a forester engaged on legitimate business.

For the Machilly-Jussy route he took the train from Annecy, and got off at the station of La Roches Foron, where there was a wait of fifteen minutes. This gave him time to go to the buffet and collect a parcel, which he left there permanently. It contained, besides his peasant's clothes, a disguise as a railwayman: cap, armlet, leather pouch, lantern and the symbolic piece of cotton waste.

As soon as the train started he locked himself in the lavatory...to emerge a few minutes later looking the typical *cheminot*. Over his city suit he was wearing the blue jacket and corduroys—the common uniform of all workmen in France—and on top of this again the accoutrements of the railwayman. The sack of potatoes and the beret remained for the time being in the parcel.

When the train stopped at Machilly he opened the door away from the platform, jumped down on the track and started walking back along it, while stopping occasionally as though to inspect the line. Naturally nobody took any notice.

After going about five hundred yards he arrived at a culvert. Here he left the track, disappeared under the arch and retrieved a woodsman's axe from its hiding-place. In its place he hid the parcel, after removing the sack of potatoes and repacking the railwayman's insignia. Then, dressed as a peasant, he shouldered the sack and the axe and set off across the fields.

Ten minutes' walk brought him to a farm, whose occupant,

a M. Paccot, was his friend. From him he learnt if any Germans were in the vicinity. When the coast was clear he crossed a couple more fields, entered the wood and soon reached the frontier.

Once on Swiss territory he went straight to the nearest customs post, where by arrangement with the Swiss Military Intelligence he was by now an accepted visitor. There he removed his peasant's clothes, and with his axe and his sack locked them in a cupboard which was specially reserved for him. Shortly after he was on his way to the station looking like any other business man.

In three years Michel crossed the frontier forty-nine times in both directions without being caught. He never missed an appointment in Switzerland and was never more than a day late. This remarkable achievement was due partly to the pains he took in planning each expedition and partly to the help he received on each side of the frontier. In particular the devotion of his compatriots—the friendly farmers who gave him shelter and reconnoitred the ground—did most to ensure his safety.

But though he was never actually caught, he had several narrow escapes. Of these the closest occurred on the Machilly-Jussy route towards the end of 1941—that is before he became known to the Swiss frontier guards in that area.

He had carried out the usual routine, done his double-change act, received the "all clear" from M. Paccot, and was in the act of negotiating the barbed wire entanglement when suddenly his knee was seized and held.

Without betraying its presence a German police dog had approached and pounced before he had either seen or heard it.

He struggled to free himself but could not move his leg. The strength of the animal was unbelievable; it was not biting, just holding, but the hold was vice-like.

Michel was unarmed—he had thrown sack and axe across the wire. Desperately he looked round for a weapon. On the ground, just within reach, was a stout length of branch, broken off and jagged at one end. He seized it and, inserting it between the jaws of the dog, thrust with all his strength.

The stick penetrated deep into the animal's throat, but still it hung on. Michel maintained the pressure until his hand was almost inside its mouth; then abruptly the grip on him relaxed as the unfortunate beast rolled over, dead.

Regardless of the barbs Michel scrambled across the obstacle. As he landed on the other side a Swiss frontier guard stepped from behind a tree with his rifle raised to his shoulder. It was not, however, pointed at Michel. The guard shouted a challenge in German and looking round Michel saw that two German soldiers were covering him from the other side of the fence with their guns.

At the summons of the Swiss they lowered their arms, whereupon Michel jumped the stream and safely gained Swiss territory.

After some further altercation the Germans withdrew grumbling, and Michel turned to thank his saviour.

"Oh, I wasn't trying to save *you*," the guard interrupted. "By pointing their guns in this direction those two were violating Swiss soil. That is forbidden by international law and it was my duty to stop it."

Brave little nation of hotel keepers! It is the fashion to make jokes at their expense, but Hitler took them seriously and many an Allied life was saved by their stubborn refusal to cede an inch of their right as neutrals prepared to defend their neutrality.

Having resisted one act of aggression, it was now the duty of the guard to oppose another. He therefore informed the invader that he was under arrest and must accompany him to the *poste*. There, after his wounds had been dressed, Michel was politely requested to return by the way he had come. It was only after disclosing his identity, and contact had been made with the Swiss Military Intelligence, that he was allowed to continue his journey.

Soon after this incident the Germans constructed a second barrier, immediately behind the first, consisting of a barbed wire fence six feet high, and clearings were made in the forest so that it could be kept continually under observation. Since it took some time to cut a breach and repair it, Michel usually climbed this obstacle, after throwing his sack and his implement.

On two occasions , however, he was accompanied by ladies, for whom climbing was out of the question. The first was his mother, whom he was conducting to Switzerland for her safety. This time all went well. Michel cut a gap to a height of five feet and when Mme. Hollard had passed through reconnected the strands.

A few weeks later he was accompanying a woman and her son. Leaving his companions to be escorted by a friendly peasant, he went on ahead to prepare the way; and had just finished cutting the last wire when a German patrol came in sight. Seizing his axe he started hacking furiously at a sapling. At that moment, to his consternation, the rest of his party appeared at the end of the path.

Making a sign to them to lie down, Michel continued to hack at his tree and so contrived things that it fell as the German were passing. The two soldiers looked at him respectfully, exchanged a few words, gave him a smile and passed on, without so much as glancing at the fence where the severed strands trailed guiltily on the ground. A few moments later mother and son were standing on neutral soil.

Usually, if he met with a mishap, it was through disobeying his own rules. One of them was never to make the attempt at night, and another not to risk it when the snow was falling. He adopted these rules after several bad experiences, of which one was nearly disastrous.

He was using a new route and had left St. Claude, which lies north-west of Geneva, with the intention of crossing the frontier at Combe du Faoug, some twenty-five miles away. After covering fifteen of them, mostly by paths, he arrived as dusk was falling at a friendly farm where he often spent the night.

It was in the depths of winter, the sky was completely covered and there was every prospect of a new fall of snow. Nevertheless he decided to push on. In front of him was a ten mile walk, mostly through woods and climbing all the way.

He had not gone far before snow began to fall; not heavily but sufficiently to cover the path, so that it was no longer possible, by searching with his foot, to know if he was following it or not.

For three hours he struggled on, sometimes stumbling into a ditch or colliding with a tree, following his instinct rather than any landmark.

Finally he had to admit he was lost. If he had been going in the right direction he should now be near the frontier, but he was surrounded by trees which gave no indication. It was quite possible, for all he could tell, that he had been travelling in a circle.

By this time visibility was reduced to nil and he was practically feeling his way from tree to tree. He had the sensation of being imprisoned by some intangible substance which extended indefinitely in every direction.

To master the panic which was beginning to take a hold of him, he stopped and rested his back against a tree trunk. He forced himself to consider the situation objectively.

There were only two alternatives. One was to stay where he was till daylight, the other to keep on trying. If he chose the first—and was not frozen to death—dawn might find him on the beat of a patrol. Somehow or other he had to find his way out.

He decided to proceed methodically. Marking his tree with a mound of snow, he started walking in a direction at right angles to that from which he had come, at the same time counting his steps. When he had counted a thousand he stopped. Nothing had changed. Still the silent anonymous forest hemmed him in on all sides.

By occasionally lighting a match he was able to retrace his steps. Having arrived back at his starting point, he turned ninety degrees and set off again. At the end of his thousand paces all looked the same.

Changing direction once more, he started on his third and last experiment. Eight hundred...nine hundred and fifty... eighty...ninety...ninety-five...it hardly seemed worth going on...six...seven...eight...nine...

He was counting aloud and as he uttered the fatal "thousand" his knee bumped against an obstacle. Michel felt for the object with his hands. It was too smooth to be a tree—probably a post of some kind. He lit a match and saw that it indeed was a post and had something painted on its surface: the badge of the Swiss Confederation!

As always when he escaped from danger, Michel's immediate reaction was to fall on his knees and offer up a prayer of thanks, together with one for the safety of his family.

Some months later he had an escape of a more dramatic kind. He had finished his business in Switzerland and towards evening found himself at Nyon, on the Lake of Geneva. There, if he had obeyed his rule, he should have stayed the night.

But it was summer, the weather was fine and there were still several hours of daylight. He decided to leave at once and make for the frontier at La Rippe, whence a walk of twenty miles would bring him to St. Claude.

From Nyon a train took him to the foot of the mountain. Normally it continued to Divonne, in France, but since the war went no farther than Crassier, the last Swiss village before the frontier. From there to La Rippe was only a few miles.

It was about seven-thirty when Michel left the train. Through open windows he could see family parties at tables and envied their security and well-being. Even the humblest dwellings had an air of prosperity; gaily painted, usually adorned with flower boxes, they were more like villas than cottages.

Soon he was beyond the village and walking briskly along the road. He passed another hamlet where shutters were being closed as the hard-working inhabitants prepared for the night's rest. Again Michel envied them their lot; how pleasant, he thought wistfully, to be indoors and to be able to sleep without fear of the nocturnal visit that haunted the dreams of every *résistant*.

Leaving the hamlet behind he abandoned the road and started to climb through the forest. Immense pine trees towered above him, swaying gently in the evening breeze. Soon it died away as darkness fell.

When he had reached a height of four thousand feet he halted and looked back. The sky was a blaze of stars. Immediately below all was black; but far away the lights of villages glimmered on the lakeside. Beyond that there was another zone of darkness, ending in a brighter glow where the lights of Hermance, on the farther side of the lake, were reflected in the motionless water.

It was a fairy-like spectacle and held Michel rapt. In spite of the war, of the occupation and all its horrors, and the constant state of tension in which he lived, his senses still responded to the stimulus of beauty. In fact it seemed that they were rendered more receptive, on the rare occasions when he had time to stop and gaze, by the extraordinary conditions of his existence. Perhaps it was the lack of security, the result of living constantly in fear of arrest, which made him savour aesthetic pleasure with a special intensity, as something he might never experience again.

He resumed his upward march, pointing to La Combe du Foug, where a deserted châlet, some eight hundred yards from the frontier, would give him his bearing for the last stretch. As he drew near he advanced with caution, pausing frequently to listen.

He had passed the châlet and proceeded a short distance when he heard, quite close, a voice in German call *Halt!* He stopped dead and remained rooted, holding his breath.

The challenge was repeated. At the same time there was the sound of a firearm being made ready.

Michel was nonplussed. He knew he was still on Swiss territory. But if it was a Swiss guard he had run into, why should he speak German? In this part of their country the Swiss spoke French.

In any case, how could the man see him? It was pitch dark under the trees and he himself could see nothing. In fact he had been steering by a pocket compass, illuminated, like a watch, with a phosphorescent needle.

Then it dawned upon him that a German patrol might have crossed by mistake to the wrong side of the frontier. At the same instant he realised what had given him away—and cursed his own carelessness.

This is what had happened.

At their periodic meetings his British contact always produced a new packet of Players, which they both smoked during the interview. On parting he would hand the packet to Michel, who although he smoked very little always accepted it as a talisman. However, he made it a rule never to light up until he was safely across the frontier. By disregarding his rule for once he had betrayed his presence to the enemy.

The end of the cigarette was still glowing brightly. Michel took a pin from the lapel of his coat and nailed the butt to a tree trunk. Then, bending double, he stole away in the opposite direction from which the challenge had come.

A few seconds later he heard it repeated again. There was a brief interval, then the sound of two shots. Since they came nowhere near him he concluded his ruse had worked, and that the Germans were firing at his abandoned cigarette.

Making a wide detour he crossed the frontier at another point, found his path and a few hours later arrived at the station of St. Claude.

Excellent Player! he thought gratefully, as he relaxed in the train that was taking him back to Paris. Only an English cigarette would have continued to burn so brightly. Lucky it wasn't a *Gauloise*—especially a war-time *Gauloise*!

Another time it was the enemy's cigarette that saved him. He had started on his journey rather late and only arrived at the frontier when night had already fallen. As he approached Swiss territory he practically trod on two Germans who were resting with their backs against a tree. Fortunately, one of them was in the act of lighting a cigarette and the glare of the match prevented either of them from spotting Michel.

When he reached the customs house half an hour later, the Swiss *douanier* was already in bed. Aroused by Michel's voice, he put his head out of the window.

"Oh, it's you," he said, not too pleased at being awakened.

"I want to speak to you," said Michel.

Grumbling, the Swiss withdrew his head and a few minutes later appeared downstairs.

"What's the matter?" he demanded. "Did you have any trouble in crossing?"

"No," replied Michel, "but I've got some bad news. My wife is in the act of being unfaithful to me."

"Why do you say that? How can you possibly know?"

"Because only a *cocu* could have the luck which has just befallen me."

8

THE LIGHTING OF THE TORCH

Early on the morning of the 8th November, 1942, Michel was sitting in a third-class compartment in the train which was carrying him from Dijon to Besançon. He had spent the night as usual, at the Hotel du Lycée and was dressed in the blue canvas jacket, brown corduroy trousers and beret which he always wore for his expeditions across the frontier. In the rack above him was the mud-stained hessian sack, half filled with potatoes, which concealed the papers he was taking to the British Embassy in Berne.

Besides himself in the compartment were three other passengers. Two of them—a fat woman of forty and a middle-aged man, both of the *petit bourgeois* class—kept up a steady conversation. The fourth passenger, who sat opposite Michael, took no part in it and appeared to be asleep.

The conversation ran mostly on the difficulties of life: rationing, shortages, and so forth. Michael paid little attention, but when the talk turned to politics he began to take more interest.

It was soon obvious that both conversationalists were de-featists. Although this annoyed Michel, he refrained for a time from intervening; but when the woman remarked it would make no difference who won the war—there being nothing to choose between the Germans and the British—he could contain himself no longer.

"What you say is quite untrue," he interrupted. "The dif-ference is between slavery and freedom. And any Frenchman who thinks otherwise is either ignorant or a traitor."

It was now about six a.m. and the train was just entering Besançon station. At the beginning of the platform there was a hut, used by the German railway police. Michel's compart-ment was right at the front, and as it passed the hut the fourth passenger suddenly roused himself, opened the window, and shouted in German. *"Friedrich, komm hierher mit jemandem!"* ("Frederick, come here with someone!")

Michel, who knew enough German to understand, immedi-ately realised his danger. As the train slowed down he got up to leave the compartment, which the other two had already vacated. At this the fourth passenger sprang in front of him and tried to close the sliding door.

Michel just had time to jam his foot in the doorway, and in the struggle that followed he succeeded in getting first his head and then his shoulder into the gap. As he was striving to wedge the rest of the body through it, the stranger, who was doing his utmost to pin him with the door, suddenly aimed a blow at his head. It caught Michel just above the eye and cut him badly, but in delivering it his assailant had to let go of the door handle. This enabled Michel to force the door open. At the same time he swung his free elbow backwards. It landed in the other's stomach, knocked him over and winded him.

As the stranger lay on the floor, gasping for breath, Michel dashed down the corridor, wrenched open the first door and jumped down the track. After crossing to the far side, he started walking down the line and in a quarter of an hour reached a small local station, where he always left his bicycle when returning from Switzerland.

Blood was still running from the cut above his eye and his clothes were stained with gore. Seeing the railway clerk eyeing him suspiciously, he explained that he had run into a pillar—it was still dark outside—and then proceed to abuse the railway company for providing such wretched lighting.

The clerk shrugged his shoulders. "You shouldn't be in such a hurry," he remarked as he handed over Michel's bicycle.

It had been a close shave. But for the fact that he was travelling in the front of the train, so that by the time it stopped there was the length of the platform between himself and the German police post, and the lucky blow which knocked out his enemy, he would have been arrested and the documents in his sack discovered.

Worst of all, it had been his own fault.

It was about eight hours later when he rang the bell at the Chancellery offices. As usual, he was received by B—— in the hall; but instead of leading the way into his own office the Englishman knocked at an adjoining door and a moment later was introducing him to his chief, whom Michel had never met.

Colonel Cartwright, the Military Attaché, although dressed like B——, in civilian clothes, was unmistakably a soldier. Ruddy and rather weather-beaten, with bright blue eyes and a red moustache, he wore the well-cut tweeds and impeccably polished brown shoes of the regular army officer seen lunching in any service club.

Advancing with both hands held out he greeted Michel cordially; but immediately spotting the cut above his eye changed his expression and sternly demanded an explanation. He then proceeded to give his visitor a thorough dressing-down. It was no part of a secret agent's business, he would have M. Hollard know, to enter into conversation with strangers, much less get involved in an argument. In fact, it was a damn fool thing to do, and had it turned out badly he had only himself to blame.

Michel listened humbly, occasionally mopping his eye, only too conscious of his fault.

Having delivered his lecture, Colonel Cartwright abruptly changed his manner again and turned on Michel with a beaming smile.

"And now," he said portentously, "I have to announce

great news. Anglo-American forces have landed in North Africa and are already firmly established."

He went to a filing cabinet, produced a bottle and poured three glasses. It was whisky, which Michel had not seen since the war. The glasses were solemnly clinked and a joyful toast drunk to the success of Operation Torch.

"And now to work," said the colonel when he had emptied his glass. "I asked B—— to bring you along because we need your help. We don't know yet what the Germans will do, but we expect their reaction to be pretty drastic. They'll certainly reinforce in Africa, and they'll probably move into the Free Zone. They may even go into Spain—or Italy. Anyhow, we shall get an idea from troop movements and that's what we want you to watch. You've given us some very useful information and I think you can get a lot more."

This was the first time Michel had received either a commendation for the past or a specific directive for the future. In spite of the cut over his eye, which was now hurting a good deal, he felt that his stock was going up with the British.

Shortly after Colonel Cartwright terminated the interview. Holding Michel's hand in both of his, he said, "Remember, we're counting on you—but no more incidents in railway carriages, please!"

As far as Michel was concerned, and for most Frenchmen, this was the turning point of the war. They had not heard of the battle of El Alamein, fought only a fortnight previously; or if they had it was only as an event of little significance. But now the war had returned to French territory, which could only be a stepping stone to France itself. It showed that the allies were determined to drive the invader from their soil.

Three days later this impression was confirmed by the German occupation of the Free Zone. That in the eyes of the French could only mean that the Allies planned to land in the south of France.

The effect was to encourage the patriots, shake the confidence of the Vichyites, and help the undecided to make up their minds. Most of the last category lived in the *Midi* and it only needed the presence of German troops to topple them off their fence and on to the right side. If prior to the 11th

November, 1942, there were perhaps twenty per cent of "collabos," fifteen per cent undecided, and sixty-five per cent pro-Ally, subsequent to it the proportion was more like fifteen per cent of "collabos" and eighty-five per cent pro-Ally. In other words, France henceforth was overwhelmingly pro-Ally, with a hard core of Vichyites forming the minority.

For Michel this shift in opinion was of capital importance. It meant that he could now depend, in a greater measure than ever, on the tacit or active assistance of the honest citizen when and wherever he needed it.

The occupation of the Free Zone had resulted in a major redeployment of German forces. While some divisions were being moved south, others were arriving to replace them. On the roads and railways there was an incessant movement of troops and materials.

As Colonel Cartwright had impressed on Michel, it was vital to the Allies to be informed of these changes quickly. Axis troops had already landed in Tunisia. Nobody knew what Hitler's next counter-stroke would be.

Since Michel had no agents working in the Free Zone, the urgent need was to recruit suitable observers on the roads and railways which the Germans were using.

For road transport the main artery to the south was *Route Nationale* 7, which goes from Lyons to Nice via Valence, Avignon and Aix-en-Provence. It was essential to have at least one agent posted on it.

One of the best hotels on this road was the Hôtellerie de Pierrelatte, about half-way between Valence and Avignon. Built in *Provençal* style, with white walls and a red roof, and famous for its *cuisine*, it was the favourite stopping place for high-ranking German officers looking for a meal or a bed.

Michel had known the place before the war and had a slight acquaintance with the proprietress, Madame Simone Boirel. A woman of thirty-five, with lively brown eyes and the features and accent of a *Provençale*, she had inherited the hotel from her father and ran it with her husband, who was also the chef. Vivacious and energetic, always smiling, she was the perfect *patronne* who makes her customers feel welcome and takes a personal interest in the needs of each.

A few days after his return from Switzerland Michel arrived at the hotel. He had already followed the movement of one panzer division from Lyons to Marseilles and had observed the installation of its H.Q. at the Hotel de Noailles. He now invited Mme. Boirel to join the *réseau* with the special mission of keeping him informed of all military traffic passing on *Route Nationale* 7, and of all important German officers who stopped at the hotel. She accepted at once.

This was the beginning of an association which, although it was to end in disaster, proved highly fruitful during the next two years. While her devotion to the cause was never in doubt, Simone Boirel was in the happy position of being able to combine patriotism with business. The more popular she became with the German Army, and the higher the reputation of her hotel with its General Staff, the more successful she was as Michel's agent.

She never had any difficulty in identifying the Generals. They were always so pleased to be asked to write in her autograph book; it made them feel they had made an impression on the attractive Mme. Boirel. And when she begged them to send her a postcard from their next address, they usually promised to do so—and did!—sometimes adding such interesting items of information as that they would shortly be moving on, or returning to Germany and would visit her again on the way.

Since it was dangerous for Michel to stop at the hotel, their meetings always took place on the train, when he was returning from his tour of the south. The train arrived at Pierrelatte at three-forty a.m. Michel always travelled in the last compartment and would open the door as a sign for Simone to get in. While they stood together in the corridor, conversing like chance acquaintances, she handed him a note-book, which he then retired to the lavatory to read. Having torn out the pages containing her report, he returned to the corridor and continued the conversation.

At four-four a.m. the train arrived at Montelimar. Simone got off and after a wait of forty minutes took another train back to Pierrelatte. Soon after five she was in her home again, where everybody was still asleep and nobody but her husband had been aware of her absence.

Having provided for a watch to be kept on the road, Michel next turned his attention to the railways. There were two main lines from Lyons to the south and they followed the left and right banks of the Rhone respectively. South of Avignon they united and then continued as one line through Tarascon to Marseilles, Toulon and the Riviera. Tarascon was thus a point of convergence for all traffic in transit for the Mediterranean whether from north, east, or west.

From discreet inquiries among station employees Michel had discovered that the *sous-chef de gare* (deputy stationmaster), by name Lemeau, was very anti-German; and had persuaded him to act as his agent. When, however, a few days later he arrived to collect the first report, Lemeau was not at the rendezvous. He would probably be found at a signal box, a porter informed Michel, about a mile down the line. Michel at once set off in pursuit.

When he arrived at the box Lemeau was talking to the signalman. At the sight of Michel he looked embarrassed but agreed to accompany him outside. It was obvious that he had changed his mind and was trying to avoid a second encounter.

After walking a little way along the track, they left it at Michel's suggestion and scrambled down the embankment to a place where they were hidden by a clump of trees.

Michel so far had said nothing. He was considering how to tackle his man. The interview, he realised, was crucial. As *sous-chef* Lemeau was responsible for the service on that sector, and probably the only person in a position to obtain the detailed information Michel needed.

If he refused his help, all would have to start again, but with the outcome prejudiced by an initial setback. Indeed, for all Michel knew, Lemeau might have denounced him already— although he thought this unlikely.

As always when the situation was critical, Michel's awareness of his surroundings was heightened. It was late afternoon and the countryside stretched in undisturbed peace to the horizon. It was a flat landscape of ploughed fields, enclosed by hawthorn hedges, only relieved by an occasional farmhouse. A few miles away a level line of poplars marked the left bank of the Rhone, while to the east the sharp spire of a church rose above the distant sky-line. Although it was winter this was the *Midi* and there was a scent of flowering rushes in the air.

Making no reference to their broken appointment, Michel pretended that he himself had been reconsidering the matter. Perhaps, he suggested, he had not sufficiently emphasised the danger. Many Frenchmen had already lost their lives doing such work, and he would not like Lemeau to take it on under any illusion as to the risk he would be running. On the other hand it was of vital importance that Frenchmen should play their part in the liberation of France.

He talked for quite a time on these lines, while Lemeau listened in silence without betraying his thoughts. He seemed to be struggling with some emotion which inhibited him from speaking.

At last Michel judged that the moment was ripe. Looking the *sous-chef* in the face with a smile he said: "Well, now you know the worst, are you prepared to work with me?"

Lemeau made no reply, but lowering his head as though in shame gave a nod of assent. This time Michel knew that he meant it.

Without exchanging another word they shook hands and separated; Lemeau to return to the station, while Michel made his way across country to the town.

The *sous-chef* kept his promise. When Michel returned a week later he was handed a complete account of every German convoy that had gone through in the interval.

From then on there was no more conscientious member of the *réseau* than Lemeau. It was as if he were determined to atone for his moment of hesitation. This, as he later confessed to Michel, had been the result of a circular sent out by Vichy, and received on the very morning after their first meeting, instructing all railway officials, under pain of severe penalties, to co-operate to their utmost in the transport of the *Wehrmacht*.

At Lemeau's suggestion Michel shortly afterwards recruited two other key railwaymen, employed at Le Teil and Portes-lès-Valance respectively. These were strategically important goods stations and between them controlled all traffic proceeding south on either side of the Rhone.

Thanks to these four new agents Michel obtained each

week a complete picture of the German trek southwards and punctually passed it on to Berne.

This, however, was only a beginning. With the enemy in occupation of the whole of France, the area of Michel's activities was almost doubled. This meant a great expansion of the *réseau*, which henceforth was to stretch from the Channel to the Mediterranean and from the Alps to the Atlantic Ocean.

His first step was to increase the number of full-time agents from six to ten. Next he recruited a further eighteen railway employees — station-masters, inspectors, dispatch clerks, traffic controllers. These were used mainly in connection with German troop movements, although they also supplied other useful information.

At the same time he enlisted the help of a new category of informant, comprising hotel personnel and domestic servants. These were the people employed to wait on the German staff officers in requisitioned hotels or private houses.

They were often very useful. Although the Germans took the usual security measures, it was not very difficult for a *valet de chambre* to discover the name of the General whose trousers he pressed every morning, and eventually to identify his command. If he failed to do so he could at least recognise, among photographs produced by Michel, the face of the owner of the trousers.

This system was soon operating in sixteen towns in the *Midi*. It not only worked well, but had the advantage of being relatively safe. There was no need for Michel to penetrate the enemy's lair; he simply arranged to meet his informant outside at a time when the latter was off duty.

Thus by the end of 1942 membership of the *réseau* was increased to over sixty persons, distributed throughout France.

In addition Michel had established at various strategic points what he called his *maisons sures*. These were the homes of patriots who, knowing him to be an outlaw, could always be relied on to provide him or his agents with safe shelter, rest and food; to give warning of danger or simply to receive and pass messages. Some were farms where Michel stopped on his way to the frontier; others were in the towns where he visited periodically. They were quite indispensable and never once let him down.

Finally to complete his organisation, there was his *voie de garage*, or "parking place", near Compiègne. This was a disused but partly equipped peat-bog, situated at Marest-sur-Matz, in the marshes of the Oise, which Michel had persuaded a wealthy friend to buy. Ostensibly producing fuel for gas engines, in fact it was a place where anyone could hide safely, while on the run from the Gestapo, avoiding forced labour, or having any other reason for avoiding the authorities.

It did produce some fuel, although at a considerable loss to the patriotic proprietor, and all the workmen were provided with the necessary documents to show that they were legitimately employed producing it. They were paid, fed and lodged, and lived in perfect security—for who would think of looking for a "wanted man" in a peat-bog?—until such time as it was considered safe for them to move.

The "parking place" was invaluable and continued to play its rôle, without ever receiving even a visit from the police, until the departure of the Germans from France. It afforded a safe refuge, as well as a means of existence, not only for the members of the *réseau "Agir"*, but for many others in temporary need of disappearing.

How much peat was actually dug is another question.

One further and important change which must be recorded here, followed the events of November, 1942. Shortly after Michel's meeting with Colonel Cartwright, B—— introduced him to another Englishman who arranged that in future he should report to an address in Lausanne.

The new arrangement was a great improvement. As representatives of the War Office the Military Attaché and his assistant were primarily concerned with military matters. Henceforth, Michel would work for the S.I.S.—Secret Intelligence Service—which served all Departments from the Cabinet downwards and was in consequence interested in everything.

Although their personal relations had always been friendly, B—— had never unbent officially and always received Michel's reports with a kind of distant acknowledgment. He studiously avoided committing himself on their value, and, apart from his original directive, never made a request or even offered a suggestion which might have assisted Michel in the work.

This reserve was quite normal, since the utmost caution needed to be exercised to avoid being duped by a "double agent"—that is, one who works for both sides, or pretends to work for one when his loyalty is to the other. An agent had to prove himself before he was taken into confidence. Until then one received whatever he had to offer, while giving nothing away. It was only when the British were convinced that Michel was entirely devoted to the Allied cause and could make a valuable contribution thereto that they were prepared really to co-operate with him.

Thus the significance of the change was that, having served his apprenticeship with the amateurs, he was now considered fit to be handed over to the professionals. At the same time he was promoted from being a casual informant to the status of a trusted ally.

His new contact—always known as "O.P"—was a charming person. In civilian life a successful businessman, with a great knowledge of the Continent and a wide culture, he took to Michel at once, appreciated his worth, and laid himself out to be as helpful as possible.

After this Michel was never left in doubt as to what was wanted of him and how far he had succeeded. He received useful advice as well as precise instructions, and at last had the feeling that in his skilled and dangerous work he was fully backed by the British.

Nor was the encouragement given to him only moral. Until almost his last visit to Berne he had never asked a penny of the British and had borne all expenses of his organisation out of his own pocket. These had greatly increased with the expansion of the *réseau*, while he no longer had any time to give to earning a living.

It was impossible, therefore, to continue without financial assistance. This was now willingly offered and henceforth he received ample funds for his work.

M. and Mme. Ponset outside the shed which they
used for signalling to Michel

Joseph Brocard (Alias Bart)
in Geneva, 1944

Cuenot's farmhouse:
(above) from the French side of the frontier
(below) from the Swiss side, with the barn door
left open as an all-clear signal

9

TRAVELLER IN TROUBLE

With sixty agents operating in as many different areas, who had to be regularly visited, briefed and in some cases paid, Michel was now almost incessantly on the move. Because of the great increase both in the volume and the urgency of his information, he had stepped up the frequency of his visits to Switzerland to once a fortnight; and in the twelve days that elapsed between his return from one visit and departure on the next he had barely time to make his round and collect his agents' reports before setting out once again.

Those in the northern and eastern sectors came to meet him in Paris, but this still left forty to be contacted in the centre and south. His usual itinerary included Dijon, Chalons-Sur-Saône, Lyons, Valence, Le Teil, Pierrelatte, Avignon, Tarascon, Arles, Aix-en-Provence, Nice, Toulon, Marseilles, Nîmes, Montpellier, Sète, Béziers, Narbonne, Carcassonne, Castel-naudary and Toulouse. He travelled by train, using a "sleeper" when possible, so as to store up energy for an emergency and for the gruelling walk across the frontier.

It might be asked how he was able to travel so freely; for

although the Germans now occupied the whole of France they still retained the old line of demarcation between the northern and southern zones, and to cross this a permit was needed.

As the representative of the *Office Téchnique du Gazogène de France*, whose business took him all over the country, Michel had no difficulty in obtaining his *Ausweis*. But once he had crossed the line from north to south, he travelled under a false name with a false identity card in order to leave no tracks of his real self.

Train journeys, of course, were always liable to be dangerous. Apart from their regular control points, the Germans made frequent searches *en route*, when the passengers had to show their documents and be prepared to open their luggage.

That was why Michel, in the early days, always left the train at Dijon and used his bicycle for entering the *Zone Rouge*. Early in 1942, however, the Germans relaxed their control to the extent of only exercising it intermittently. Through friends on either side of the line Michel received warning of the date on which it was to operate and had merely to avoid travelling on that day.

On one occasion, however, he was misinformed, and only discovered five minutes before his train was due at Auxonne, where the control was carried out, that it was to take place that day. Since he was returning from Switzerland with compromising documents—including a new batch of photos of high-ranking *Wehrmacht* officers—and in any case had no permit to be in the *Zone Rouge*, the consequences if he were discovered would be serious. The only hope was to find a hiding-place quickly.

After traversing the length of the train through crowded corridors he reached a luggage van immediately in rear of the engine. It was of an antique type which he had not seen in use since the First World War. At one end there was a little cubicle for the guard, and at the other a boxed-in section, occupying the whole width of the compartment, whose purpose was not apparent.

The guard was sitting in his cubby-hole. At the appearance of Michel he glanced up.

"I'm in trouble," said Michel breathlessly. "I have no permit

and if the Germans find me they'll arrest me. Is there anywhere I can hide?"

The guard shrugged.

"Not here, as you can see for yourself."

Michel looked round desperately. Except for a few pieces
of luggage the van was bare.

"Then I'll have to jump off," said Michel and moved towards the door.

"But that's forbidden," said the guard sharply, getting up
from his seat.

Before he could intervene Michel had opened the door and
was standing on the step outside, ready to jump as soon as the
train slowed down.

At that moment he noticed close beside where he stood a
small door low down in the side of the van. He recognised
this as the entrance to a dog kennel, which explained the
boxed-in section of the van. It was closed from the outside by
a bolt, kept in position by a padlock.

The guard was standing at the window, uncertain what
action he should take.

"Can I hide in there?" Michel asked. Already he could see
the outskirts of the town and a signal-box ahead.

The guard hesitated.

"Nobody will look inside," Michel urged. "But you must
act quickly or it will be too late."

"All right. I'll get the key."

The door was opened and, after Michel had climbed inside
he heard it bolted and locked behind him.

A few minutes later the train drew up in the station. While
he crouched on all fours in his cramped and dirty hiding-
place, Michel, peeping through the ventilating holes, could see
the jack-booted legs of the German railway police preparing
to board the train. A little later he heard them enter the
luggage van. There was a kick on the side of the kennel
followed by the sound of the guard's voice, then the tramp of
retreating footsteps.

At last the Germans left the train, whistles were blown and
the coach began to move. When it was well clear of the
station the guard let Michel out, took one look at him—and
burst into laughter. The kennel could not have been used for

years and its accumulated grime now covered Michel. His hands, face and clothes were black with soot and he looked as though he just emerged from a coal mine.

But he was safe and had been saved once again, not only by his extraordinary luck—it was probably the only luggage van fitted with a kennel still running on the French railways—but by the combination of luck, a cool head and boldness. This is probably what people mean by a "charmed" life.

There was another occasion when his escape was even more sensational. He had been asleep on the train and only awoke in time to discover that some German police, conducting a search had already arrived in the next compartment. Michel sprang up and without even waiting to collect his haversack from the rack started off down the corridor. Before he had reached the end of the coach he heard a shout and looking round saw that the Germans were in the pursuit. He hurried along and reached the rear of the train where a passenger was seated with his back to the door. Fortunately, at that moment the train slowed down to negotiate a curve. Michel said "Excuse me" and, as the passenger moved aside, opened the door, got down on the step and jumped onto the track.

He took a tumble, rolled down a slope, and although not hurt was momentarily dazed. By the time he had picked himself up and taken stock of the situation—he was in open country with no cover close by—the train had drawn up and he could see the two Germans descend on the line and start looking round. While he was considering his next move— whether to run along the track or strike across the fields— another train appeared round the tail of the first. It was a long goods convoy and, like the other, had slowed down in order to negotiate the curve. Michel took a quick decision and as the last vehicle—an empty guards van—drew level with him, he jumped for the step, grabbed a handle and retained his hold.

Half an hour later the goods train stopped at a small station. Michel abandoned his perch and sought out the station-master whom he had never seen before.

"Listen," he said. "There's something I wish you'd do for me. I had to change trains hurriedly and I left my haversack in the one that arrives at Tarascon at eleven twenty-two. Since it goes no farther the people there should be able to find it. Would you telephone through and ask them to hold it till my next visit? It contains nothing of value except a new raincoat which I would not like to lose!"

The station-master promised to do his best and in due course Michel recovered his raincoat. But he had to wait until after the war for an opportunity to thank the station-master.

Some months later he was travelling again on the Auxonne line. This time he had his permit, but, as on the previous occasion, was carrying compromising papers. They included a letter which a French woman had given him in Switzerland and which he had promised to deliver to her husband in Paris.

Shortly before the arrival of the train at the control point he made a packet of the papers and hid it under the foot plate connecting two of the coaches. He then walked to the other end of the train and stood in the corridor while the Germans carried out their search. When all was over he returned to the hiding place—only to find his parcel gone.

Since there was nothing in the missing document which could be traced back to him, Michel, though annoyed, was not unduly alarmed. On arrival in Paris he apologised to the husband and thought no more of the incident until a few days later, when he found himself in Switzerland again. He was then informed by the lady that her letter contained, among other compromising matter, the name and address of the farmer who was sending food parcels to her husband.

This was dangerous. If the Germans found the letter and followed it up by questioning the farmer, they could discover the destination of the parcels, and from that it was only a step to discover the bearer of the letter.

Michel decided he must try to forestall them. If he could reach the farmer first and warn him, the man would know what to say if the police called.

The farm was in Ain Department, about twenty miles on the French side of the border. To reach it Michel had to return to the frontier, cross it without being seen and follow a mountain track through the snow. Although night had fallen, it was mid-winter and there was little hope of completing the journey by daybreak, he decided to set off at once.

That march was a nightmare. It was pitch dark, snow fell incessantly, and his feet, encased in ordinary boots, soon became numbed with cold. After frequent falls and losing his way several times, he arrived at the River Valserine, which constitutes the frontier, not far from the French village of Mijoux. A quarter of a mile beyond, at the top of a steep slope, was a farm-house which he always used as a place of departure and return when crossing the frontier at this point.

The farmer, M. Ponset, and his wife were good friends of Michel's. On the outgoing journey they would watch the river where the Germans patrolled and let him know when the coast was clear; and at his return a white panel displayed outside a shed, which was visible from the woods on the Swiss side of the boundary, was an indication that it was safe to cross.

This time, however, as his journey was unpremeditated, there was no signal and anyhow he could not have seen it in the dark. Although it was not his destination, and in spite of the risk of encountering a patrol, he decided to make for the farm house and rest there till daylight before continuing his journey.

It was about four a.m. when he arrived under the Ponsets' window. Although he was utterly exhausted and suffering from the first stage of frost-bite, he could not bring himself to wake up his hard-working friends and was preparing to wait till they got up, when a light appeared in the room and M. Ponset put his head out.

A few minutes later Michel was sitting in front of a blazing fire sipping a steaming cup of coffee liberally laced with rum. When sufficiently revived to speak he explained the purpose of his journey. He was then put to bed after extracting a promise from the Ponsets to wake him in two hours' time.

When he awoke it was dark and Mme. Ponset was shaking him gently by the arm. Michel jumped up, looked at his watch, and, seeing that he had slept for ten hours, began upbraiding his hostess for not waking him, when she interrupted.

"Don't worry. My husband carried the message. It took him all day to get there in this weather on his skis. I've been waiting at the post office and he's just telephoned to say that all is well."

No better example could be given of the kind of help which Michel could count on, usually from the humblest people.

The operation of the *réseau* and liaison with the British, which might have been considered the administrative side of Michel's work, was not by any means the end of it. On the contrary, he never hesitated to undertake a mission himself if the situation demanded it.

After the Allied landing in North Africa, for example, it was important to find out what was happening in Toulon. Through Admiral Darlan at Algiers the Allies were making desperate efforts to persuade the French fleet, if not to join them, at least to place itself out of reach of the Germans. The latter were equally determined to gain control of it.

Finally the question was settled by the French sailors. On 27th November, 1942, while the German troops were closing in, they scuttled their ships in the harbour.

As it happened, Michel was in Switzerland at the time. No sooner had the news come through than he was requested by his British contact to go to Toulon immediately, in order to find out the exact extent of the damage and what chances there were of any of the ships being salvaged.

This, he knew, was not going to be easy. Immediately after their invasion of the Free Zone the Germans had put a cordon round Toulon and all traffic in and out was rigorously controlled. Following the scuttling of the fleet, these measures were tightened up. Annoyed by the loss of such a valuable prize, the Germans reacted by making life still harder for the Toulonese.

When Michel arrived on the evening of the 28th—having walked in from the country through lanes and side streets— the atmosphere was tense and oppressive. Germans were everywhere and the few Frenchmen to be seen had the cowed look of people who have suffered a disaster. Like Portsmouth or Plymouth, Toulon existed for the navy and its destruction was a tragedy that touched every inhabitant. Even the waterfront, normally the centre of attraction, was deserted.

As he debouched on the quay Michel could see on all sides the tops of masts and funnels marking the grave of the fleet.

From the partly submerged hulk of a beached battle cruiser thick columns of smoke were still rising. A film of fuel and grease covered the waters of the port, in which the last light of the dying day was reflected in lurid colours.

It being too dark to investigate further, Michel started to look for a bed. He soon discovered that every hotel had been requisitioned either by the *Wehrmacht* or the *Kriegsmarine*. After trying a dozen unsuccessfully he decided to adopt a bold policy. Ignoring the large swastika hung outside, he entered the *Terminus*, the big hotel near the railway station, marched up to the reception desk and asked for a room.

Before the receptionist could reply a German N.C.O., who had overheard his request, brusquely demanded his business.

"I'm a mechanic," Michel replied. "I'm in Toulon to repair some machinery."

The German looked slightly less hostile.

"Could you repair a radio set?"

"Certainly."

"Then follow me."

The German led the way to a reception room, in the corner of which stood the defective set. Michel made a brief inspection, saw what was wrong and turned to the German.

"Supposing I do mend it, what will you give me?"

"I'll pay you a good fee."

"I don't need that."

"What do you want, then?"

"A room for the night in this hotel."

"I promise you shall have it."

"Which one?"

"I'll show you."

Thereupon the German summoned the manager and demanded the best room that was vacant for Michel. The manager having proposed *"Appartement No. 2"*—a self-contained suite on the first floor—the German gave his approval and Michel set to work.

An hour later he had repaired the set and tuned in to London to test it. The news bulletin in French had just finished and was being followed by the usual innocent-sounding messages, which in fact were signals in code.

With the N.C.O. standing beside him Michel was listening

without much interest when his attention was riveted by a phrase which was somehow familiar. "The beer is good," the announcer repeated, and then repeated it again.

There was no longer any doubt. By an extraordinary coincidence he had been listening to a code message put out at his own request. It was the message giving warning of the bombing of Abbeville aerodrome that his agent, Louis Villette, had asked him to arrange.[1]

Thinking of the "plastering" the German airfield would soon be receiving—possibly that very night—and of the pleasure this would give Villette, Michel could hardly contain his joy. He longed to impart the news to his stolid German friend, to slap him on the back, and tell him to cheer up. Instead he started humming his war song: *Tout va très bien, Madame la Marquise*.

He switched off the set.

"That was London," he informed the German, "and the fact that we heard it so well in spite of your jamming shows what a good job I've made of it."

Pleased and grateful, the German offered to stand him a drink and would have taken him off to the bar. But Michel was exhausted and only wanted to sleep. He therefore excused himself; whereupon the German insisted on showing him to his room, unlocked the door and himself drew the curtains before bidding his guest good night.

The room with its private bath was luxurious, the bed magnificent and there were even towels—which had practically disappeared from French hotels since the war. It was the fact, however, that he was enjoying it at the expense of the *Wehrmacht* that gave such unwonted comfort its particular relish.

When he left the next morning, bowed out by the hotel staff, and without having even filled in the usual form, he was repeating to himself one of his favourite slogans: *De l'audace, encore de l'audace, toujours de l'audace*. It had certainly paid off on this occasion.

As he approached the naval dockyard Michel saw that the entrance was guarded by a German sentry. He was unprepared

[1] See page 76.

for this and was considering what pretext he could use when the soldier came to attention and saluted. Too astonished to react, Michel smiled feebly and passed through.

(Later it occured to him that there was a possible explanation: if the soldier was billeted at the *Terminus* he might have recognised Michel as the honoured guest of his *Feldwebel*.)

In broad daylight the spectacle of the sunken fleet was heart-rending. One battleship, two battle cruisers, seven cruisers, twenty-nine destroyers and sixteen submarines had been scuttled, as well as many smaller craft; but since only the upper works were showing it was difficult to identify the wrecks.

Over all there was an air of desolation. The dockyard, usually a hive of activity, was silent: the jetties deserted, the ferry and pilot boats abandoned, the cranes idle and even the power station stilled.

Some distance away two solitary individuals were standing by the statue to the "Genius of Navigation," gloomily contemplating the scene of devastation.

As Michel approached he saw that one was an elderly man, the other quite young. He went up to them and in reply to his inquiry the younger man started to point out the wrecks, giving each ship its name. The partly submerged ship, he explained, which was still on fire, had engaged the Germans on shore to keep them at bay while the scuttling of the fleet was completed. They had replied with shells, killing many French sailors.

While this conversation was going on the older man said nothing, only nodding from time to time to confirm some remark of his companion. There was something in his bearing, however, that impressed Michel favourably. Tall and lean and rather grizzled, dressed as a workman, he possessed both dignity and authority.

After a time Michel invited them both to a café. He then asked the older man, a foreman artificer employed in the dockyard, to do him a small favour. He had, he explained, some occasional business in Toulon, but it was difficult to obtain the necessary authorisation. An inter-zone postcard, posted in Toulon and requesting his presence to repair a gas engine, would enable him to obtain a permit to return. Would

his new acquaintance oblige by dispatching such a card—
which Michel then produced already written and addressed—
a fortnight from that day?

The foreman artificer having agreed and pocketed the card,
Michel shook hands and left. He was well satisfied with the
morning's work. He had got the information he wanted,
knew what ships had been sunk and which could be salvaged,
and in addition had established contact with a likely new
recruit, well placed for acting as his agent in Toulon.

Following the same route in reverse, he slipped out of the
town without being stopped and an hour later was safely in
the train.

Punctually on the agreed date the card arrived in Paris.
Armed with it Michel obtained his permit, and the following
day was back in Toulon. Going straight to the address of the
foreman artificer, he was lucky enough to find his man at
home and alone. The latter had already guessed what Michel
was up to, and in a very short time they reached an understanding. It was thus that Alexander Roman became a member
of the *réseau "Agir"*.

Married, with two children, devoted to his family (for
whose sake he often went hungry himself), and showing signs
of the hardships imposed by the Germans as a reprisal, Roman
was the best type of skilled artisan. As a senior foreman
employed in the armaments section of the dockyard, which
had started to function again under German supervision, he
was also the ideal person for Michel's purpose. From now on,
thanks to his vigilance, nothing of importance that occurred at
Toulon failed to reach the British Intelligence Service.

One of his earliest and most important reports concerned a
new type of torpedo, invented by the French, plans of which
had been seized by the Germans on taking possession of the
arsenal. By a lucky chance Roman had worked immediately
under the inventor and was able to produce a complete description of the torpedo—it ran on hydrogen peroxide—and
send it through Michel to the Admiralty in London.

In the summer of 1943, when the battle of Sicily was
raging, the Axis patrol boats damaged in the campaign docked
at Toulon for repairs. By virtue of his functions Roman

always knew the date they were due to sail, and included the information in the fornightly report which Michel took to Switzerland. This was passed on to London and as a result the enemy craft were usually attacked as soon as they left port. Their losses were known immediately in the arsenal and included by Roman in his report.

One day when he was lying on his stomach on a cliff, sketching a new naval supply base constructed by the Germans near La Seyne, a German soldier who had been watching him from the branches of a tree jumped down and demanded what he was drawing.

Roman had his explanation ready. He was planning, he said, to build a house on the waterfront, and was making a sketch to assist him in choosing the site.

This incredible story was not accepted by the soldier, and he hauled Roman off to the guard-room. Fortunately the N.C.O. was more credulous; and after the prisoner had produced proof that he was an inhabitant of Toulon he was released with a caution.

He continued his valuable work for a year. Then something happened to place him in danger.

Michel had an agent called Louis Maiffret, who was employed as a surveyor by the municipality of Nice. Maiffret had been introduced to Roman by a third agent, who was occasionally used by Michel to collect their reports on his behalf. This agent thought it useful that Maiffret and Roman should meet, so that in the event of his being unable to visit Nice, Maiffret could come to Toulon and hand his report to Roman.

As soon as Michel heard of the arrangement, he realised that it was undesirable, since if either of the two was arrested the other would probably be compromised. He therefore left at once for Toulon with the object of putting and end to it.

When he arrived at the Romans' house Mme. Roman let him in and he saw at once that he had come too late. In a distraught voice the poor woman told him what had happened. Two days before, early in the morning, some Germans in plain clothes had called at the house and removed her husband in a car. Since then no more had been seen or heard of him.

Both for his sake and hers Michel did not prolong the interview. After making certain that she had enough money for immediate needs, and promising to do what he could to discover her husband's whereabouts, he took his departure with a heavy heart.

Weighed down by a presentiment of worse to come, he took the first train to Nice. There, without going farther than the station, he learnt the full extent of the disaster. Louis Maiffret's father, Jean, chief controller of traffic at Nice station, who also worked for Michel, had been found with a list of military movements which could not be explained by his official functions. He and his son had both been arrested and had been seen as they were put on the train for Marseilles. Inevitably the arrest of Roman had followed.

His disappearance was a bitter blow to Michel. Utterly loyal, disinterested, fearless and conscientious, and hiding those qualities under the same unassuming manner that had taken Michel's fancy at their first encounter, he was one of the most effective members of the *réseau* and the value of his information had been proved time and again.

As always when he lost an agent, especially if the latter was a family man, an agonising question arose in Michel's mind. Was he justified in exposing another to mortal danger? Could the victim's dependants ever forgive him?

The question was never answered to his satisfaction; but when his own turn came it was a consoling thought that he was sharing to some extent the martyrdom of those for whose fate, as their chief, he felt responsible. In the darkest days of Neuengamme it was this thought that sustained him more than anything else.

One day in the summer of 1943, during a meeting between Michel and his new British contact, the sympathetic "O.P.," the question came up of the whereabouts of Von Rundstedt.

"O.P." declared firmly that he was still commanding the Mediterranean section of the German Army of Occupation. This was the Army Group whose headquarters were at Avignon and it controlled all German troops in the south of France.

Michel was not so certain. He had heard rumours of changes and since he had no agent in Avignon he volunteered to go and find out himself.

"No point," said "O.P.," "since we know it is Rundstedt."

Michel was still not happy about it and after leaving Lausanne decided to investigate. A few days later, having completed his tour of the *Midi*, he arrived at Avignon station.

It was some time since he had been there and he was struck once again by the charm of the ancient city. In the late afternoon the air was pleasantly cool and charged with the scent peculiar to Provence: a mixture of thyme and fig-tree, vines and olives. Plane trees in full foliage spread their shade over the street and there was an atmosphere of relaxation after the heat of the day.

There was, however, one jarring note. As he strolled across the square adjoining the station, he glanced at the twin turrets which fomerly guarded the walled town and saw that the Germans had mounted A.A. guns on top of them!

A few minutes' walk brought him to the Hotel Terminus, where the German commander had installed his headquarters. Planted in front of the entrance was the flag—a black and white centre surrounded by red—denoting an Army Group. A wooden barrier, extending to the middle of the road, prevented any approach. This was guarded by three French policemen, while the space inside was patrolled by German soldiers under the command of an N.C.O.

Immediately opposite the hotel was a café. Michel went to the counter, ordered a coffee, and, after engaging the *patron* in conversation, lowered his voice and said, "Tell me, your neighbour across the way...is it still the same one?"

The *patron* did not reply, but moved away and busied himself with crockery. Taking the hint, Michel left the café.

The three French policemen were still lounging by the barrier. Michel observed them, undecided on his next move. Then he told himself that after all they were Frenchmen. Anyhow he had no time to waste. In an hour his train would be leaving.

He approached the nearest of the three and repeated the question he had put to the *patron* of the café.

"No," replied the policeman without showing any surprise, "there's been a change in the last two weeks."

"Do you know the name of the new one?"

"No," said the policeman and turning to his colleagues he asked if either of them knew it. Both shook their heads.

Then one of them said: "Why don't you ask the proprietor of the hotel? He's still living there and he's a very good chap."

"What's his name?" Michel asked.

"Pamard. Monsieur Pierre Pamard."

Michel thanked his informant, the barrier was lifted and he passed inside.

As he approached the entrance a German sentry stopped him and asked him for his pass. He replied by requesting to see the N.C.O.; and when the latter arrived explained in German that he only wanted to see M. Pamard, for whom he had an urgent message.

"I'm sorry," said the N.C.O. politely, "but nobody is allowed to enter without a pass and if I let you through I shall get myself in trouble."

"But nobody will see me," protested Michel. "M. Pamard is an old friend and I know the hotel well. I shall see him in his private office."

He produced some American cigarettes and pressed them into the hand of the sergeant. The German gave a shrug and he hurried through the door.

He had never been in the hotel before, but assuming the confident air of one who knows his way about, he marched straight ahead. The hall was full of German and Italian officers, to whom he smiled and made a slight inclination as he passed. When he had almost reached the point where he could go no farther without stopping to inquire the way, a young woman appeared in his path.

Michel stoped and asked for M. Pamard.

"Who shall I say?" the girl demanded.

"My name will mean nothing to him," replied Michel. "Just say it's an old comrade from the regiment."

The girl disappeared and a few moments later Michel saw approaching him a tall dark man of about thirty-five, dressed in the conventional black coat and striped trousers of the high-class *hôtelier*.

Before he had time to speak Michel seized his hand and shook it vigorously. At the same time he whispered: "I'll explain everything—but not here." He then led the way to a place where they could not be seen from the hall, and after apologising for his subterfuge explained that for private reasons it was essential for him to know the name of the General who had succeeded Von Rundstedt.

"General Von Felber," replied M. Pamard. "But that was some time ago. Since then Von Felber has been replaced. I don't know the name of his successor but my wife will know and if you'll excuse me a moment I'll ask her immediately."

A few minutes later he returned and handed Michel his card. On it was written the name: Von Sonnenstern.

"Thanks," said Michel. "Now there's something else. I want to know where Von Rundstedt and Felber were moved to and where Von Sonnenstern came from. Also the towns where his subordinate commands have their headquarters — and anything else you can find out."

As though this was the most natural request in the world, M. Pamard nodded understandingly. Some of the information, he thought, was already available. The German Generals who had left the hotel nearly always wrote to his wife to say how comfortable they had been. It was a question of checking up and might take a little time.

"Good," said Michel. "Then I'll return in a few days. Choose a rendezvous and give me a number where I can leave a message in safety."

After arranging to meet at the bar of another hotel — which being kept by a *milicien*[1] was above suspicion — and to telephone to fix a day and a time, Michel took his departure.

While Pamard was seeing him out with all the marks of the warmest friendship, the German N.C.O. looked on with approval, as though to show his pleasure that Michel had succeeded in finding his old friend.

A few days later Michel collected Pamard's report and took it straight to Switzerland. "O.P." accepted his defeat with a good grace.

"But," he added, "*somebody* is going to look pretty silly."

There is a tragic epilogue to this story. Pamard continued to work for Michel and provided some useful information; but after the latter's arrest he was approached by another resistance group with a request to work for them. For fear of

---

[1] Member of the hated Vichy militia, largely employed to suppress opposition.

compromising the *réseau* "*Agir*" he declined. He was in consequence labelled as a "collabo" and after the liberation of France shot by his compatriots as a traitor without being given the opportunity of vindicating himself.

10

THE EXPERT COMES TO-MORROW

In the summer of 1943 Michel was requested by his British contact to investigate the aerodrome at Cormeilles-en-Vexin. This was a very large airfield not far from Paris used by the *Luftwaffe*. It had twenty miles of runway and was believed to be divided into three sections. One of them, skilfully camouflaged, was used for operations; a second appeared to be out of service; while a third, surrounded by fencing, was equipped with searchlights and A.A. The directive given to Michel was to plot the limits of the three sectors, and to discover the exact function of each.

He decided to entrust the job to Bart. The latter had distinguished himself by his work, particularly on the Channel coast, and was now based on Paris and available to be sent on special missions.

Although partly enclosed, the aerodrome was too vast to guard, and Bart had no difficulty in approaching its perimeter. Carrying a large-scale map in one hand and a pair of field glasses in the other, he proceeded methodically, noting the various features.

After fixing the boundaries of the neutral sector and shading it in on his map, he reached a part of the ground where there were some curious buildings. Nobody being in sight he decided to explore it. The results were interesting. For example, a church steeple made of wood surmounted a large storage tank, while what looked like a row of cottages were in reality repair shops.

A little farther on two haystacks next aroused Bart's curiosity. Scraping away the soil he discovered at first a layer of concrete and then a padlocked manhole. He guessed these were ammunition lockers and was just proceeding to mark the position on his map, when suddenly a German soldier concealed in a silo landed on the ground and covered him with his rifle.

There was no question of flight. The German was only a few yards away and must have been watching him for some time. With his hands above his head he was marched off to the guard-room; and from there taken before an officer wearing air force uniform.

Bart had already prepared his story. He was cycling past the airfield when he noticed a church and some cottages that had not been there when he was last in the neighbourhood. Obeying a natural curiosity he had stopped to investigate.

What about the map—and the glasses?

Well, the glasses had been given him by a friend in the neighbourhood whom he was visiting (this was true, he had borrowed them for the occasion from the *curé* of the next village), and he was taking them back to Paris.

As for the map, why he had picked it up off a bench on arriving at the station. It was already marked—in fact it was that which had aroused his curiosity in the first place.

During an hour's interrogation, accompanied by some knocking about, Bart stuck to his story. Finally he was informed that the explanation was not accepted and that he was to be sent to Maissons-Laffitte for questioning by the Sicherheits-Dienst.[1]

That night he spent in a police post at Pontoise. Towards

---

[1] Security Police to be distinguished from the Gestapo (*Geheimnis Staats Polizei*) or Secret State Police. The latter however worked with the Security Police and were always called in for cases of espionage or subversive action.

dawn, seeing that his escort were asleep, he rose and crept towards the door. He had stepped across two of the men without disturbing them when the third sat up. All he could do then was to request to be taken to the lavatory.

At Maisons-Laffitte he was mercilessly "grilled" all day. Different interrogating officers succeeded one another with progressive brutality: at first face slapping and blows of the fist, then beating with various implements. With desperate courage, Bart stuck to his story. He had found the map at the station; the writing on it was not his.

Paper and pencil were put before him and he was ordered to write down some sentences which his interrogator dictated. Guessing the purpose of this he wrote in a faked hand, but weak as he was with pain and exhaustion the effort was not very successful.

"Right," said the German. "Now we'll send for the hand-writing expert. He'll soon tell us if you're speaking the truth."

As it happened the expert could not be found. He would not be available, apparently, until the next day; but if the writing on the map was identified as his, Bart was informed, he would be shot immediately as a spy. He was then conducted to Houilles, a small town just outside Paris, and locked up for the night.

His cell was on the third floor of the building, about fifty feet above ground. High up in the wall there was a small rectangular window protected by a network of wire. The wire was stretched taut across a wooden frame which was secured by wire lashings to bolts in the wall. In the door was the usual spy-hole enabling the guard to look in.

All thought of escape seemed hopeless. And yet one phrase spoken by his interrogator kept recurring in his head: "The expert comes to-morrow." He was convinced his faked hand-writing would not delude the expert. Unless he got away, there could be only one end to it.

He looked at the window again. It appeared inaccessible— and yet perhaps not quite. The guard had just looked through the judas, and Bart had heard his retreating footsteps. Presumably he would hear them coming back. He had the impression that he was the only prisoner on that floor, so visits to it might not be very frequent.

Placing the truckle bed on its side, he stood on it and just managed to reach the window. He started to unravel, strand by strand, the wire lashings which attached the frame to the opening. With only his hands to help him it was a slow and painful business and soon his nails were ripped and his finger-tips bleeding. But he worked on steadily, only pausing to listen for footsteps outside. Once the guard returned and he just had time to drop on the bed and feign sleep before the judas was opened. By midnight he had the frame dismounted.

The opening measured about sixteen inches by twenty inches—large enough for the slight form of Bart to pass through. But what then? A drop of fifty feet—in the dark—on to what—not to mention the noise of the fall?

At that moment the sound of a train could be heard in the distance. This gave Bart an idea. He had already heard several pass quite close, making the night hideous with their clatter. If he could time his leap to freedom when this one approached, the noise of it would deaden that of his fall.

It might be suicide, but the alternative was to face the expert—and it was not as though the Germans would shoot him at once, either. Convinced of his guilt they would want some more out of him, and by now he knew enough of their methods to feel that death was preferable to another "grilling."

Anyhow, there was no time to calculate the risk. The noise of the train was growing louder every moment. In a few seconds it would have passed. Without a clear idea of what he meant to do with it, Bart seized his blanket and pulled himself up to the window. He squeezed through the opening feet first until he was sitting on the ledge outside. Then he spread the blanket above his head to act as a parachute, kicked with his heels to take him clear of any obstructions...and jumped.

By a miracle he was not killed—nor even knocked unconscious. He had fallen into a garden on to soft ground. As he lay on his back in an agony of pain, groaning audibly, he heard the train go by in a shattering inferno of sound.

Soon after he heard footsteps approaching. Pushing inside his mouth a corner of the blanket which he was still holding, Bart succeeded in rolling to a hedge. The sentry, as he guessed it must be, was patrolling on the other side. When opposite the place where Bart was lying, he stopped...and relieved himself, almost on top of the injured man! Then he resumed his beat.

By a supreme effort Bart managed to get on all fours, and, sometimes crawling and sometimes dragging himself on his stomach, reached the end of the hedge, where there was an opening. This led to another garden at the end of which was a small house.

How he got there Bart never knew, but he eventually arrived at a door, under which he could see light. He had just sufficient strength to knock feebly before collapsing; and as the door opened his unconscious form fell across the threshold.

When he came to he was lying on a couch in a sitting-room. Two elderly people, a man and a woman, were standing over him. The woman had a cup of coffee ready and raised his head to help him drink. His back hurt atrociously—although he did not know it yet, he had broken his spine in three places—but it got some support from the rough bandages made of sheets with which the occupants of the house had bound up his torso.

Bart's first question was to ask the time.

His hosts tried to calm him. There was nothing to worry about. They would look after him, and he must just lie still until they could send for an ambulance.

"Impossible," said Bart, "I've just escaped from the *boches*. They will be looking for me now. Unless I can get to the station I shall be caught and shot."

"But you can't move," the man objected. "We think your back is broken."

"Yes I can if you'll support me. I feel stronger now. Anyhow, it's my only chance."

After some more argument it was agreed to try. It was about 5.30 a.m. and there was a workers' train from Houilles at 6.45.

With one arm round the neck of his Good Samaritan, and the other leaning on a stick, Bart set off for the station. To avoid passing in front of his recent prison it was necessary to make a wide detour; and although the station was only a short distance away it took them nearly an hour to reach it.

But they caught the train—Bart's companion buying the

tickets—arrived in Paris, took the metro to the Gare de Lyons, and eventually reached a small hotel near the terminus where Michel had a room permanently reserved.

He used it occasionally to sleep in, and also to keep the reports brought to Paris by his agents in northern and eastern France. These were hidden on top of the wardrobe and he only collected them just before leaving for Switzerland.

It was here that he found Bart later in the day, stretched on the bed and exhausted with pain.

By this time the injured man was not making much sense, but his speech was sufficiently coherent to convey roughly to Michel what had happened to him. When he had finished his story Michel looked at him sternly and said: "Did you tell them anything?"

"Of course not."

"Are you quite sure?"

"Nothing. I swear."

"Good," said Michel. "In that case we'll attend to your affair."

Fortunately he knew of a nursing home whose surgeon, Raoul Manod, was a cousin and friend of his. It was run by the Protestant *Association Diaconnesses*, and was not far away, at 18 Rue de Sergent Bauchat.

There Bart was taken the same evening and operated on immediately. An X-ray revealed three broken vertebræ. These were set by the surgeon and the injured man escased in plaster.

By what seemed not one miracle, but a succession of miracles—the second being the failure of the Germans to discover his escape, and the third his getting to Paris with no spinal column—Bart had so far survived.

But his escape was not yet assured, and every day he lay in the nursing home the risk of discovery increased. The problem was first to find a safe place for him, and then to move him to it.

One of the difficulties was that he would take months to recover and meanwhile would need to be nursed. For this reason he could not be sent to the "parking place," where there were no facilities for the injured. On the other hand, an invalid always attracted attention and this made Michel's friends reluctant to harbour him. To complicate matters further, Bart was liable for conscription in the labour force.

After considering various alternatives—including a hiding-place in the country—Michel decided that the only solution was to remove Bart to Switzerland, and proceeded to make his plans accordingly. Fortunately it was summer, so he could use the original route across the frontier, where there was no barbed wire to negotiate.

After a week in bed the patient was considered well enough to be moved. It was arranged that his mother should collect him at the clinic and conduct him to the Gare de Lyon where Michel was to meet them. All went well until they were passing the barrier, when the ticket inspector demanded their *fiches d'admission*. These were special passes with which passengers had to provide themselves to gain admission to a particular train. Michel had not had time to obtain them.

"This young man is seriously injured," he explained. "He has to leave Paris for urgent treatment."

"Then you should have brought a medical certificate," the inspector replied.

At this Bart, who had overheard, pulled up his shirt and displayed his plaster cast. The effect was sensational. Drawn on the white surface with a violet pencil and covering it from neck to waist line was a large Cross of Lorraine—the emblem of the Free French. Below was printed a title:

IST REGIMENT OF PARACHUTISTS

The drawing was the work of Bart's neighbour at the clinic, who had waggishly added the title as a tribute to his original method of descent from a third storey window. Michel, who had not seen this artistic effort before, was horrified; but the inspector took one glance, discreetly looked away, and motioned the three to pass through.

Thanks to a friendly guard a corner seat was secured for Bart and he passed a reasonably comfortable night in the train. There was no longer any control at the line of demarcation and the journey passed off without incident.

At Besançon, where they arrived early the next morning, Bart's mother said good-bye to him. He and Michel then continued on the single line railway which runs between Besançon and Morteau.

At La Grande Combe, five miles from the terminus, they left the train to continue the journey on foot. Bart could walk, but only slowly, and the plaster cast weighed painfully on his hip-bones. Michel usually travelled by paths and across country, but this was too difficult for Bart, so they had to keep to the road where the risk increased of meeting a German patrol.

After walking for two hours they arrived at Derrière-le-Mont. Cuenot had been warned and his wife was waiting for them with a meal. Bart had so far stood the journey well, and after the meal and a short rest he was ready to go on.

Now began the real test. The mountain path, which Michel had travelled so often, became progressively steeper and narrower. After a time there was no room for two people and Michel, who had been helping his companion, had to abandon him to his own devices.

The pain caused by the plaster pressing on Bart's hips soon became unbearable. To ease it he took the weight with his hands. This meant abandoning his stick and he had difficulty in keeping his balance. Step by step, sometimes inch by inch, Bart struggled forward, while Michel looked on helpless in an agony of doubt whether his plucky comrade would ever make it.

At last the climb eased as they reached the plateau and hit the track which led to Cuenot's farm. The carter had gone ahead to reconnoitre and Michel saw in dismay that the door and window were closed. This meant that it was not safe to cross the valley.

He looked at his watch. There were five minutes still to go till the agreed time. He watched the farm anxiously, while Bart lay on the ground desperately trying to recuperate his forces.

At last the door opened. Inside he could see Cuenot looking out. It was the "all clear" sign.

Revived by the news, Bart struggled to his feet and with Michel again supporting him they resumed the march.

From the edge of the forest there was an easy descent of about a hundred yards to the stream at the bottom of the valley, and this was accomplished without too much difficulty. But when they started to climb the farther slope Bart soon began to show signs of distress. For a little way he struggled on and succeeded in reaching the shelter of the trees. Then he stopped. For the time being his strength was finished.

The worst was still ahead—a quarter of a mile at least of stiff climbing through scrub and rock. Dropping on his knees Michel took his companion on his back; then advancing on all fours, a foot at a time, half carried, half dragged him the rest of the way. By the time they reached the wall which marked the frontier, he had just enough strength to lift Bart over and pull him under cover of some trees before he himself sank down completely exhausted.

There they lay together, without an ounce of strength left, but savouring the sweet taste of another victory, gained by sheer "guts" over an all-powerful enemy.

When they had recovered their strength sufficiently, they resumed their walk and eventually arrived at La Brevine. From there Michel telephoned one of his friends in the Swiss Army, who immediately left by car to meet him. A few hours later he and Bart were both installed comfortably at a hotel in Neûchatel.

The next day Bart was admitted to hospital, while Michel returned to Paris. He had made many secret and dangerous journeys to Switzerland, but none had taken more out of him than this, nor afforded him so deep a satisfaction.

Part Two

11

A WARM SCENT

Shortly after his return from escorting Bart to safety, Michel received an intriguing message. One of his agents, a railway engineer at Rouen called Daudemard, had overheard a conversation in a café between two building contractors. They were discussing some new and unusual constructions which were being carried out on German orders at various points in the *Seine Inférieure* Department. What made them unusual was the amount of material required and the extreme accuracy demanded for the siting of certain buildings.

As always when it seemed that the matter was important, Michel decided to investigate himself.

Arriving at Rouen one day in August, he went straight to the local Labour Office and asked for the welfare section. To the official who received him he explained that he was the representative of a Protestant welfare organisation and was anxious to get in touch with some of the workers recently engaged for the Occupying Authority.

He then produced from his brief-case several bibles and a number of religious and moral tracts. The official glanced at the titles — *Christian Marriage, The Scourge of Disease* — and appeared to be favourably impressed. It was an excellent thing, he thought, that someone should be concerned with the spiritual life of the workers. Uprooted from their families, living in conditions that left much to be desired, but with plenty of money in their pockets, they were obviously exposed to grave moral dangers. He would therefore be glad to assist in any way he could. What did Michel want?

"If you can tell me the names of the places where the construction is proceeding, I will visit them. It is always best to get the men when they are working."

"Well, I don't know them all, but here are one or two you could start with," said the official.

He wrote some names on a slip of paper and handed it to Michel, who thanked him warmly, repacked his brief-case, and withdrew.

An hour later he got off the train at Auffay, a small place about twenty miles north of Rouen. He had changed *en route* and when he emerged from the station was wearing his workingman's clothes over his city suit, and a black beret on his head. He had left his brief-case behind and carried on his shoulder a well-worn haversack containing his maps.

He had chosen Auffay from among the places whose names had been given him because it seemed the most accessible; but inquiries in the village produced no result. Nobody seemed to have heard of any important construction being carried out in the neighbourhood.

There were four principal roads leading out of Auffay. In his usual methodical way Michel decided to explore each of the them for a distance of five kilometres.

After drawing three blanks he tried as a last resort the road which led westward towards Bonnetot le Faubourg. It took him through gently undulating country, with hedged fields, occasional copses and green meadows in which cattle were peacefully grazing.

He had gone about three miles and reached a point where the land flattened, when he came on what he was looking for. On a large open space immediately adjoining the road several hundred labourers were busily employed. While some of them were erecting buildings, of various shapes and sizes, others were laying roads or putting down concrete. The din of bull-dozers, mechanical mixers and pneumatic drills was incessant.

The site was about four hundred yards square, but looking at it from the road told him nothing. Somehow or other he had to gain admittance and inspect it at closer range. Except on the north-east, where it was bounded by a copse running at right angles to the road, the site was open on each side, and sentries were posted all round at short intervals. Other Germans in uniform could be seen on the ground; presumably they were engineers supervising the work.

Clearly there was no hope of sneaking in unobserved. He had to find a plausible pretext for entering the site.

Looking round for some tool to give him countenance, he noticed a wheelbarrow lying in the ditch beside the road. After hiding his haversack under a tree, he pulled the barrow out, wheeled it to the entrance of the site, and marched boldly in under the unsuspecting gaze of the guards.

He had already marked down a group of labourers, who were working on one of the buildings in the middle of the ground, and he now directed his wheelbarrow towards them. Arrived in their midst he dropped the barrow, and busied himself, as they were, shovelling sand and cement.

Nobody questioned his presence and he was soon in con-versation with one of his mates.

"What's all this for?" he asked after a while.

"We don't know exactly," the man replied, "but they say the buildings will be used as garages, for their transport."

This struck Michel as fantastic. The building they were erecting was much too small to shelter vehicles, and none of the others, as far as he could judge in their unfinished state, was any larger. It was obvious that the garage story was invented by the Germans to conceal their real intentions.

Making some excuse to his mate, Michel retrieved his barrow and after half filling it with bricks set out on a tour of exploration. As far as he could make out without appearing too curious, there were ten separate constructions, none more than one-storey high. Concrete paths and roadways were being made to connect them.

What particularly intrigued him was a wider strip of concrete, about fifty yards long, which had been laid along the edge of the site nearest the wood and at the corner farthest from the road.

Still more intriguing, there extended down the middle a row of wooden posts on which was stretched, a few feet above the ground, a single length of blue string. This continued beyond the strip for another hundred yards, and to make it easier against the landscape there was a metal disc attached to the top of each post and a strip of white sand running across the grass.

The more Michel looked at the concrete strip, and especially the length of string stretching away into the distance, the more convinced he was that it held the key to the mystery. But what was it?

The string did not seem to serve any purpose. It was too light to carry a weight or stand any strain. Where had he seen anything similar before? Bricklayers used a line when building a wall. It was not that. What about the metal discs? They reminded him of something he had seen used by surveyors when lining up the direction of a new road. But, of course, that was it: a line direction. Otherwise why prolong it so far beyond the site?

With a sudden intuition he walked back to the concrete strip and placed himself so that he was in line with the direction of the string. There were some men working nearby, but they weren't taking any notice of him, and the nearest German was some way distant.

He always carried a pocket compass, and it had often helped him find his way when crossing the frontier. Bending down and pretending to do up his bootlaces, he placed the compass on the ground and read off the magnetic bearing of the string—which was that of the axis of the concrete strip.

As he stood up he noticed one of the workers looking at him. Michel went up to the man and said: "Tell me, what's this emplacement in aid of?"

The man gave a shrug. "I have no idea. You'd better ask the foreman."

"Which is he?"

The man looked round, then pointed at another worker, who was talking to one of the German engineers.

"That's one of them," he said.

Michel waited till they separated, then followed the foreman, who was heading for a canvas screen at the far end of the site. He disappeared behind it and when Michel arrived was already ensconced on one of a row of rudimentary earth closets. With what must have appeared somewhat unnecessary "mateyness," Michel pulled down his trousers and took his place on the next seat. Then he pulled out a packet of American cigarettes and offered one to his neighbour. After a slight hesitation the foreman accepted.

After they had puffed away in silence for a time Michel repeated his question. Instead of answering the foreman glanced at him and said: "You're new here, aren't you?"

"Yes," replied Michel, "they sent me out from Rouen. Said you were short-handed."

"Well, then, my advice to you is not to ask questions. Our bosses don't like it."

"Really. It's so mysterious?"

"They don't tell us anything. We haven't even seen a plan. There's a *boche* in charge of each section and he simply tells us what he wants. It's a funny way of working."

"It must be something important then?"

"I don't know about that, but I can tell you they're in a hell of a hurry to finish. We're working in three shifts all round the clock."

"And this isn't the only one?"

"I should think not. They're all over the place."

"Do you know where exactly?"

"Well, there's one at Tôtes and another at Yerville, then at Le Bosc Melet, Brauquetuit, Abbémont, St. Vaast-du-Val..." The foreman broke off and looked at Michel curiously. "But why should that concern you," he asked, "since you've been sent here?"

"Well, I've got a pal who's looking for work. I told him I'd let him know if there was anything doing."

"Looking for work? That's funny. Most of them are trying to avoid it."

The foreman by now was ready to leave. Michel waited till he had gone before following. His barrow was standing outside. He wheeled it once more past the cordon of sentries, reached the road, recovered his haversack and was soon on his way to Auffay. There, after a short wait, he caught a train for Rouen, and late that evening arrived back in Paris.

He was sleeping at the small hotel near the Gare de Lyon where he rented a room permanently. It was on the first floor overlooking the *cour* and had a ledge outside the window which gave access to the roof and afforded a means of escape in an emergency.

Among other things he kept his maps there. They included one of the English Channel which showed Northern France and Southern England as far as London. Spreading it on the floor he drew a line from the approximate position of the site near Auffay along the bearing he had read off his compass. As he had guessed, it passed through London. In other words, whatever it was that the Germans were building, its axis pointed at the English capital.

It seemed that he was on to something good.

When he reported his find in Switzerland a few days later, "O.P." was not particularly impressed. Reports of "curious constructions" and "suspicious buildings" were common, and it often turned out that they were something quite innocuous, like a field laundry or recreation centre. The mission of which he was a member was expected to act as a filter; cluttering up the wires with useless information would not make it popular in London.

Had it been another informant, he might even have hesitated to pass the report on. The fact that a certain strip of concrete happened to be laid with its axis pointed at London—or so appeared from a very approximate calculation—could be as easily accident as design; and to draw any conclusions therefrom was the sort of thing officially frowned on.

But coming from Michel it was rather different; the latter was now in the privileged category of agents whose information, however improbable, is treated with respect because in the past it has always proved reliable. He had only attained this position after a long period of trial and it had recently been confirmed by an outstanding exploit.

During the summer he had reported that work was proceeding at Marseilles on the construction of a new naval dock.

This was dismissed by the British as pure fantasy. Since he had seen the thing himself, and at considerable risk, he was furious; and after promising to return with proof, left immediately for Marseilles.

The dock was being built under cover of an enormous shed, normally used as a warehouse, at the northern extremity of the Quai de la Joliette, and every approach was closely guarded. Michel arranged to arrive, disguised as a workman, just as the day shift was leaving and the night shift taking on. Mingling with the latter he entered the site, picked up the nearest tool and started excavating industriously under the watchful eye of the S.T.O.[1] foreman.

When the midnight break came he found a shadowy corner, and while the rest of the men crowded round the food trolley, proceeded calmly, under cover of a newspaper spread on his knees, to take photographs of the scene—with a "Brownie" Kodak which he had carried concealed under his jacket.

At the end of the break he resumed his labours and in the morning filed out with the rest of the workers when they returned to the barracks where they slept.

The next day he was back in Lausanne once again, and with a roll of film to support his statement. This was duly forwarded to London. A few days later the area was heavily bombed. After that no report of Michel's was ever questioned.

As a consequence, when he described his latest discovery, although his British contact knew no more than Michel of flying bombs, he took it seriously enough to forward the report to London.

If Michel knew nothing about the *Vergeltungswaffen*—the "revenge" weapons which were to turn the tables on the Allies—the British Government at this stage were equally ignorant about the manner and direction of the coming attack.[2]

Since the end of 1942 there had been rumours of secret weapons and in April a report was received of an experimental

[1] S.T.O.—initials of the Todt Organisation shown on the armlet worn by its employees.

[2] For a full account of the "V" weapons, *see The Second World War,* by Winston Churchill, Vols. V and VI, and *The Royal Air Force,* 1939–1945, Vol. III (H.M. Stationery Office).

station at Peenemunde, on the Baltic. But what the weapons
were and how and against whom they were to be used,
nobody outside Germany as yet knew. Some sort of rocket
was thought most likely and this view prevailed for a considerable time.

The Government took the threat seriously and at the insti-
gation of Mr. Churchill a committee was set up to study it
under the chairmanship of Mr. Duncan Sandys.

In June there came the first report of an "air mine with
wings." Two months later the report was confirmed by further
information. By a curious coincidence it was through "O.P."
that this came to the knowledge of the British Government
and in the following circumstances.

Shortly after the visit of Michel mentioned above, "O.P."
was in his office one Sunday afternoon when an unannounced
visitor was shown in. Dressed in workman's clothes, dusty
and unshaven, the visitor explained that he had walked from
Luxembourg and carried a message which he had to deliver to
the head of the British Intelligence Service.

"O.P." replied that this was not possible but offered, if his
visitor cared to leave the message, to see that it reached its
destination.

The Luxembourgeois shook his head and repeated that he
must deliver the message personally to the head of the Intelligence. There followed a two hours' argument, during which
"O.P." tried to overcome the man's suspicion, and the latter
obstinately refused to be persuaded. Finally his confidence
was won and he agreed to relinquish the message. This, as it
transpired, was concealed in the heel of his boot and a screw-
driver was required to disclose it. Having handed it over and
refused any payment, the visitor then took his departure, after
nailing on the heel of his boot.

The message, written in German and scrawled in pencil on
a grubby bit of paper, was very short: it merely stated that a
"cigar-shaped missile with wings" had been fired from the
ground a distance of 250 kilometres into the Baltic.

This sounded so fantastic that "O.P.'s" chief, when the
message was shown to him, was reluctant to forward it to
London on the grounds that such stuff would be regarded as a
joke, and discredit them both. "O.P.", however, who had a

hunch that it was important, insisted; and eventually obtained permission to send a telegram on condition it went with a low priority. The following day an acknowledgment came back sharply demanding the reason why such vital information had not been handled as urgent!

Shortly after—that is, about the middle of August, 1943—any doubt about the existence of the new weapon was removed, when a Danish gentleman, walking on the Island of Bornholm, came upon a curious machine embedded in the sand, and courageously made a sketch of it. This in due course reached London. The machine was a prototype of the V.1, or flying bomb, probably launched from the air, as was originally intended by the inventor.

At the time the British did not connect it with Peenemunde, since the latter was still supposed to be concerned exclusively with rockets.

Thus at the date when Michel discovered the site at Bonnetot le Faubourg all the British knew was that the Germans were experimenting both with a rocket and a pilotless aeroplane; they could safely assume that these were intended for use against England, but did not know from where or how they would be launched. Apart from attacking Peenemunde[1] and the centres of production, there was, therefore, no means of taking effective counter-action.

Meanwhile the War Cabinet and the Chiefs of Staff, without giving way to alarm, were increasingly concerned by the prospect of a new "blitz" of unknown ferocity which might seriously disrupt plans for invading the Continent. Mr. Morrison, responsible for Civil Defence, was naturally the most agitated of the Ministers and was having plans prepared for the evacuation of a million women and children.

It can be imagined, therefore, with what interest Michel's report was read in London. It was the first definite indication that whatever was threatening would be arriving from bases in Northern France and would be aimed at London.

Instructions were sent immediately that he was to follow

---

[1] Bombed by the R.A.F. on 17th August but with only partial success.

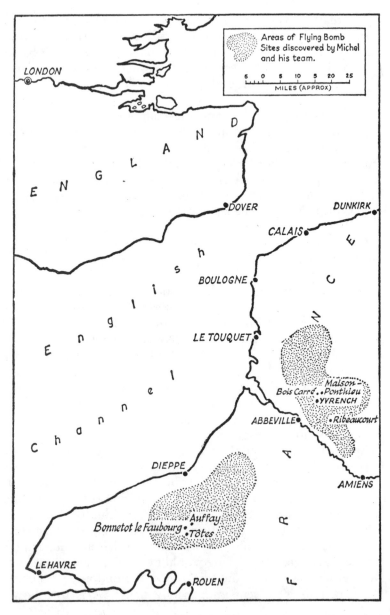

The groups of launching sites discovered by Michel's team

up his discovery and concentrate all his resources on finding out more; and this was the directive he received from "O.P." on his next visit to Switzerland.

In the meantime, with the assistance of one of his agents, Pierre Carteron, he had inspected several other sites, the location of which he had ascertained either from the Labour Office or from the foreman at Bonnetot le Faubourg. The constructions and the lay-out were always the same, and seemed in every case to converge on the concrete strip which Michel felt must hold the key to the mystery.

The only difference between one site and another was the direction of the axis of the strip, as observed by compass. But if the direction was different the aim was the same. When he had plotted the lines on his map, they all converged on one point—London.

His hunch that he was on to something good had been justified, but he was still far from realising just how good it was.

Back in Paris Michel gave all his energy to the new task. The directive given to him specified two objectives: to locate all sites similar to those he had discovered, and to obtain a complete plan of the installation. As regards the latter, he was given no clue; nobody had even mentioned a possible connection with new weapons, and he himself was still ignorant of their existence.

The first need was to organise a search of the Channel area. The sites he had inspected were all within twenty miles of the coast and it was safe to assume that the others would be about the same distance from it. He also knew that there had been a special recruitment of labour in the *Seine Inférieure* and *Pas de Calais* Departments. Thus a fairly well defined area existed in which to conduct the search.

Collecting a team of reliable agents, he provided each of them with a bicycle and allocated him a zone covering a stretch of the coast to a depth of twenty miles. Experience soon proved that this was not enough and the depth was subsequently increased.

Each agent was also provided with a map, and a description of what to look for. All he had to do, when he discovered a site, was to mark the exact position.

The results surpassed Michel's wildest expectations. In three weeks his team had located over sixty sites, distributed along a corridor nearly two hundred miles long and thirty miles wide, and running roughly parallel to the Channel coast.

Michel toured the whole area weekly in order to meet his agents and collect the information, which he then took with him to Switzerland. Later the search was extended as far as Valognes, near Cherbourg. By the end of October a hundred sites had been discovered.

"O.P." was delighted by such prompt and effective action, but Michel was far from satisfied. For he was still without a clue to the purpose of the sites, and had no plan to obtain it.

All inquiries had come up against a blank wall. German security was making certain there should be no leakage of the secret and none of the thousands of Frenchmen working on the sites had the remotest idea for what they were intended.

The problem seemed insoluble, but unless he could solve it Michel knew that he would have no rest.

12

VICTORY

As so often happens in life, Michel's greatest opportunity came to him by chance. This does not mean that the result was pure accident. On the contrary, he had done everything possible to ensure it. But, like the most successful generals, he needed luck as well to achieve a really resounding victory. His merit was to be in the position, and have the will, to exploit good fortune when it came his way.

He and his team had discovered a large number of sites, and confirmed that they were all designed for an attack on London; but he had not yet succeeded in penetrating their secret. It was a problem which obsessed him day and night, and with increasing urgency as his agents reported the rapid progress of the sites and he envisaged the danger if the British were found unprepared.

Then one day something occurred which was to set in motion a whole train of fruitful events. One of his informants, a railwayman, known as Jo-Jo, employed at the Gare du Nord, introduced him to a young man called Robert Rubenach, who was anxious to join the Resistance. Of independent means but with business experience, temperamentally gay and carefree, Robert took a small boy's delight in pulling the master's leg; his favourite pastimes were to scribble ribaldry on German posters and to let out the air from German tyres. Now he wanted to help with something more serious.

As it happened, Michel had recently seen an advertisement by a German contractor for personnel to be employed at Cormeilles-en-Vexin. It was here that the unfortunate Bart had been arrested while taking notes of the aerodrome, and Michel was still looking for someone to replace him. He therefore suggested that Robert should answer the advertisement and if successful act as his agent.

Robert, only too delighted, agreed. Duly enrolled as a member of the *réseau*, he took the *nom de guerre* of Robert de Vic, after his native town of Lorraine.

He then answered the advertisement and was engaged as an accountant, not at Cormeilles-en-Vexin, but at Bernes, twenty miles north of Paris. Since this was also an important enemy airfield which the Germans were in process of developing, Michel was quite content.

The work had only just started, and more technicians were needed. This gave Robert the idea of proposing to a friend of his, a young engineer called André Comps, that he should apply for one of the vacancies, so that they could be together.

André, who had just taken his degree, was not very keen to start his career under German auspices; but when Robert hinted that it could be a means of helping the Allies he agreed to apply, and was engaged as draughtsman.

A few days later Robert met Michel in Paris to report on the progress of the aerodrome. He found his chief *distrait*: obviously his mind was elsewhere. After a while Michel interrupted to ask Robert if he had heard anything of special sites being constructed near the Channel coast; and drew a rough plan to show what he meant. This was news to Robert and he promised to keep his eyes open.

On return to Bernes he stopped by the board where notices were posted of interest to the employees. Since his departure earlier in the day a new notice had been posted. It was an appeal for certain categories of technicians, who were asked to volunteer for urgent work at an unspecified place, where they would be boarded and lodged on the spot.

Although there was nothing to indicate it, his instinct told Robert that this was connected with the matter in which Michel had shown so much interest. Among the personnel required were draughtsmen. Why shouldn't André volunteer?

The two were living at the same billet and it was there that Robert found his young friend.

"Listen," he said, "have you seen the new notice—the one where they ask for volunteers?"

"Yes, I did read it," replied André without much interest. "Why?"

"I've a hunch it's something important I've been asked to investigate. If you took it on you could probably find out."

"Do you think so?"

"Well, you could try, at least."

André was dubious. It was the first time he had been asked to do something illegal and he had never met Michel. Although he had come to Bernes because Robert had appealed to his patriotism, there had as yet been no opportunity to show it. Quiet and studious, and excessively shy, he was more interested in winning his spurs as an engineer than in engaging in clandestine activities against the Germans.

However, Robert continued to press him, and in the end he agreed to put his name on the list.

A few days later he was given his orders. With the other volunteers he was to report next day at one of the Paris termini. Without yet knowing his destination, he said good-bye to Robert. It was agreed that as soon as he had anything to report he should ask for a day's leave and come to Paris.

Nothing happened for a week, and then Robert, who had meanwhile informed Michel what he had done, telephoned to say that André was on his way and to suggest that the three of them should meet for lunch at his flat.

It was Michel's first meeting with André and he was not very favourably impressed. The young man struck him as immature and timid, without any strong convictions or real heart in the Resistance, and more interested in his profession than helping his country.

This impression was soon to be belied. The truth was that

André had not yet adapted himself to the double life into which Robert had inveigled him, and which he had accepted without an idea of what it might entail.

He had arrived, he explained, from Yvrench, a village about ten miles north-east of Abbeville, and was employed on the construction of a site at a place called Bois Carré which answered the description given him by Robert. It was, in fact, one of those already discovered by Michel's team.

He then produced a few rudimentary sketches, which were scarcely more informative than those Michel had made himself; and with the air of one who is relieved to have finished an uncongenial task and hopes not to be asked to do any more, announced that he must be going.

"Wait a minute," said Michel quietly. "I'd like to ask you some questions."

Looking rather unhappy André sat down again.

"First of all, what is your job at Bois Carré?"

"Well, I was engaged as architectural draughtsman."

"And what does that mean exactly?"

"It means that I have to draw up the plans for the constructions."

"And how do you do that?"

"Well, there's a master plan, showing the general lay-out. My job is to draw up detailed plans for our site. Naturally they vary with each one—according to its size, surroundings, means of access, etc. I can tell you it's quite a business, and I don't get any help. However, I'm managing all right—at any rate the *boche* seems quite pleased with me."

"The boche? Who is he?"

"The German officer in charge."

"There's only one?"

"Only one permanently. The others come and go."

"So really you've got quite a responsibility."

"Oh, yes," said André proudly. "In fact, you could say that I'm the man who is doing the work."

"Very interesting," commented Michel dryly.

In his enthusiasm for the new job—after all, it was his first since graduating as an engineer—André had lost his timidity. But now the anxious look reappeared in his face.

"I hope that will help you," he remarked nervously, glancing at the sketches. "Because I really ought to be getting back now."

"Not much, I'm afraid," said Michel. "In fact, it really takes us little farther forward. What I need—and you are probably the only Frenchman who can obtain it—is a complete and detailed set of plans; in fact, a copy of those you are preparing."

André looked aghast.

"I'm afraid that will be difficult," he stammered.

"Why—since you have legitimate access to them? I should have thought you were the one person for whom it would be easy."

"That's true," André admitted with increasing embarrassment, "but—well—you see—since Robert asked me to do this the Germans have made us all sign an undertaking . . . not to reveal what we were doing."

"That means nothing," Michel snapped. "We are at war. Your labour is conscripted. You are not a free agent. An undertaking given in such circumstances is not binding."

André gave a dispirited shrug. "I suppose you're right. I hadn't thought about it."

"Is it perhaps that you are afraid?"

André kept his eyes on the ground.

"I hadn't thought about that either," he answered after a while, "but since you mention it, I must confess it seems to me that you are asking me to do something very dangerous."

"Good," said Michel. "Now we know where we are. Besides it's perfectly natural. We are *all* afraid, and I more than any."

He got up and started to walk about the room. Robert had gone out to talk to his wife and he and André were alone.

In principle he never tried to coerce an unwilling person. The exceptions were when there was no alternative, and this was one of them. By a combination of luck and initiative he had secured an agent who was in a position to obtain the most vital information. The chances were slight of finding anyone else as well placed as André for his purpose, since on the other sites he knew of no Frenchmen employed above the rank of foreman. And time was running out. It was André or no one.

"Listen," he said. "I must speak frankly. You have the

opportunity—possibly unique—of rendering a great service to our country. It is your duty as a Frenchman to do it—and I'm sure if you reflect you will see that. But I must warn you that if you refuse you will be just as guilty as a soldier who runs away in battle. And you will be treated accordingly. You understand?"

André nodded.

"Well then?"

"Put like that I see it leaves me no choice."

"So you'll do it."

There was a pause before André murmured, "Yes."

"Good. I'll give you a fortnight. At the end of that I want you to meet me again here bringing copies of all the plans. The more detailed the better. Agreed?"

André nodded, but he still looked doubtful.

"It's going to be difficult to get away," he said. "The Germans won't give us any leave. I came to-day without telling them and I shall have to make some excuse when I get back."

"Then this is what you must do. During the second week you will start complaining of pains in the stomach. These will become more and more severe until you are unable to continue your work. You will then ask permission to come to Paris to be treated by your own doctor. Once you are here I'll arrange the rest."

"All right. I'll do what I can."

"I'm sure of it," said Michel. "I have confidence in you. And now you'd better be getting back."

For two weeks there was no news. Michel was away from Paris doing his round of the *Midi*, and heard nothing from Robert, who was his link with André. He had taken the latter's sketches of the site to Switzerland, where once again his British contact had impressed on him the urgency of obtaining more precise information.

By this time knowledge of the V.1 in Britain was advanced to the extent that it was known that a pilotless aeroplane similar to the machine found by the Dane on Bornholm was being experimented with at Peenemunde.

This established the connection of the new weapon with the

experimental station, which hitherto had only been associated with rockets; but it did not link up with the sites in France, so that from the point of view of defence against the threat the British Government were not much further forward.

Meanwhile, Michel speculated anxiously on the progress made by André. Had he been wrong to stake everything on such a young and, apparently, timid person? Or had he perhaps midjudged him? True, the first impression had been unfavourable; and yet when at the end he had professed confidence in André, it was only for the purpose of *giving* it to him. There *was* something in André which inspired confidence, if it was only his sincerity in admitting that he was scared. A less honest person would have made some other excuse.

Michel had arranged to return to Paris on the morning of the day fixed for their next meeting. As soon as he arrived he contacted Robert to find out if the meeting was on. The answer was reassuring: yes, André had sent a message the night before to say that they could expect him for lunch at Robert's flat.

When Michel arrived at the flat, André was already there. Before they had exchanged a word, his face showed Michel that he had succeeded. Although his manner was still shy the anxious expression had gone. In place of the timid boy there was a man with confidence in himself.

While they ate their lunch André told his story. To copy the plans he had already seen presented no difficulty. They were those he had made himself, based on the German master plan but adapted to local requirements. Except when required on the site, they were kept in the hut which he used as office and where he was usually alone. He had merely to wait for a quiet moment when he was resonably secure from interruption and take a tracing. This he had done within forty-eight hours of returning from Paris.

Unfortunately they were not complete. There was one piece of the jig-saw missing and it was the most important of all, for it alone showed what was to be erected on top of the concrete strip.

That a separate plan for this existed and had not been shown to him, André was well aware. Except for the excavation of some square holes down either side of it, no work had been begun on the concrete strip; but he had frequently seen the German engineer examining it with a blue-print in his hand. He had also noticed that, after completing his inspection, the German always returned the blue-print to the inside pocket of his overcoat.

As the days passed André was more and more convinced that here was the missing link. Somehow or other he had to obtain that blue-print.

Exactly how, he could not see. As far as he could observe, it never left the possession of the German, who wore his overcoat even in his office, which was next to André's.

There was, however, one exception to this rule. Every morning at nine o'clock precisely the German left his office *without* his overcoat, walked to the edge of the site and disappeared behind the canvas screen shielding the latrines. Some time later he reappeared and returned to his office.

André could watch this proceeding from his window and he took to timing its duration. It varied between three and five minutes; the longer period was when the German took a newspaper with him.

For two or three days after making this discovery, André was seized with a sort of mental paralysis. He could not bring himself to accept the inescapable conclusion: that if he was not to fail in his duty, there was no alternative but to steal the blue-print and that this could only be done during one of the brief daily interludes when the German was separated from his overcoat.

But as the dead-line given him by Michel drew closer, fear of facing the latter with an admission of failure became a stronger motive than fear of the consequences if he was caught by the German; and two days before he was due again in Paris he took a firm resolution to make the attempt.

As luck would have it, it was one of the days when the German refused to be parted from his newspaper. He even started reading it before he reached the screen. This emboldened André, as if were, to jump the gun. Without waiting till the German was out of sight, he nipped into the next office, saw the overcoat hanging from a hook, put his hand in the inside pocket, and grabbed the blue-print.

Back in his own office, he made a rapid tracing of the plan, jotted down the essential measurements and made some short-hand notes. He had allowed himself three minutes for the operation, and by the time he had finished there were thirty seconds still to run: just long enough to walk to the next room, replace the blue-print where he had found it, and return to his place. When the German reappeared, after another minute had passed, André was working calmly at his drawing-board.

The next day he had reported sick, with vomiting and pains in the abdomen. The German doctor was sceptical; but, when André started retching in his surgery, agreed to his request to be treated at home and authorised four days' leave.

"You have done well," said Michel, when André had finished his story, "and justified the confidence I expressed in you. But you haven't finished your work yet. We'll need several days to interpret these drawings and produce an intelligible plan. Then I'll have to take it to Switzerland and there will be a further delay sending it to London. It is essential that you remain in Paris until it is received over there. We'll have to get you an extension of leave."

Thanks to Raoul Monod, the surgeon of the clinic in the Rue du Sergent Bauchat, where Joseph Bart had been treated, this was arranged. A certificate was dispatched to the German doctor at Yvrench stating that the patient required ten days of complete rest and requesting extension of his leave for another week.

The next problem was to find a safe place where André and Michel could work on the plans undisturbed. This was solved by André, one of whose relations owned a house, for the time being unoccupied, at La Varenne St. Hilaire, just outside Paris.

Here for the next four days the pair of them went to work. For security reasons, André had kept his material to the minimum, so that if it was found on him, or at his billet, he could have explained it away as "home work." It consisted of an assortment of rough sketches, tracings and notes, the latter in a shorthand of his own. Out of this, assisted by his memory and technical knowledge, as well as that of Michel, who was also an engineer, there had to be pieced together a coherent plan of the site as it would appear when all construction was completed.

It was a formidable task and they were frequently baffled. Several times André, easily discouraged, came near despair. But Michel kept him at it, going out to buy the food and cooking it himself; and gradually a plan emerged, accurately drawn to scale, which revealed the whole scheme. One of André's rough sketches will give an idea of its principal features. Since his notes were written in French a key to the plan in English is provided below it.

Rectangular in shape, and representing an area measuring approximately three hundred and fifty yards by two hundred yards, it showed a number of small buildings and concrete platforms connected by a network of communicating roads. As Michel had already noticed, the roads converged on a larger emplacement at the northern corner of the site: that is, the corner nearest to England. This was prolonged by the concrete strip, which had first attracted his attention at Bonnetot le Faubourg, and which he had always felt held the key to the mystery.

But now at last one could see for what it was intended. The copy of the blue-print stolen by André showed that its function was to support an inclined runway, or ramp, about a hundred and fifty feet long, rising at an angle of fifteen degrees, and carrying two metal strips rather like a small-gauge railway. With its axis, as André had confirmed, pointed at London, a hundred and thirty miles away, there could no longer be any doubt that it was designed for the launching of some missile aimed at the British capital. A rectangular structure at the foot of the ramp was obviously the firing point. The other buildings, including one designed on the non-magnetic principle, were respectively for assembly, storing, fuelling, etc.

There was also a curious feature whose significance for the time being remained obscure. Some of the buildings were extended by a curved section which, seen from the air, made them resemble a ski on its side. It was this that gave their name to the "ski sites," as they were subsequently called by the R.A.F. The ski-shaped building were, in fact, intended for the storage of the flying bombs, although they were also used as shelters to which the personnel could retire when the bomb was launched.

Armed with the sketch and the plans which accompanied it, an expert could reconstruct the complete procedure for assembling and launching the flying bomb, even though some of its details were only disclosed much later, after the capture of the sites and of some bombs intact.

Briefly the procedure was as follows, the number in brackets referring to the key to André's sketch.

When a bomb was to be launched it was first assembled and checked, with its war-head in place, on the Checking-out Platform (1). It was then moved to the Waiting Platform (2), at the side of which stood the office (3) of the chief technician. From here it was taken to the *Richthaus* (4), a non-magnetic building whose axis was exactly parallel to the direction of the ramp.

In the *Richthaus*, which the bomb entered on rails, there was a sort of turntable which enabled it to be rotated before being brought into alignment with the axis. Its gyroscopic compass was then set at zero. If during its subsequent flight there was any deflection from course, the compass would send out electronic signals which corrected the error.

With its controls set the bomb was next moved to the foot of the ramp (5), fuelled and placed in position. It was now ready for launching.

Welded to the ramp were two plates with guide rails, along which the bomb travelled, its tail being supported on a sledge. Immediately below the rails there was a long cylinder—the firing tube—in which a dumb-bell shaped piston fitted. This piston had a protuding lug which engaged with the fuselage of the flying bomb, so that when fired it travelled at great speed up the tube carrying the missile forward with it.

As soon as the bomb left the ramp and became airborne it continued under its own power—it was driven by a simple type of jet propulsion engine—while the piston and the sledge described a parabola through the air before falling to the earth some two or three hundred yards away, whence they were recovered to be used again.

Power to launch the bomb was provided by a "steam gun" embedded in a massive block of concrete (6) to take the recoil.

While the pressure behind the piston was building up, the missile was held in leash by means of a bolt secured to a bracket at the base of the ramp. When the pressure was sufficient to shear the bolt, piston and bomb were released and shot forward together.

During the firing operation the crew retired to a bomb-proof shelter and firing cabin (7), from which the mechanism was operated by remote control. A narrow slit with a thick layer of glass enabled them to observe the operation. (In spite of this precaution, during the early stages many casualties occurred and it was reckoned that as many Germans were killed by their own weapon as in all the Allied bombing of the sites.)

When the final picture emerged, Michel and André felt something of the wonder of the archæologist who, from some scattered remnants, by dint of patient measurement, reconstructs the magnificent building of which they once formed part. It was difficult, in fact, to believe that between them they had pierced the mystery; and yet Michel was certain that, even if he did not understand it all himself, he had in his hands the essential data which the British Intelligence Service had been so desperately seeking.

However, there was no time for self-congratulation. The four days' leave granted to André had expired and there had been no acknowledgment of his request for an extension. If the Germans started to investigate they might easily become suspicious. It was essential for Michel to get to Switzerland first.

After instructing André to make himself scarce, but on no account to return to Yvrench until he sent him a message, Michel returned to Paris. The same evening he left for the Swiss frontier, carrying the plans in his brief-case.

13

EXPLOITATION OF VICTORY

Michel's rendezvous with his British contact was never fixed in advance. He simply telephoned that he was on his way as soon as he had crossed the frontier. These conversations were always conducted in a code agreed at the previous meeting.

On this occasion he announced that he had bought the tickets and that the performance began at two o'clock. Then he added: "I've got very good seats."

"O.P." was therefore prepared for something exceptional, bet even so he was staggered by the richness of Michel's haul. Consisting of a dozen architect's drawings and a master plan, it was a complete blue-print of a "ski" site, such as a construction engineer would have required to build one.[1] Rapidly Michel told the story of its acquisition.

"O.P." was triumphant. "This is terrific. It's the biggest thing we've brought off. We'll send the whole shoot in the

---

[1] Models were, in fact, made from it and used, among other purposes, for target identification by the R.A.F.

bag." He looked at his watch. "My God, they close it at four."

He dashed out of the room and a few minutes later returned to say that all was arranged. The diplomatic bag, in which papers were sent to England and which was obligingly carried across enemy country by a neutral courier, would be delayed for two hours to give time for the precious parcel to reach the Embassy in Berne. This, as "O.P." explained, was unheard of.

"Now I must draft a cable," said "O.P." "You'll have to help me with that."

For an hour or so they worked together on the draft, trying to put into plain English the mass of technical detail which Michel had brought with him in notes and sketches. When finally "O.P." was satisfied and the cable had been sent for enciphering, he asked Michel what his plans were.

"How long will the bag take to reach London?" Michel asked.

"We must allow four days."

"And they'll acknowledge immediately?"

"Presumably."

"Then I'll return here in four days. Until I hear it's been received untampered I cannot allow André to return to Bois Carré. It would be sending him to his death—in fact worse. I told him to wait in Paris till he heard from me."

"Okay. I'll expect you."

Four days later Michel was back in Lausanne. He had used the interval to make a short tour of the *Midi* for routine contacts and collection of reports from his agents.

He was met by a beaming "O.P.," who, without saying a word, thrust a telegram under his nose.

"Booty received safely. Congratulations." Michel read.

"If we'd never done anything else," said "O.P.," "and never do anything again, this has justified our existence."

It was no exaggeration. The exposure of the V.1 threat in all its details, long before the first flying bomb was fired, was a gigantic combined operation for which the British Government used all their resources and in which thousands of people were involved, from the Prime Minister feeding his energy into every branch of the public service, down to the humblest secret agent pedalling his bicycle through the dusty French lanes.

When all due credit has been given to others, however, there is no doubt that the plan of the site at Bois Carré had a decisive influence on the operation. When it reached London at the end of October the British Government already knew of the existence of the flying bomb—although it was still referred to as the "pilotless aeroplane"—and they also knew that it was being tested at Peenemunde. But they did not yet connect this knowledge with the sites discovered in France.

Some weeks after the receipt of the plan a photograph of Peenemunde taken by the R.A.F. revealed an installation similar to that at Bois Carré in all respects, including the curious ski-shaped construction. Thus the connection between Peenemunde and the sites in France was for the first time definitely established and the suspicion that they were to be used as launching platforms for the new weapon—to which André's drawing of the inclined runway had given colour—deepened into near conviction.

This became certainty a few days later—to be exact, on 28th November—when another aerial photograph of Peenemunde showed a pilotless aeroplane actually sitting on its runway.[1] The final link in the chain of evidence had been forged.

Leading from Bornholm to Peenemunde, from Peenemunde to Bonnetot le Faubourg, from Bonnetot le Faubourg to Bois Carré, and from Bois Carré back to Peenemunde, it had been produced by the joint effort of ground and air intelligence, and in the former, as the Prime Minister acknowledged at the time,[2] the rôle played by the *réseau "Agir"* was of capital importance. It had found the first site, located most of the others, and produced the first complete plan of a site.[3]

[1] See *Royal Air Force*, 1939–1945, Vol. III, p. 147. (H.M. Stationery Office, 1954).
[2] In a letter to President Roosevelt dated 25th October, Churchill wrote: "We have an excellent system of intelligence in this part of N. France and it is from these sources as well as from photographs and prisoners that the story is built up."
[3] One other patriotic organisation also handled by "O.P." made a smaller but valuable contribution by locating some of the sites. Its gallant eighteen-year-old leader was afterwards captured and shot by the Germans.

Later Churchill was to pay a personal tribute to the agents—and they included, of course, not only Frenchmen but also Poles and other nationals—who risked their lives to save England from its peril. Summing up his account of the defeat of the V.1, this is what he wrote:

"Our Intelligence had played a vital part. The size and performance of the weapon, and the intended scale of attack, were known to us in excellent time. This enabled our fighters to be made ready. The launching sites and the storage caverns were found, enabling our bombers to delay the attack and mitigate its violence. Every known means of getting information was employed, and it was pieced together with great skill. To all our sources, many of whom worked amid deadly danger, and some of whom will be for ever unknown to us, I pay my tribute."[1]

Of all this, of course, Michel knew nothing. Like everyone else he had heard rumours—they had appeared in the Press—of new weapons; but he was quite ignorant of what had been discovered at Peenemunde and elsewhere, and how it fitted in with his own discoveries.

His British contact was probably not much wiser—it was not the policy of headquarters to share secrets with their subordinates—but, even if his superiors had seen fit to put "O.P." "in the picture," he would have been barred by the rules from passing it on to Michel.

There was a good reason for this. If an agent in the field is given a hint of what to look for, there will be a strong temptation to colour his reports accordingly. Moreover, to put him in possession of other information is to risk the enemy finding out that you have it.

In consequence, apart from the congratulatory telegram, which was at least an indication of its value, Michel had no idea of the crucial importance which was attached in London to the plans of Bois Carré. It was just another job done. He had completed one more mission and it was time to return for the next.

---

[1] *The Second World War*, Vol. VI. p. 43.

It was too late for him to reach the frontier before dark, so he decided to spend the night at Neuchâtel. Having just brought off one of the biggest coups achieved by any intelligence service in the war, he might well have thought it an occasion to celebrate. The idea never entered his head. He drank very little anyhow, and the knowledge that he had succeeded and could sleep without danger was sufficient reward for his labours.

The next day he crossed the frontier and returned to Paris. He had telephoned earlier and found Robert and André waiting for him in Robert's flat. On Robert's insistence a bottle of champagne was now opened. Then André, whose extension of leave expired that day, had to depart to return to Bois Carré.

"The congratulations sent by the British are primarily for you," Michel said. "But that's not a reason for slacking. I shall expect you to keep me fully informed of all new developments at Bois Carré."

André smiled. He and Michel understood each other now.

"What are the English going to do with what we've given them?" he asked.

"We must wait and see," said Michel diplomatically.

It was a question often asked by his agents. Having risked their lives to obtain some information, they naturally liked to see results; and if it took the form of a heavy raid by the R.A.F., so much the better.

More often nothing happened at all; and then, to maintain morale—perhaps the hardest of all his tasks—Michel could only assure them of the great value attached to their work by the British Ally.

On this occasion he had asked "O.P." the same question.

"I suppose they'll bomb the sites," was the reply, "but goodness knows when. They wouldn't tell us, anyhow."

For the time being he and André and the other members of the team had to be content with this.

Soon afterwards, Michel received another message from Rouen. It came from the station-master, Pierre Bouguet, who was a friend of Daudemard, the informant who had put Michel on the track of the sites. The message was to the effect that some unusually shaped crates had recently arrived at

Rouen in a goods wagon and had been sent on to the station of Auffay.

Michel was always interested in Auffay, which had been the starting point of his most rewarding enterprise up-to-date. He therefore decided to investigate, and instructed one of his agents, Pierre Carteron, who had been highly successful in locating other sites, to meet him on the spot.

The station-master at Auffay, a M. Bourdon, to whom they first addressed their inquiries, was not known to either of them, but he was quite willing to talk. He informed them that the wagon, with its mysterious contents, had been shunted into a shed belonging to the local sugar factory, which was almost next door to the station but on the other side of the railway. The shed had been requisitioned and was closely guarded by German sentries.

A preliminary reconnaissance confirmed this news. The shed stood in a corner of the factory premises and was connected by a loop line to the railway, from which it was separated only by a footpath running parallel to the track. A sentry was walking his beat in front of the entrance.

After observing for a while from the platform of the station, where they pretended to be waiting for a train, they noticed that the sentry sometimes prolonged his beat. Instead of stopping when he reached the corner of the shed, he turned ninety degrees and continued about half-way down its side. From there he could see anyone approaching on the path.

It was therefore arranged that Pierre should walk along it and distract the sentry's attention at the moment when he was at the maximum distance from the entrance of the shed and no longer in sight of it. Michel would then cross the railway and slip inside the shed before the sentry returned to the front. All went according to the plan. Michel entered the shed without being detected, and after taking the precaution of unbuttoning his trousers—so that if caught he would have a ready-made excuse—set to work to examine the crates.

Their contents, whatever they were, were in three sections, and as far as he could make out, for he was working almost in darkness, consisted of a cigar-shaped body and two flatter parts. With a tape measure, which he had concealed under his shirt, he measured such portions as were accessible and made a mental note of their form. This took him nearly an hour, at the end of which he had a pretty shrewd idea of what the crates contained.

When he had learnt all he could he waited for the propitious moment, and then made his retreat by the way he had come.

A week later one of the first sketches of the flying bomb to reach England, with its dimensions accurately given, was on its way to London.

Meanwhile the team waited with increasing impatience for the retribution to come. André was reporting regularly on the progress at Bois Carré, which by now was practically ready to go into operation, and agents in other localities confirmed this impression. The first bombs had arrived and were being assembled under cover, and some of the sites were already being camouflaged. At any moment, it seemed, they would be ready. Were the British never going to take action?

At last the great moment came. On the 25th December, 1943—five days after Michel's return from Auffay—the R.A.F. struck. The effect was devastating. At least a dozen sites, accurately pinpointed by agents' reports and aerial photography, were destroyed in the first raid. A few nights later Bois Carré was attacked; and to his enormous satisfaction on arriving for work the next morning, André was able to see with his own eyes the result which he had done so much to bring about.

He could see at once that the site was beyond repair. The news had got around and only a few French workmen turned up. They were employed cleaning up the mess. The offices, though badly damaged, were still standing, and André was given the job of repairing them.

At La Loge (Somme) Pierre Carteron was actually present when the bombers dropped their load. He himself was lifted by the blast and lucky to escape with a broken arm. Casualties of both French and Germans were heavy. More serious from the German point of view, the workmen panicked and refused to return to the site. This reaction was general and was one of the reasons why the Germans abandoned the idea of repairing the sites, and concentrated on building new and smaller ones which could be hidden in woods or otherwise concealed from the air.

By the end of December fifty-two sites had been hit, and during the first half of January seventy-nine were attacked, including Bonnetot le Faubourg and Le Bosc Melet.[1]

On 7th January, Colonel Wachtel, commander of *Flak* Regiment 155W, which had been specially formed to operate the V.1 weapon, wrote in his war diary: "If Allied bombing continues at its present rate for two more weeks, the hope of ever using the original site system operationally will have to be abandoned."

He was not being over-pessimistic. According to the enemy's own admission, between 15th December, 1943, and 31st March, 1944, nine sites were totally destroyed, thirty-five severely damaged, twenty-nine partly damaged, and twenty lightly damaged, out of a total of one hundred and four.[2]

The effect was to put the majority of sites out of action before they could be used. Long before the end of March, however—in fact, at the end of February—the Germans realised that their original scheme was in ruins, and turned their attention to improvising another, which in the event proved quite inadequate. About forty new sites were constructed on the same principle but much smaller and more easily hidden, and it was from these that the attack on London was eventually launched without any real success. What could have been a serious, and possibly decisive, threat to the Allies, was reduced strategically to not much more than a nuisance.

For the effect of the bombing of the sites was two-fold: it both delayed and mitigated the flying bomb atack.

Hitler had given orders for the attack to start on 15th December, with an onslaught of five thousand bombs a month. Had this plan been carried out—even assuming it made no difference to the Allied invasion of France—something like fifty thousand flying bombs would have been launched in the nine months before the capture of the sites by Montgomery's army in September, 1944. Of these, on the basis of actual experience, over fifteen thousand would have got through, as compared with the two thousand four hundred which actually

---

[1] See *Royal Air Force*, 1939–1945, Vol. III, p. 150.
[2] *War Diary of Flak Regiment* 155.

arrived between June and September.[1] In other words, the attack would have been six times as severe and lasted six months longer. This might well have sufficed to alter the course of the war.

Here it may be appropriate to quote the opinion of a man who was in as good a position as any to estimate the effect had Hitler's original plan succeeded. Writing in his *Crusade in Europe,* this is what Eisenhower had to say of the V.1:

"It seems likely that if the Germans had succeeded in perfecting and using these new weapons six months earlier than they did our invasion of Europe would have proved exceedingly difficult, perhaps impossible. I feel sure that if they had succeeded in using these weapons over a six months period, and particularly if they had made the Portsmouth-Southhampton area one of their principal targets, "Overlord" might have been written off."

The Germans had, in fact, sustained a major defeat; they had played their last trump card and lost. They were, moreover, in no doubt of the reason: through his spies the enemy had got wind of their plans and countered before they were ready. Wachtel himself attributed his failure to the British Intelligence Service, asserting that their agents were swarming everywhere, especially in the launching area.

"Swarming" was an exaggeration. During the whole period of his investigation Michel never had more than six men working in the area, including himself, and his rival organisation probably not so many. The fact that the Germans came to see spies behind every hedgerow is a tribute to what was achieved by so few.

They reacted by redoubling their security measures. Wachtel, convinced that he was marked down for assassination, changed his name, wore a false beard, and dressed in a different uniform. Although most of them were now useless, the sites were more closely guarded than ever and most of the French workers, if they had not already taken flight from the bombing, were discharged.

---

[1] The total launched against London, according to German official sources, was 8,564. Of those which failed to reach the target approximately 4,000 were destroyed by defences and another 1,000 crashed soon after launching.

At the same time the counter-espionage services, which had doubtless come under heavy criticism, intensified their efforts to track down the spies.

Although there was nothing for André to do at Bois Carré after he had repaired the offices, he had not been released from his engagement and had not asked for release for fear of arousing suspicion. Later he was employed patching up other sites, including one or two of the modified type which eventually came into action.

The fact that the Bois Carré site had been one of the first to be bombed, and that most accurately, was likely, he realised, to attract inquiries; these would inevitably lead to himself as the only Frenchman employed in a position of responsibility. Thus he waited with the sword of Damocles suspended over him. When another young Frenchman was put to work with him, whom he instantly guessed to be a *mouton*—i.e., a stool pigeon—it was clear that the net was closing in.

At the time he was staying in a billet about half a mile from his work, to which he walked across fields every morning. One day as he was approaching he saw two large cars drawn up outside the offices. They were black limousines of the type used by the Gestapo, and he had no doubt what they were there for.

Turning round, he hurried off and avoiding his billet took refuge with another family about two miles away. Shortly after, the Gestapo arrived at his late habitation and searched it without result. After remaining in hiding for a month he returned to Paris and eventually found a safe retreat at Epinay-Sur-Orge, where he remained till the Liberation.

Soon afterwards, Robert was also in trouble, but this had nothing to do with the V.1 sites. A Frenchman called Forly, a "collabo," also employed at Bernes, had been killed by a grenade thrown by a *résistant* while he was drinking in front of a café with two Germans. On his body was found a notebook containing a list of people known to be hostile to the Occupying Authority. It included the name of Robert, who never concealed his feelings and who was described by the informer as a "dangerous terrorist."

Robert, with two others, was arrested and taken to Maisons-Laffitte for interrogation. He defended himself by discrediting Forly; there had been a theft from the safe in his office and he was able to convince the police that Forly was the thief. He was not maltreated, and in consideration of the fact that he had volunteered to work for the Germans was released with a caution at the end of the day.

The other two were tortured savagely, and one of them subsequently died as a result.

To complete the story of Michel's work on the V.1, one other incident must be recorded here.

Soon after the attack on the sites had begun, he arrived in Switzerland with a report that the top German scientists employed on the new weapon were staying at the Château de Ribeaucourt. He had only heard the news just before his departure, and had not time either to check it, or to locate the place, which he thought was somewhere in the Pas de Calais.

For an hour he and "O.P." poured over maps trying to spot the name, but without success. Then Michel had to return to France where he had an urgent appointment the next day.

"O.P." continued the search, but still without success. Maps, guide books, directories, were all of no avail—the name of Ribeaucourt, or anything like it, was not to be found. It seemed useless to persist—probably Michel had got the name wrong, although this would be most unlike him.

It was a Saturday and "O.P." was due to join his wife at their châlet for one of his rare week-ends off duty. He had got as far as the station when he realised that he would have no peace of mind until he solved the enigma. Telephoning an excuse to his home, he returned to his office and got out his maps again.

It was long after midnight when he at last found his quarry. In an ancient guide book a page was devoted to the Abbeville district, and there, on a small map printed opposite, was the name: Château de Ribeaucourt.

The Swiss telegraph office was open all night. "O.P." put his message into cipher, took it round, and at 3.00 a.m. dispatched it.

At 9.00 a.m. he received the reply from London. "Your 0300 acknowledged," it said. "At 0600 Château reconnoitred. At 0800 Château bombed. Excellent staff work."

Some months later, when the British Army advanced into

the area, a building near the Château was found in ruins; and to the Intelligence Officer visiting it French peasants pointed out a row of graves in which the Germans who lost their lives in the raid had been buried. They included the commandant of the establishment, Colonel Siebel.

As an example of good liaison between "I" and "Ops," this would be hard to beat.

It was, however, only one instance of "O.P.'s" devotion. Anybody who is engaged in Michel's kind of work knows the importance of the man who acts as his contact. It was "O.P." whose understanding and encouragement gave Michel the material and moral support without which he could not have achieved what he did.

Like all high-mettled animals Michel needed handling; and with his intelligence, tact and wisdom "O.P." was the perfect manager for this *cheval de race*.

14

ARREST OF MICHEL

Anyone who leads the sort of life that Michel had been living knows that sooner or later it must end in disaster. It was more than a risk—almost a certainty—which he had accepted from the beginning, and of which he was constantly reminded, not only by the daily toll of arrest, but by the very circumstances of his existence.

Constantly moving, never sleeping two nights running in the same place, travelling under a false name with forged papers, alternately hunting and being hunted, he had something in common with a fox, who one day is breaking into a chicken run and the next flying for its life before the pack.

But after two and a half years, during which almost all the links with his former life had been broken, he had come to accept the present almost as normal. That he should never see his family, except for rare and fleeting visits, or go to an office, or meet friends, or spend an evening listening to music or reading a book, no longer struck him as extraordinary.

In the same way he had become accustomed to living with danger. He had taken so many risks, had so many close escapes, that risk and escape seemed to belong to the natural order. He had got away with it every time, why not again?

Yet in his inner consciousness he knew it could not last. One by one some of his best men had already gone: Olivier Giran, Roman, the Maiffrets, Léopold Turcan—tortured beyond belief in a Blois cellar—and a dozen others who had endured a similar ordeal before being shot or deported. The surprising thing was that he, the most exposed of all, should have avoided the same fate for so long.

By the end of 1943, and especially after the flight of André, he could not believe it would be postponed much longer. Like a man condemned to death by his own doctor, he began to look at people and things as though he was seeing them for the last time.

For some time he had had the feeling of being followed in Paris. To get rid of his "shadow" he found it best to use the Metro. On arriving at the station he would loiter about the subway till a subterranean rumble announced the approach of the train. Judging the moment to a nicety he would then run down the steps and reach the platform just as the automatic gate was closing. While Michel squeezed through and flung himself on the train, anyone following was left immobilised on the wrong side of the barrier.

Unfortunately the enemy possessed a weapon against which no amount of courage or cunning could prevail. Like so many others, Michel was to be betrayed by treachery.

Towards the end of the year 1943, Mme. Simone Boirel, the proprietress of the Hôtellerie de Pierrelatte and one of Michel's most effective agents, received a visit from her old friend, Laure Lescane. A woman of thirty-five, pretty, elegant and well educated, Laure had known Simone since their schooldays, and the latter was delighted to see her.

In an exhange of news and confidences, Mme. Boirel revealed the work she was doing for the Resistance, mentioned the name of Michel, and suggested that her friend should join the *réseau*.

Laure Lescane was thrilled. As it happened, she informed her friend, she was engaged to a certain Comte de Kergoat, who was anxious to get in touch with the Allies in connection with an invention of his. Could M. Hollard help him?

Mme. Boirel replied that she was sure he could and promised to do her best to arrange a meeting.

Michel was not keen on the idea, but allowed himself to be introduced to Laure Lescane. As a precaution he would not commit himself to a meeting with her fiancé, and instead called on Kergoat unexpectedly.

He found the self-styled Count installed in a luxurious flat close to the Bois de Boulogne. Kergoat[1] was a man of forty, of middle height, with abnormally broad shoulders and an enormous square, fleshy face. He received Michel seated behind a large desk, in an expensively furnished drawing-room which he also used as an office. His coarse appearance and vulgar manners made a bad impression on Michel.

He explained his invention: a new kind of air brake which enabled aircraft to land with a much shorter run. After years of experiment he had now perfected the device and was anxious, he said, to offer it to the Allies. As he understood that Michel was in touch with them, would he act as an intermediary?

Michel, who had taken an instant dislike to the man, saw that he was only interested in money. He was therefore extremely "cagey," made no promises, but suggested that Kergoat put his proposal in writing.

"If I do that," Kergoat objected, "they may take my idea and not pay me anything."

"You'll have to take the risk," said Michel. "Anyhow you don't have to go into details."

After some more discussion Kergoat agreed and asked when they could meet again. Michel was evasive, said that he was seldom in Paris, but that his secretary would receive any communication. The interview then ended.

During the next weeks Kergoat and an unknown woman made repeated attempts to contact Michel and several times called at his office. Michel's secretary, Madeleine Boulanger, herself a member of the *réseau*, invariably told them he was away.

This was usually true, for in addition to his usual round of visits, there was the special team observing the V.1 sites to

[1] His real name was Henri Marette. An informer working for the Gestapo, he was convicted of treachery after the war and sentenced to a long term of imprisonment.

look after. Although they had accomplished their main task, they still had plenty to do, reporting on bomb damage and looking out for new sites.

In the last week of January he paid his routine visit to Lausanne, bringing the usual bulky dossier of reports from every part of France, including the V.1 area. By this time it was known that the Allied bombing of the sites had been highly successful; and reports of German despondency were already coming in. Hitler's high hopes lay in ruins.

It was the climax of Michel's achievement. He had covered himself with glory, and was being recommended, "O.P." told him, for the highest decoration they could get him.

Now he needed a rest—and deserved it. Would he spend a fortnight in Switzerland as a guest of the British Government?

Michel was sorely tempted. He was sick with accumulated fatigue and anxiety. But his men were still at their posts, and he could not abandon them. Deeply touched by "O.P.'s" offer, he thanked him warmly...and refused.

It was 8.00 p.m. when he reached Lausanne station. His intention was to take the train to Geneva, spend the night in a hotel and cross the frontier between Jussy and Machilly at dawn. Thereafter it would be the familiar round: Lyon, Avignon, Toulon, Nice, and then on to Nîmes, Sètes, Béziers, Narbonne, Carcassonne and Toulouse.

As he followed the subway which led to platform three, he was overcome by an immense tiredness of body and spirit. His feet were like lead, and there was a burning pain in the soles (which had been revived by the heat of "O.P.'s" office), while his back ached with rheumatism. He thought wistfully of the invitation to take a holiday and wondered if he had been wise to refuse it.

Never had the prospect of returning to France looked so bleak: the interminable journeys on overcrowded trains with perhaps two nights a week when he slept on a bed; the inadequate meals; absence of heating; and general atmosphere of depression produced by a shabbily dressed, under-nourished and cowed people.

By contrast, everything around him spoke of happiness and prosperity: healthy looking men and women dressed in good clothes, gay young things and children with a glow on their cheeks, and all with that air of comfort and security, and unconcern for the morrow, which was so notably lacking in his own life.

While he waited on the platform for his train, a woman in a neatly starched apron came pushing a trolley and ringing a bell to attract attention. The trolley was loaded with every good thing: cigars, cigarettes of every variety, chocolates, caramels, nougats, thickly buttered sandwiches with generous portions of ham, and, best of all, *uncensored* newspapers which printed the Allied communiqués.

Contemplating all these treasures, Michel was seized once again with an overwhelming desire to put off his journey, and to enjoy a short space, in the safety of a neutral country, the pleasures of a normal life.

To resist it he closed his eyes and thought of his family, and all the hardships they were suffering; of his team of cyclists, eating badly and going without sleep to do the jobs he had given them; of Gendron, one of his three deputies, tramping the roads in all weathers; of Jean-Henri dodging the sentries at Bosc-le-Hart. He thought of Pierre Carteron with his broken arm—blasted by a British bomb—wheeling his bicycle with the other; of Louis Villette roaming the aerodome of Abbeville, and Loius Margot freezing in the winter dusk as he watched the mounting of a German balloon barrage.

That was enough: the temptation was mastered. Michel worked his team hard, as hard as he worked himself, and the more he demanded of them the more they responded. One could not desert such people, even for a day.

However, the devil had not finished with him yet.

The train for Geneva came in. Michel was about to board it, when he felt both his arms seized, and the next moment he was being impelled away from the train and towards the exit.

His two captors were two Frenchmen living in Lausanne, whom he had met on previous visits. They had happened to see him arrive earlier in the day and had remained at the station to intercept him with a view to inviting him to dinner.

The elder, Georges, had come to Switzerland to recruit French refugees for the *maquis*. He was a jovial individual, as well as a genuine patriot, who enjoyed the good things of life; and knowing the work that Michel was doing, and the kind of existence he led, was detemined to give him an evening out.

The other, younger and less talkative, but equally devoted

to the Resistance, was a friend of Georges and engaged on the same mission.

It was useless for Michel to protest. In any case, as he told himself, since he was crossing the frontier at daybreak, it made no difference whether he spent the night in Lausanne or Geneva. It seemed that for once he could allow himself a diversion; it would be the first since the day he had offered his services to the Allies.

They dined at the Auberge de la Sallaz, a first class restaurant overlooking the town. It was the first time since the war that Michel had been in such a place. The pleasant warmth of the room, the aroma of succulent dishes and expensive wines, the enormous chimney where fat chickens were being roasted on the spit, the gaily chequered curtains and tablecloths, and the soft hum of carefree conversation, filled his starved soul with a glow of well-being.

Later in the evening a talented pair entertained the diners. The man, famous in Switzerland for his anti-Nazi skits, was a brilliant comedian of the *boulevardier* type; his partner—red-haired with porcelain complexion and enormous eyes—a gifted *diseuse*, by turns witty and sad, with that mixture of tenderness and gaiety which is so uniquely French. Together they sang the songs which evoked the France that had been, and which Michel had not heard for four years; *La Closerie des Lilas, Le Mot de Cambronne, Quatorze Fuillet*. Michel was entranced. It was as if a long nightmare were suddenly dissolved and one awoke to a world of sanity and laughter.

When they left the place in the early hours of the morniing, he was still under the spell of the evening. Since the invasion of France nothing had brought home to him so poignantly the difference between the free and the oppressed. Like a man who has lived in darkness, he was dazed by the sun...and now he must return to the darkness, which would seem only blacker after his glimpse of the light.

It was snowing when he reached the customs post after a two-hour walk from Geneva. The guard, a genial giant who knew him well, proffered a steaming cup of coffee.

As he was taking his leave of this friendly person, Michel was unable to hide the anguish in his soul.

"Oh," he exclaimed, "if only I didn't have to cross this accursed frontier to-day!"

The guard had never heard him express such sentiments. He looked concerned and said: "Perhaps that's an omen. Who knows but you wouldn't do better to postpone your journey!"

"Oh, it's only a passing weakness. I don't suppose I'll think of it again."

They shook hands and then Michel took the path into the woods.

A little later he met another customs guard, standing in a clearing close to the stream which marked the frontier. This was a taciturn individual not usually friendly, but for once he greeted Michel almost cordially and wished him good luck.

Again Michel felt the need of unburdening himself, as if by communicating it to another human being he could rid himself of the sense of doom which weighed him down.

"This time," he said, "I'd give ten thousand Swiss francs not to have to cross that stream."

"It's a lot of money," was the guard's only comment.

As Michel reached the French side of the boundary he recalled that it was his ninety-fourth crossing.

Something told him that it was also his last.

A few days after his return to Paris, Michel had a rendezvous with two of his agents and his secretary at a little café near the office in the Rue Beaubourg. The rendezvous was for 9.00 a.m., the date being the 5th February, 1944.

As it happened—a rare occurrence—he had spent the night with his family in the little house at St. Rémy Les Chevreuses to which he had moved them a year previously. Since he saw his wife so seldom and there was much to discuss, he was delayed in starting; and realising he could not keep the appointment he rang up his secretary to cancel it. Instead, he fixed a meeting for the evening at a different place, where he already had an appointment with two other agents.

During the morning, while Madeleine Boulanger was alone in the office, she received another visit from the Comte de Kergoat and the same unknown woman. She said that Michel was not available and invited them to leave a message.

But this time they were taking no excuses. It was absolutely essential, the woman pleaded, that she should see M. Hollard that very day. Somebody very dear to her was in danger and only M. Hollard could save him. It was a matter of life and death.

Remembering Michel's injunction never to betray his whereabouts, especially to this pair, whom he did not trust, for a long time the secretary resisted their entreaties. But finally she was persuaded that the request was genuine.

She could not get hold of M. Hollard during the day, she told them, but she knew where he would be that evening. She then gave the time and the place: 6.15 p.m. at the Café aux Chasseurs, 176 Faubourg St. Denis, opposite the Gare du Nord.

Michel had chosen the time and place for the evening rendezvous because it was convenient to the two agents who were to meet him. One was Robert Rubenach—known in the *réseau* as Robert de Vic—and the other a man called Mailly. Robert was coming from Beaumont, to which he had recently been transferred from Bernes, and Mailly from Le Bourget, where he was employed as a railway clerk.

Both of them were due at the Gare du Nord by train which arrived at about six o'clock, and they only had to cross the road to reach the meeting place.

The other two, whom he was to have met in the morning but had put off till the evening were Joseph Legendre, alias Gendron, and Henri Dujarier.

As Michel entered the café he had a sudden presentiment of danger. The place was full, as usual at that hour, but something about the scene struck him as abnormal. There was a man leaning against the bar at the corner nearest the street, and another standing in front of the door to the *Lavabo*, who did not look like the ordinary customers.

It was not a definite impression but something he sniffed in the air, like an animal scenting an enemy.

Three of the people he was meeting—Legendre, Dujarier, and Mailly—were already seated at a table. At the sight of Michel, Mailly stood up and handed him a small parcel containing his notes.

Before Michel had time to sit down, he heard his name

called, and, looking round, saw a strange woman standing in the end of the room. This was something he did not like the look of. He had no idea that his secretary had given her the rendezvous and a stranger was the last person he wished to meet at that moment.

As he joined her in the little vestibule, she started to pour out some story about a friend who was in danger of arrest, and whom she was trying to get out of the country. Michel cut her short. "Listen, madame, it's impossible to discuss such things here. You must give the details to my secretary and I will do what I can."

Then, out of politeness and in the hope of getting rid of her, he invited her to join him for a drink and led the way to another table.

They had just sat down when one of the two men, whose presence had already aroused Michel's suspicion, suddenly produced a revolver and shouted: "Hands up, everyone! German police."

In a moment the whole café seemed filled with armed men. Michel was still carrying the packet given him by Mailly, and as he raised his arms he dropped it behind the bench.

He was set on by several police in plain clothes and his hands handcuffed behind him. The other three, as lesser fry, were handcuffed in front. All four were then bundled outside, where several cars were waiting. Michel was put in the back seat of the first, with a guard on either side; the other three with their escort followed in another car.

As the cortege moved off Michel caught a glimpse through the window of the stranger struggling and screaming with two policemen. This was the usual pantomime which the Gestapo played when they pretended to arrest the decoy. It was intended to protect the traitor from reprisals, but seldom took anybody in.

The three other people who should have been at the rendezvous—Robert Rubenach, Lucien Francois and Madeleine Boulanger—fortunately arrived late. Seeing three cars stationed outside the café, they smelt danger and retired to the post office opposite, from the windows of which they watched the drama.

15

RUE MALLET STEVENS

The car sped along the boulevards, crossed the Place de la Concorde and turned right to follow the river. From time to time it was stopped by traffic or lights. Michel looked at the door and wondered if he could open it with his shoulder and make a dash. He quickly abandoned the idea. The two plain clothes men, with revolvers in their hands, kept him pressed against the seat; with his hands locked behind him any move would have been hopeless.

On reaching Auteuil, the car turned and started to climb steeply. Michel could see the other one following. They were now in one of the richest quarters of Paris. Large blocks of modern flats, with spacious balconies and magnificent views over the Seine, were interpersed with private houses standing in their own grounds.

The road wound as it mounted, then straightened out. A little farther on the car turned sharply to enter a narrower road, which was also a cul-de-sac. As it turned, Michel read the name of the street: Rue Mallet Stevens XVIIIe. Two wooden-faced Paris policemen were stationed at either corner.

A few yards down they stopped outside a large square building. Its severe grey façade, only broken by iron-shuttered windows, looked more like a fort than a private house.[1] A short flight of steps led to massive double doors enclosed by a heavy iron grill. Over the entrance was engraved the number "5."

A moment later a large iron shutter in the wall was raised, revealing a garage big enough for several cars. Michel's car drove inside followed by the other. Then the shutter closed behind them with a crash, which to Michel was like a crack of doom.

The four men were hustled out, pushed up a short staircase, and locked together in a room without light. Michel had the impression that it was on the ground floor, as this was raised some distance above street level.

For a moment or so nobody spoke. It is always a depressing experience, to say the least of it, to be taken prisoner; and when the enemy is the Gestapo—for that's what it really meant, though they were technically in custody of the *Abwehr*[2]—the situation is still less enviable.

Even Michel, for once, was aghast, not so much for himself as for his three companions. He felt responsible for their arrest and was deeply disturbed by the thought that other members of the *réseau* might by now have suffered the same fate. How had it happened, he kept on asking himself.

It was Legendre who broke the silence, with his irrepressible cheerfulness.

"Well, here we are, chaps, and I'd give a lot to be somewhere else."

Michel's mind was already working again. By leaving them together the enemy had given him a chance which he might seize.

Before he could act, however, the door was flung open and the names of Gendron (Legendre's pseudonym) and Mailly were called out. They stumbled out, another person was pushed inside, and the door locked again. For all Michel knew their

---

[1] It was, in fact, a private house, the property of a French millionaire, requisitioned by the *Abwehr*.

[2] Counter-espionage branch of German military intelligence.

companion could be a *poulet* (police spy) and he therefore decided it was safer to keep silent. He had often rehearsed with Legendre and Dujarier what they should say if questioned: they were employees of the *Gazogéne* company and knew him only as manager of the business. As long as they stuck to this story they still had a chance. Mailly was different; as a railwayman employed at Le Bourget it was difficult to explain why he should be meeting Michel in Paris.

For himself Michel had no illusions. He could not hope to deceive the Germans, they knew too much about him. It was the logical end of his adventure and he had only one more duty: to shield his accomplices.

Five minutes passed, which he spent collecting his thoughts for the coming ordeal; then it was his turn.

As he emerged from the *cachot* he found himself in a hall, from which a flight of stairs led to the floor above. Propelled by his guard he mounted the stairs, until he could see through an open door the back view of Legendre standing in front of the table. At the same instant, Legendre, hearing Michel approach, raised his voice and almost shouted: "I repeat I am only an agent for the *Gazogéne* company."

Realizing that this was intended for him, Michel took new heart. He knew now that Legendre had adhered to the plan agreed on.

As he entered the room, Legendre was brought out, and they had a chance to exchange glances of mutual encouragement.

It was a long high room with a cinema screen at one end and a gallery with a cabin for the projector at the other. The curtains of the two windows were drawn.

Seated at a long table were the four interrogators. Michel's impression was that they were all fairly young and well dressed in their civilian clothes. One of them, a man of forty, who did not look German, was not unsympathetic in appearance. The other three struck him as cold-blooded and cruel.

One in particular, who appeared to be the chief, was horribly repulsive. In his thirties, with a long oval face, a prominent cranium going bald, and bad teeth, he had the rat-like expression of a small time criminal. The others called him Rudi. It later transpired that he was a Belgian.

In the background, standing, were the two plain clothes

policemen who had provided his escort in the car. One of them, the more brutal of the two, appeared to be French.

Now that at last he was faced by the actual apparatus which for four years had kept half Europe in submission, Michel felt his courage waning. It was the deadly coldness of these men — a coldness as of reptiles — that for a moment chilled him in spite of himself.

To resist it he concentrated on preparing his "line" — which was to take everything on himself and admit all facts that would not compromise anyone else. In this way he hoped not only to cover the other three, but to divert attention to his own misdeeds. He found that thinking what to say gave him back his courage, and he awaited the first question calmly.

It was Rudi who conducted the interrogation.

"What were you doing at the Café aux Chasseurs this evening?"

"I was having a business meeting."

"Why should you hold it at such a place?"

"Because it was convenient to the other three, who live out of Paris."

"You're lying. You were meeting them in connection with your secret activities as an enemy agent."

"On the contrary, they know nothing whatsoever about that. Legendre is my senior salesman and I wanted him to meet Dujarier, whom we have just appointed as our representative at provincial fairs. Mailly was bringing me information about the cost of sending our goods by train. Until now we have always delivered by road — but, you understand, with the difficulty of obtaining fuel..."

"I'm not interested. So you don't deny that you are a British agent."

"I'm a French patriot and I work with our Ally."

"Why?"

"As the most effective means of continuing the war against you. I regret that it's not possible to fight you openly."

"Well, you see that we're stronger and that you've lost."

"*I've* lost, yes, but *you'll* lose the war."

"Are you disposed to tell us what your secret action consisted of?"

Michel made no reply.

"You might just as well. You see, we know all about you. That you travelled all over the *Midi* as a spy and took your information to the British in Switzerland."

The mention of the *Midi* was a useful clue. If the informer, as he thought, was the woman in the cafe, she must have revealed what she had been told by someone in contact with the part of his organisation in the south, which was limited to a few agents and from which reports were collected on behalf of Michel. Simone Boirel had been arrested in November, and although he did not suspect it at the time he now realised that it must have been due to the activity of the informer.

"I don't deny it. I collected all the information I could that I thought would be useful to our Ally, and made regular visits to the British Embassy in Berne. My reports were handed to Colonel Cartwright, the Military Attaché. If you doubt my word, you can look up his name in the telephone book. It is no secret that he acts as the receiver of intelligence. That is the function of a military attaché, as you must know."

"And are you disposed to give us the names of your collaborators?"

"I had no collaborators. I worked on my own."

"We know that's a lie. You had many people helping you. We want their names."

"It would be of no interest to you. Most of them were simple people who did not even suspect my rôle."

"Nevertheless, we would like their names."

"I'm afraid I can't help you."

"You are really not disposed to tell us?"

"Absolutely not."

"You realised that may cost you dear?"

"It would not surprise me."

"And that is your last word?"

"I'm afraid so."

"All right. You won't sing. Well, to-night you shall sing like a little bird."

Rudi turned to one of the Germans and still speaking in French said: "You'd better prepare one electrode—no, both."

Then he turned again to Michel.

"Is that really your final decision?" he asked.

Michel nodded. Rudi fixed him with eyes as cold as a cat's, and said very slowly and softly:

"I tell you that to-night you'll talk. Yes, you'll talk so that there will be no stopping you."

When Michel returned to the *cachot* the other three had been removed and he was shut in alone in the darkness. Groping around he found an iron bar and for a time tried rubbing his handcuffs against it. Soon he abandoned the attempt. There was nothing to do but wait.

Everything had been taken from Michel, including his watch and the diary in which he noted his appointments. So he had no means of telling the time, but he reckoned it was about midnight when they came for him again.

He was taken through passages to another hall, where the *mise-en-scène* seemed deliberately designed to inspire terror. Leather whips and rubber hose, a length of rope and several pairs of handcuffs were strewn on chairs and tables in careless profusion.

Michel assumed this was the place where he was to be made, in Rudi's words, to "sing like a little bird"; but the sinister procession continued until it arrived at a ground-floor bathroom. Besides Rudi, the party consisted of the French *policier* and three other powerfully built individuals.

While the bath was being filled with ice-cold water his handcuffs were removed and he was ordered to strip. Then his ankles were attached and his hands tied behind him.

A punch in the face, delivered by the Frenchman, caused him to stagger backwards against the bath. In doing so he overturned and fell on his back in the water. For a moment he was completely immersed but managed to get his head out and came up spluttering.

Rudi was standing over him with Michel's diary in his hand.

"I see," he said, "that you have an appointment for to-morrow, 6th February, at 9.0 a.m., at the Gare d'Austerlitz, with a person whose initials are 'C.G.' You will now tell me the name of this person."

"C.G." was a certain Charles Guillard, an ex-officer of the Swiss Army who kept a wine shop at Etampes. He was employed by Michel to make plans of the new aerodrome of Mon Désir and to report on German air movements. He came regularly to Paris and was always met by Michel, either at the station, or just outside, or at the entrance of the Jardin des Plantes nearby.

"You won't tell me?" said Rudi as Michel made no reply.

Michel shook his head, and was immediately hit on it from above, causing him to immerse again.

Having been caught by surprise, he had not taken in much air and was soon forced to surface.

The question was repeated.

"Who is 'C.G.'?"

This time he was hardly given time to shake his head before an avalanche of blows forced him under again.

For the third time he came up gasping, only to receive the same treatment.

This went on for about half an hour, but with progressive effect as the beating became more severe and he was given less and less time to breathe before plunging. After the fifth or sixth round he began to drink water, his struggles became more frenzied and he felt his strength diminishing.

He lost count of the rounds, but at the end of a certain time he was dragged out and given a ten minutes' rest. Then the process recommenced.

It was repeated four more times, each session lasting roughly half an hour, but at increased intervals as it was judged that his failing strength required longer to recover.

In the later sessions, when he had drunk a lot of water, there came a moment when he was too weak to struggle any longer. At the first sign of this, for which his tormentors watched carefully, they would drag him half out, with his head over the side of the bath, while he retched himself free of water.

Eventually the time arrived when he was too weak even to retch. Then the French *policier*, who throughout the proceedings took a leading part, put his knee in Michel's stomach and forced the water out of him.

Of all the tortures used, if not invented, by the Gestapo, that of the *baignoire* was by far the most effective, for the simple reason that if skilfully applied the victim never lost consciousness; whereas, under beatings and other brutalities he usually fainted fairly soon.

The object of the exercise, of course, was to keep the victim alive, while doing everything short of actually drowning him. The instinct of self-preservation is so strong that it forced him to resist and the resultant struggle was such agony that in ninety-five cases out of a hundred he ended by doing what was required of him.

Michel himself has expressed the opinion that one more session would have succeeded. If he could have killed himself by drowning he would, but he was not allowed to. As it was he endured five, which, with intervals, lasted for at least three hours.

While he was resting after the fifth, literally more dead than alive, with his head supported on the side of the bath, he heard, through the mist of pain and dizziness and vomit, the exasperated voice of Rudi: "We're wasting our time with this pig-headed fool. We've better things to do."

Then he heard the gang troop out and the door slammed.

After a while he managed to summon enough strength to roll out of the bath and on to the floor. There he was lying, shivering with cold and weakness, when some time later the door opened and an elderly woman appeared. She was carrying a hunk of bread, which she proceeded to break into small pieces and offer him a piece at a time.

Gratefully, Michel allowed himself to be fed. When the last piece was swallowed he smiled his thanks—he was still incapable of speech—and the unknown angel withdrew. He afterwards discovered that she was one of an Italian couple employed as concierges in the building.

Nothing was better calculated to revive Michel's spirits. It was not only the nourishment, welcome as it was, that cheered him; but the gesture of humanity in a place from which all humanity seemed to have been driven.

Later, the guards returned, released him, and allowed him to dress. He was then handcuffed again and shut in a different *cachot*. He was in pretty bad shape, but comforted himself with the thought that he had won the first round and the match was not yet lost.

The well-known Resistance leader and author, who writes under the name of "Rémy," although he himself was never tortured, has made some pertinent remarks on those who were.

"A *résistant*," he says, "who fell into the hands of the enemy and who lacked the force to remain silent under torture was far from being a traitor. On the contrary, between him and his compatriots who remained passive there was all the difference between a combatant and a shirker.

"As for those who had the courage to resist to the end... who in other words remained indomitable, they belong to a small and exclusive *élite*. The memory of their struggle should be sacred and it should fill us with both astonishment and reverence."

This perhaps comes nearest to expressing what we all must feel about the very few who, like Michel, resisted *jusqu'au bout*.

His own comment on the performance was characteristically much more modest.

"*En effet le bon Dieu m'a donńe une délivrance formidable en les fatiguant plutôt que moi*"[1]

At eight o'clock he was brought a cup of coffee, and soon afterwards the French *policier* and one of the Germans came to fetch him. Michel was quite expecting to return to the bathroom, but instead he was led to the garage and placed in the back of a car, with his two escorts on either side.

As they were driven off the Frenchman said: "We are taking you to the Gare d'Austerlitz. We shall stop opposite the exit and you will identify "C.G." as he comes out. If you fail to do so before the last passenger emerges our orders are to shoot you on the spot. It will be to stop you escaping, you understand, and no questions will be asked."

Five minutes before the train from Etampes was due, the car drew up in the station yard slightly to the side of the exit. The engine remained running and the two escorts had their revolvers ready.

Michel had no fears as long as Guillard adhered to the rule: never to stop or look round if he wasn't there to meet him, but to proceed along the street toward the Jardin des Plantes.

It was nine o'clock by the station clock. Michel looked

---

[1] "Indeed God Almighty gave me a wonderful deliverance in tiring them out before me."

straight ahead and, as far as he could with his hands handcuffed behind him, tried to settle back in the car in an attitude of relaxation, knowing that it only needed the slightest reflex to betray him.

One minute past nine. A man came out of the exit carrying a brief-case. It was Guillard. The fact of his being the first passenger to emerge was so unexpected that in spite of his preparedness Michel visibly started. Had the two *policiers* been watching him instead of the exit he would undoubtedly given himself away.

Fortunately they too had not counted on their quarry appearing so soon and Michel's slip passed unobserved. He saw Guillard cross the yard without looking to right or left and disappear into the street which led to the gardens. Meanwhile the other passengers were coming out, first in ones or twos, and then in a crowd.

When the last had emerged the French *policier* turned on Michel and struck him a blow in the face with the barrel of his gun.

"You filthy swine," he shouted. "We'll teach you to make a fool of us."

The other joined in and together they hammered him about the head and face, until both eyes were closed, his lips cut, and blood was streaming down his face.

After that, the party returned to the Rue Mallet Stevens and Michel was locked in again

Later that morning he was taken up to the cinema room again and interrogated by another Gestapo officer. This time the interview was quite short.

"If you will reveal your organisation we will release you at once."

Michel merely shrugged.

That night he could hear through the walls of his *cachot* three other prisoners being submitted to the torture of the *baignoire*. Two of them surrendered after one ducking, but the third held out as valiantly as Michel himself; and for three hours the latter had to share vicariously in a repetition of his own experience.

The victim, as he learnt later, was a young Frenchman, a

naval officer called De Pimodan, of aristocratic family: as Michel described him, "a *noble* by his birth and *un homme noble* by his conduct." He was later deported, survived the war, but with health undermined, died in France a few years ago.

These nocturnal goings-on were naturally not calculated to raise Michel's morale. Hungry and shivering—it was snowing hard in Paris—he awaited his own turn, which he was convinced must soon come. One thought only sustained him: he had beaten the enemy once, and was the stronger for it.

But the night passed and he was left alone.

In the morning he decided he must try to escape before another night came round. He requested to go to the lavatory and was allowed his hands free while the guard waited outside with the door ajar. By standing on the seat he could just reach a small window overlooking a court on the side of the house. He had got his head and shoulders through and was stuck when discovered.

The only result was another beating up.

That night again he waited interminable hours for the foot-steps which would announce a further session with Rudi. But for once the building was quiet and in the small hours of the morning, when he was finally convinced it was not for that night either, he got some sleep for the first time since his arrest.

The next day, the third, he was taken for interrogation to a different room. The man behind the table was one he had not seen before, and from the respectful attitude of the others Michel gathered that he was a senior officer just arrived from Berlin.

His manner was courteous, almost friendly. Michel's hand-cuffs were removed and a chair was provided for him.

The interrogation proceeded on much the same lines as before, except that the German did not press him to reveal the names of any accomplices. Michel had made a clean breast of his relations with the British, although he had not given away any of his contacts except Cartwright—which, in any case, was no secret to the Germans—or the place of his meetings other than Berne.

His tactic, in fact, was to expatiate on this aspect of his activities, which involved no one but himself: but the German seemed anxious if anything to mitigate it.

When, for example, Michel declared that his visits to Switzerland had been bi-monthly, the German replied, "That is every two months," and appeared to make a note accordingly; and when he stated that the British paid him 68,000 francs a month, the German repeated the "eight" but not the "sixty," as though he had not heard the first figure.

As the interview was concluding, Michel said: "I suppose this will cost me my head."

"Unfortunately, yes, Monsieur," replied the German gravely, almost as though he regretted it.

That was Michel's last experience of the Rue Mallet Stevens. The same evening, with his three companions in misfortune, he was removed to the Rue des Saussaies, the Gestapo head-quarters, to be officially charged and registered as an enemy agent before being imprisoned at Fresnes. He and Legendre travelled in the same car, while Mailly and Dujarier arrived shortly afterwards, chained together.

Except for Mailly, whom he had glimpsed once at a distance, looking haggard and totally demoralised as he was dragged along by two guards, Michel had seen nothing of the others since his first interrogation.

Now, while they were waiting for the formalities to start, there was a brief opportunity to exchange news. Mailly was still too shaken to tell his story, but the other two were in relatively good spirits.

Apart from a routine beating-up, Legendre had not suffered. Dujarier had been suspended for several hours, head down, from the projector cabin in the cinema room, and in this position beaten intermittently. He had continued to protest his innocence and after this was not maltreated any further.

Their conversation was cut short by the arrival of an elderly officer and several soldiers, who took over charge of the prisoners from their plain clothes escort.

As the officer was entering their names in the register, Michel said: "You've no right to detain these three men. They were arrested unjustly and are completely innocent."

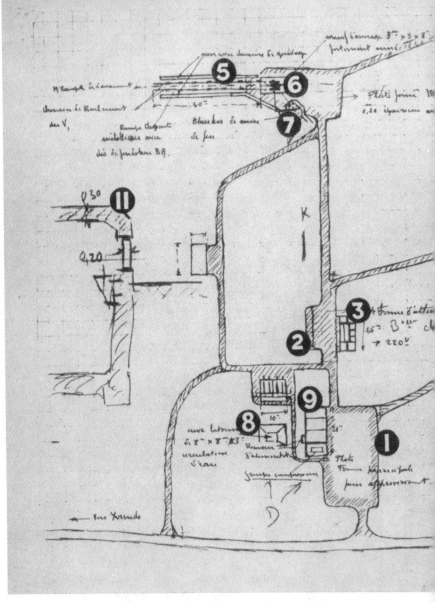

André Comps' sketch of the V.1 site at Bois Carré

KEY 1. Checking out platform
     2. Waiting platform
     3. Chief technician's office
     4. Non-magnetic building for setting gyro-compass
     5. Launching ramp
     6. Firing Unit

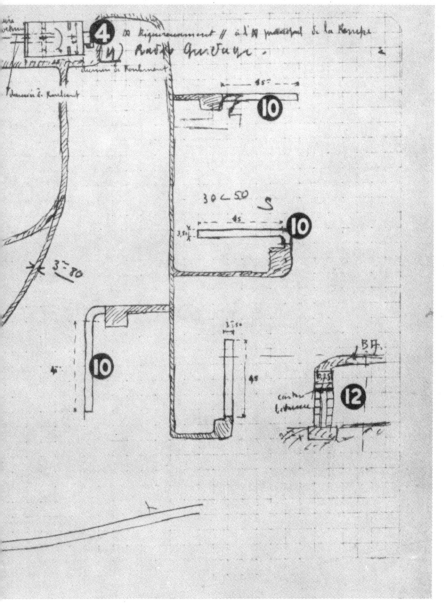

—it was smuggled to England via Switzerland

Michel Hollard

Joseph Legendre

ICI
ONT ÉTÉ ARRÊTÉS
LE 5 FÉVRIER 1944
PAR LA GESTAPO
LE CHEF DU RÉSEAU "AGIR"
Michel HOLLARD
LES CHARGÉS DE MISSION
Joseph LEGENDRE
Henri DUJARIER
ET
Jules MAILLY
MORT POUR LA FRANCE
LE 1ER JUIN 1944
A MAUTHAUSEN

The plaque outside the Café aux Chasseurs, where Michel and the three other members of the *réseau* were arrested

Henri Dujarier

Jules Mailly

A V.1 (flying bomb) photographed immediately after launching

Auffay station. The shed in which Michel discovered
a flying bomb is indicated on the right

"Then they have nothing to fear," replied the German politely and in good French. "Those who have done no harm will be released."

Legendre and Dujarier were, in fact, to be released three months later, no evidence being found against them. Mailly, on whom incriminating documents were discovered, was shortly deported to Mauthausen, where he died from his treatment a few months later.

16

FRESNES

A "Black Maria" was waiting in the courtyard. Michel and his three companions climbed inside and were locked in separate compartments. There was just room to sit down and it was pitch dark. The van started and Michel could feel it descending a slope, turning right and then accelerating as it set out for Fresnes through the silent Paris streets.

Half an hour went by, then the van slowed down, turned right and stopped. There was the sound of heavy iron gates being opened. The vehicle started again, jolted over some *pavé*, swung round, reversed and finally came to rest. The doors of the compartments were unlocked and the four men descended, surrounded by German soldiers. As they moved away Michel noticed that the driver of the "Black Maria" was wearing the blue cap of the *Préfecture de Police*, and that the small open car which escorted it was occupied by two French policemen. It always saddened him to see his countrymen doing the enemy's dirty work.

They were taken down a staircase into a basement passage,

dimly lit and immensely long. From there another staircase led to a vast central hall. Rising to the full height of the building, it was surrounded on all sides by galleries. These were at four different levels and at each level a narrow bridge spanned the width of the hall. Beyond could be seen the serried rows of cell doors, each pierced by a circular peephole.

The handcuffs and chains of the new arrivals were now removed and they were conducted to different cells. Michel's was on the ground floor. Before locking him in, an elderly German N.C.O. asked whether he was a "terrorist."

"No," replied Michel. "A patriot."

"Then you go in here, Mr. Patriot," said the German.

Producing an enormous key he opened a heavy door. Michel stepped inside and the door closed behind him.

It was quite dark but he could hear somebody moving on the ground. He introduced himself and received from his unseen cell-mate a cool but polite acknowledgment. Judging by the voice, he imagined a man in his fifties.

"You'll find some straw in the corner," said the stranger, "and here's something to cover yourself with."

Groping around, Michel found the straw, and the apology for a blanket which his companion had ceded him. He wrapped his feet in the blanket, pulled his light overcoat around him, and settled down to his first night in prison.

Long before dawn the cold awakened him, and for what seemed an interminable time he waited for the coming of day. When it was light enough to see, he perceived that his cell-mate was a much younger man than he had thought. Tall and dark, with a three-days beard, he appeared to be an educated person.

Before they had exchanged many words, the door of the cell was opened and Michel was called out to join a column of other prisoners. Among them were Mailly, Legendre, and Dujarier. The column was conducted through underground passages until it arrived at a room fitted with showers and an enormous steam steriliser. Here they were ordered to strip and make a parcel of their clothes before washing under the shower. The parcels were then removed for sterilisation.

As the latter process took longer than their ablutions, there was an interval while the prisoners waited naked for their clothes. The door was open and through it Michel could see a small courtyard and, beyond, the outer wall of the prison. In between there was a building with a sloping roof, whose lower end was not much higher than a man, while the upper end rose nearly to the top of the wall. It occurred to him that two men, acting as ladders for each other, might scale the roof, reach the wall and drop the other side. The escort had withdrawn and the only Germans present were the two N.C.O.s in charge of the sterilising arrangements.

While they were dressing he managed to whisper a word to Legendre. The Breton, always game, gave a nod of assent; but at that moment the escort returned to conduct the prisoners to the cells. Any attempt to get away was then out of the question. All the same, the discovery of a possible escape route gave Michel something new to think about and raised his spirits considerably.

They were next taken to a row of box-like cells, each about the size of a telephone kiosk, and locked in again, one man to a box. From time to time a prisoner's name would be called and he was then released to be conducted to his permanent abode in the prison.

Michel's turn came after a wait of several hours, during which he was brought some nameless but hot liquid and a small piece of bread. A long walk through passages and stairways brought him and his escort to the third floor of the third division. A door bearing the number 394 was unlocked and he entered his new home. It was Wednesday, 9th February, 1944.

The cell was very light and scrupulously clean. Daylight entered through a large window of frosted glass, the top section of which only could be opened to admit air. In the lower corner, however, a tiny portion of the glass had been cut out and could be removed or replaced at will. This enabled the occupants of the cell, by closing one eye, to obtain a restricted view of the outside world. As the third division was in the block nearest the prison wall, and cell 394 was on its outer side, there was a glimpse of fields and trees, of a road and houses, where people were still living in freedom. Anyone who has been in prison will know how much this meant to Michel.

In the corner nearest the door there was a water closet with a tap above it. Otherwise the furnishing consisted of two shelves attached to the wall and a single iron bed with four mattresses, artistically arranged to make it look like a divan. It was here that the four occupants of the cell, which was intended to house one prisoner, spent the greater part of the day.

When Michel arrived to join them only two were there. The third, they explained, was doing duty as *Kalfactor:* that was the prisoner who assisted in the distribution of meals and performed other small jobs for the guards. He was allowed out of the cell every morning and only returned to it later in the day.

The younger of the two was a boy of eighteen, by name Jacques Dognin. One of a large family, four of whom had escaped from prison camps to join the Resistance, he had been arrested at Rouen on the information of a Frenchman called Dordain. The same traitor had also betrayed one of Michel's agents, J. H. Daudemard, the informant at Rouen, whose tip had led to the discovery of the V.I site near Auffay.[1]

The older man, in his fifties, was a rather flabby-looking individual called Bougras. Proprietor of a small provincial café, he had no idea why he had been arrested, and looked forward confidently to being released. It seemed probable that his wife, who was also imprisoned at Fresnes, had been implicated somehow with the Resistance, and that the Germans, as usually happened, had assumed the guilt of the other partner.

The fourth prisoner, whom Michel did not meet till the evening, was a young career officer called Gardiol. Member of a Resistance group organised by the army, he was small, dynamic, and imbued with a burning patriotism.

Michel was still showing, on his face and head, and also on his wrists, where the handcuffs had scored them, signs of the treatment he had received from the Gestapo; and this was the best introduction he could have, at least to two of his new companions.

They welcomed him as a fellow fighter, and as a mark of solidarity insisted on his sharing the precious remains of a

---

[1] Dognin and Daudemard both survived deportation and it was through their efforts that in 1947 Dordain was finally convicted of treachery.

parcel of food delivered at the prison by Dognin's family.

To find himself in such company was a great comfort to Michel. The good order in the cell, the friendliness of his cell-mates, and the high morale which they evinced, made him feel more like a member of an exclusive club than a prisoner; and almost allowed him to forget that in all probability he would only leave it to go to his place of execution.

At night three of the mattresses were spread on the floor, while the fourth remained on the bed. Michel slept under the window. At regular intervals the light was switched on from outside as the guard looked in through the peep-hole.

At about six the prisoners were roused and the day's routine began. Each of them rolled up his bedding and washed in turn under the tap. Then they swept out the cell with a home-made broom, composed of a handful of twigs tied together. This was followed by fifteen minutes of physical jerks, in which they all took part except Bougras.

At seven the sound of wheels announced the arrival of breakfast. This consisted of a warm, brown liquid, not entirely tasteless, with which the *Kalfactor* filled their mugs from an enormous container. At the same time each received his day's ration of bread: 200 grammes, about half a pound.

This was the one moment of the day when the prisoners had some contact with life outside their cell. Although the proceedings were supervised by a German soldier, the *Kalfactor* was usually able to pass on any item of news he had picked up: for example, that there was to be a search of the cells that day, or that parcels were being delivered for "E to H" (i.e., for prisoners whose names commenced with the letters E, F, G or H); or, what was more usual, that they were forbidden till further notice.

Besides breakfast, two more meals were served during the day. The menu was always the same: a mug of soup which was never inedible and on rare occasions distinctly appetising. These occasions coincided with the gifts of food which from time to time were made by the French Red Cross, and other charitable organisations, to the inmates of the prison collec-tively. They were always distributed fairly by the Germans.

The administration of Fresnes was not, in fact, inhuman.

Although over-crowded, it was one of the most modern prisons in France and the prisoners on the whole were treated normally. The guards, mostly reservists of the *Wehrmacht*, were with few exceptions, decent men who did not maltreat their charges. The torturing and other brutalities went on elsewhere, mostly at the Gestapo headquarters in the Rue des Saussaies.

The beginning and end of the day were always marked by a ritual exchange of greetings with the neighbouring cells. This was conducted by tappings which could be heard through the walls without attracting the attention of the guards. The greeting consisted of seven taps: a long, three shorts, a long and two shorts. It was followed by a further series indicating the number in the cell. Those to whom the signal was addressed then replied in the same code. After communicating with the cells to right and left, the tappings were transferred to the floor or the ceiling, where they could be heard by those above or below.

In this way the inmates of cell 394 considerably enlarged the frontiers of their world. Not only were they kept informed of comings and goings among their neighbours—always a matter of interest to prisoners—but they were less isolated and had the sense of belonging to a community united in spirit and purpose.

Michel's family had suceeded in tracing him, and on the first day that it was allowed he received a parcel of food and linen. He also received from the German chaplain, a Lutheran pastor called Peters, the gift of a bible and a hymn book. The latter contained his favourite hymn, and he spent the rest of the day memorising the verses. That evening, about an hour after dark, the silence of the prison was broken by the voice of Michel singing "Nearer my God to Thee." He had known the tune since childhood and had been told by his parents the story of its being played by the band of the sinking *Titanic*.

The next evening, with Jacques Dognin joining in, he repeated the performance. The following evening the other two copied them. Soon the habit spread to the neighbouring cells and by the end of a week it had been taken up by all the inmates of the eastern half of the third division. Thereafter, every night the solemn and moving chant rose from a hundred voices of men and women, and the Germans never interfered with it.

During the next six weeks, Michel was twice taken out of his cell, handcuffed with his hands behind his back, and driven in the "Black Maria" to the Rue des Saussaies for further interrogation.

The second time he was simply informed that he had been condemned to death and that his defence had been conducted by a German advocate. He was then pressed to make a "complete confession."

"I have nothing to confess," replied Michel.

It was now that, for the first time, he gave way to despair. Through the hole in the window of his cell he could see the first signs of spring. The little field which rose beyond the prison wall looked green and lush in the sunshine, and the hedge beyond was already in blossom. He could hear the song of birds and sniff the sweet breath of the reawakening earth.

At the thought that he was to die and see none of this again, something like panic seized him. He had thought himself resigned to his fate and had accustomed himself to contemplate it coolly. But now that it faced him his calm for once deserted him; he felt his self-control breaking down.

Looking round desperately for something to distract his thoughts, his eye lighted on a bar of chocolate which had come in the last parcel brought by his daughter. He was saving it up to use as currency: either to bribe a guard to accord him some small favour, or to exchange with another prisoner for something he needed more.

He started to nibble at a corner; the taste was exquisite but it vanished too quickly. He nibbled another corner, then another...Soon the mutilated bar was past offering to anyone, and there was no longer any point in saving it. With deliberate greed he ate the rest, extracting from each bite the maximum of pleasure. By the time he had swallowed the last delicious morsel his moral crisis had passed. Satisfied physically, his mind recovered its strength. Once again he was master of himself.

Ever since his arrest he had not ceased to worry about the *réseau*. Left without a head, what would become of its members? They would know, from his non-appearance at the rendezvous, that something had happened to him. He hoped the deputies he had appointed would be in touch with them; but one of the three, Legendre, was in prison, and there was nobody designated, or qualified, to maintain liaison with the British.

His obvious successor was Legendre, the most enterprising of his agents and also the closest in his confidence. From the way the Breton's case had been handled—he had not been questioned again since leaving the Rue Mallet Stevens—there seemed some hope of his release. In this event he would need instructions from Michel, particularly in regard to contacting the British.

But how to communicate with him? No writing materials were allowed the prisoners. Paper could be obtained from the wrappings of food parcels, but there was absolutely nothing to write with. One day, as he was scouring the floor for something sharp, Michel discovered a minute length of lead, formerly part of a pencil. This was riches beyond the dreams of avarice. Armed with it, he spent a day writing in microscopic letters, on scraps of newspaper, the essential orders for Legendre.

The next problem was to get the message to him. He had discovered that Legendre occupied a cell on the same floor and not very far away. One way would be to give his letter to the *Kalfactor* and ask the latter to deliver it as he was doling out the soup, but he decided this was too dangerous: the German soldier who was always present would be sure to spot it.

One day, as the German N.C.O. in charge of the division was inspecting the cell, Michel, addressing him in German, asked if there was any job he wanted doing. The German, who was not unfriendly and was pleased at hearing his own language, received the request favourably; and the next morning Michel was called out, handed a broom and told to sweep the gallery outside the cells.

He applied himself to the task energetically, taking particular care to sweep under the doors, where most of the dust accumulated, and even using his hands to assist the broom when necessary. He thus had no difficulty, when he reached the cell of Legendre, in slipping his note under the door without arousing the suspicions of the German guard who was supervising the work from a distance.

A few days later, on the pretext of lending his friend some underclothes, Michel obtained permission, under escort, to visit Legendre's cell. There he learnt to his intense joy that the Breton had been released that very morning.

This was the best news since the day of their arrest. It meant not only that the beloved "Gendron" was free, but that the line to Switzerland would reopen, and the *réseau* resume its function of supplying information to the Allies.[1]

It would be difficult to exaggerate the comforting effect this knowledge had on Michel. It set the seal on the victory he had won over his opponents in the bathroom of the Rue Mallet Stevens. Had he lost that fight—and talked—his whole organisation would have been destroyed. As it was, he knew now that it would survive; whatever happened to him, his work would go on.

Moriturus vinco, he could have proudly claimed at this moment.

The nights were the worst. During the day a resourceful prisoner could usually find something to do, if it was only putting a point on a minute fragment of metal by rubbing it on a rough bit of a stone. But when he lay on his mattress in the dark, with nothing to occupy his mind or his hands, he cold only think of his wretched condition. None of the others, except Bougras, slept any better than Michel, and during the long wakeful hours, after conversation had finally died down, he could hear them tossing and turning on their pallets.

Sometimes they would ask him to recite some poetry; then he would declaim the *Mort du Loup* or *Maison du Berger* of De Vigny, Victor Hugo's *Waterloo*, or Valéry's *Cimetière Marin*. This acted like a soothing drug, calming the spirits of men whose nerves were stretched to breaking point, and enabling them at last to forget their misery in sleep.

Not that the prison was ever peaceful for long. Almost

---

[1] Shortly after his release Legendre arrived in Switzerland with the full story of Michel's arrest. Thereafter he assumed the leadership of the *réseau*, which continued its useful work until the Liberation of France. This was largely made possible by the initiative of Bart, who, after nine months in hospital, recovered sufficiently to assume the liaison between the *réseau* and the Swiss, which enabled agents to cross the frontier.

every night the quiet was shattered by some disturbance; a woman sobbing hysterically; a son or husband shouting a message of love or despair across the blocks; guards entering a cell to suppress some irregularity.

There were air-raids too, when the guards made a tour of the cells, double-locking the doors, as it was believed, against a rescue attempt by parachutists. The British had, in fact, a plan to repeat at Fresnes the successful bombing of the prison at Amiens, when several hundred prisoners, members of the Resistance, escaped; but it was never put into execution.

Once, however, Michel and his comrades were overjoyed to hear, above the droning of engines and rattle of *flak*, the distant explosion of heavy bombs, and to see the window of the cell momentarily lit up. The next day they heard from a new arrival that the petrol dump at Vitry-sur-Seine had been successfully attacked.

In the morning a guard made the round of the galleries informing prisoners who were required for "tribunal." This was the most dreaded moment of the day. "Tribunal" meant questioning at the Rue des Saussaies, where torture was almost invariably applied if the answers were unsatisfactory. Until the guard had passed a cell nobody inside breathed freely; when he had gone by they all knew they were safe for another twenty-four hours.

But Michel had not even this certainty. Prisoners under sentence of death were more often removed in the evening, to spend their last night in one of a row of condemned cells. Every day for a hundred and five days he awaited the fatal summons.

There was no regular period for exercise, but from time to time the prisoners were taken out in small groups and given a ten-minutes airing. This took place in a small courtyard, surrounded by a raised walk, on which the sentry kept his watch. Michel always spent the time doing physical exercises.

One day, Dognin found a small dandelion sprouting from a crack in the pavement. Removing the plant by the roots he hid it under his jacket with some earth, and on returning to the cell replanted it in a little pot made of tinfoil. The weed grew and flourished for many days, obstinately curling its petals towards the window. Lovingly cared for by Dognin, it relieved the drabness of the cell and brought to the lives of the occupants something of the freshness of the country.

The two German chaplains, one a Catholic priest and the other the Lutheran pastor already referred to, did their best to comfort the prisoners. They were allowed to see them alone, in a cell set apart, which was used as a confessional and for the giving of communion. Occasionally they brought messages from families; they also undertook to deliver the last wishes of a condemned man. Through this channel Michel sent to his wife the last letter he ever expected to write to her.

It was also thanks to the Lutheran that Mme. Hollard was put in touch with the family of Jacques Dognin. This had a happy consequence. The Dognins had found a means of communicating with their son by messages concealed inside a biscuit. Henceforth, whenever a parcel arrived for Dognin there was also a message for Michel.

A little later they contrived a method for replying. Since food containers were scarce prisoners were allowed to return them. A cardboard jam pot was sacrificed to provide a double bottom for another pot, which was then used to convey outgoing messages. Thus a regular two-way correspondence was established, which was a great solace both to the men and their families.

Towards the end of March, with heavy hearts they said good-bye to Gardiol. He was being sent to a concentration camp in Germany. His place was taken by a boy of eighteen. A student at *L'Ecole des Eaux et Forêts*, the latter had been arrested, with the whole of his class, who, while ostensibly taking a lesson in practical arboriculture, were found preparing a ground for parachutists in the forest of Fontainebleau.

After a fortnight the new arrival was removed—a bad sign— and they never heard of him again. He was succeeded by an unlikeable character, a timber merchant, who had obviously been arrested in error. A pretentious self-righteous individual, he did not conceal his disgust at being imprisoned in a cell with "terrorists," whom, as a "collabo," he clearly regarded as little better than common criminals.

However, he did make himself useful to his cell-mates by assisting them in a project which they had long been nurturing.

Foreseeing that he would shortly be released, Michel and Jacques Dognin gave him the addresses of their families, and charged him with a message for them. This was to indicate the position of the cell, and to request them to make an appearance outside the prison at a certain hour on a given day.

The plan worked marvellously. Five days later the timber merchant was released, and on the first Thursday following Michel and Jacques completed their preparations. Using the broken-off handle of a spoon, they had succeeded, with infinite labour, in prising open the lock which secured the window. A little before the hour stipulated for the apparition, Jacques took up his watch at the small hole in the pane, while Michel stood with his back to the door so as to prevent the guard looking in. A few minutes later, Jacques's two sisters appeared, walking along the path which crossed the field beyond the prison wall. He opened the window wide enough to wave to them, and saw them wave back to him.

He then exchanged places with Michel. After a short interval Michel observed two figures strolling along some way behind the other two. He recognised his wife and his daughter. On a man who never expected to see his own again, the effect was overwhelming. That the two people dearest to him should be there in the flesh, before his eyes, not a dream but a concrete reality, and both looking, as it seemed to him, more youthful and appealing than ever, struck him as something bordering on the miraculous.

When he had waved and received a discreet acknowledgment—for it was important that the visitors should not attract attention—Michel blew them kiss after kiss for as long as they remained in sight. When at last they disappeared from his view, he sat down on the bed and closed his eyes as though by doing so he could retain the vision a little longer.

Shortly after, the inmates of cell 394 were transferred to another cell, No. 312. Although in the same division, it faced inwards and the window was screwed down immovably. When they had succeeded in making a small hole in the corner, all they saw was the face of the opposite block.

As a condemned man who daily expected to be taken out for execution, Michel's thoughts ran ceaselessly on the idea of escape. He had already missed one chance and could not forgive himself for his stupidity. A guard had entered the cell and asked if his name was Robart. When Michel shook his head, the guard repeated the name and spelt it out. Again Michel replied in the negative. The next day he learnt that a prisoner called Robart had been released. Had he possessed the presence of mind to answer in the affirmative, he would probably have obtained his freedom. Nor would this have prejudiced the real Robart's chance, as he could not have been blamed for the mistake.

After that he resolved to make an attempt, come what may. The best, in fact the only, opportunity arose when the prisoners left their cells for a bath. This occurred about once a fortnight, and warning of it was given by the order to "prepare for the showers." They then had to undress in the cell, keeping only their shoes and an overcoat, and wait till a guard came to fetch them.

Having decided to make his attempt at the next bathing day, and realising that a beard would make him conspicuous outside, Michel persuaded Jacques to shave him with a razor blade which the latter had succeeded in concealing. When the time came, instead of undressing like the others, he hid his socks inside his shoes, rolled up his trousers till they were hidden by his overcoat, and buttoned the coat tightly round his neck to conceal that he was dressed underneath.

The guard arrived to escort them to the shower room, and they proceeded ahead of him in single line. Michel was at the tail of the queue. The shower room was situated in the basement and was in charge of a German N.C.O. As they reached the bottom of the stairs leading to it, their escort turned back to fetch another group. Michel waited a second or so, then turned back too and silently mounted the stairs.

This brought him back to the central hall. From here an inner staircase, hidden from the hall, communicated with the galleries above. Michel's plan was to reach the third floor, from which a service lift, used for bringing up food, descended to the basement. From there an underground passage led to the kitchens, and to the little courtyard which Michel had observed when taking his first shower, and where he had noticed a small building whose roof reached nearly to the outer wall of the prison. If he could reach this courtyard there was a good chance of his not being seen from the kitchen, whose windows were obscured by the fumes of cooking, while he climbed across the roof to the top of the wall.

He reached the third floor without being seen. The service lift was half-way along the gallery, where the women's section of the division began. Just beyond it, with her back to Michel, was a female wardress—one of the "grey mice" as they were called. Michel stole forward on tiptoe. The lift was there with the gate open; he had only to step inside, press the button and be whisked safely out of sight.

He was within three paces of his goal when the wardress turned and saw him. Immediately suspicious, she shouted for a guard. In a few seconds a soldier arrived. Keeping his head, Michel explained that he was returning from the showers and had lost his way. The guard looked sceptical, but said nothing and unlocked the door of cell 312.

The plan was well conceived and with a little luck could have succeeded. The only consolation for its failure was that he had not been punished for attempting it. But this was not much to set off against the bitter disappointment of seeing his last hope vanish.

17

DEPORTATION

One morning, towards the end of May, Michel was taken out of his cell alone. Except for his two visits to the Rue des Saussaies, this was the first time he had been separated from his cell-mates. Had the fatal day arrived, he wondered?

He was conducted to the prison doctor, treated to a summary auscultation, and then returned to his cell. Later in the day he learned from the *Kalfactor* that this was the usual prelude to deportation. His sentence had, in fact, been commuted.

The reprieve did not affect him so much as it would have done in the early days of his imprisonment. The passing of time without news of his impending execution had made the prospect of death recede. On the other hand, between death and deportation there was not very much to choose; so often the one was but a stepping-stone to the other. But at least it provided a respite; he could still make plans to escape.

A few days later the N.C.O. in charge of the division brought his brief-case and other possessions, and told him to get ready to leave. This was the friendly sergeant who had

done him several small favours—for example, by turning a
blind eye to such breaches of the rules as the receiving of
cigarettes, playing cards, etc. A reservist in his fifties, formerly
a cashier at Cologne Town Hall, he had always treated the
prisoners with humanity. After giving Michel his instructions
he added with a sad smile, "I'm sorry. They are taking the
best of my charges."

Michel had little to pack—a few articles of clothing, a New
Testament, and some photographs. When all was ready
he grasped the hands of his two companions and together the
three sang a farewell chant to the tune of "Auld Lang Syne."
Only one of them was he to meet again. Jacques Dognin,
though crippled in health, survived deportation and returned
to France after the war. The unfortunate Bougras, still protesting his innocence, was swallowed up in Germany and seen
no more.

At two o'clock he joined a group of twenty other prisoners.
As their names were called out, Michel thought he heard that
of Daudemard, his former agent at Rouen, but before he
could check up the party were marched outside and loaded on
board a motor bus. Four Italian soldiers armed with tommy-
guns provided the guard.

The bus started off, passed the great iron gates—which
immediately closed behind it—and swung on to the road to
Paris. Michel gazed hungrily on the passing scene. The untidy
straggling suburb, with its scattered houses, open fields and
waste land, was not particularly beautiful, but to him it had
all the freshness of an undiscovered world.

The bus soon arrived at the Porte d'Orléans and headed for
the centre of the city. At the Place Denfert-Rochereau there
was a little *bistro* where Michel had often stopped for a coffee
and a cigarette after arriving by train from St Rémy-les-
Chevreuses. As they passed the place he glanced nostalgically
towards it and recognised the *patron* in his usual place behind
the bar.

On Boulevard Raspail the bus stopped to pick up some
passengers from the prison of the Cherche Midi. A crowd
soon collected but were kept at bay by German soldiers. This,
however, did not prevent two of the prisoners dropping
messages, which were immediately picked up by passers-by.

With all its seats now filled, the bus set off again, travelling in a northward direction. Leaving the Gare du Nord on the left, it passed through the suburbs of Aubervilliers and Le Bourget before striking the main road for Senlis. There was little traffic. Private motoring had practically ceased and the only vehicles to be seen belonged either to public transport or to the occupying forces. For taxis people used bicycles towing tiny trailers.

Beyond Senlis the road entered the forest of Compiégne. After a long lonely stretch with woods on either side, they passed through another village, and almost immediately came in sight of their destination: a vast enclosure, partly covered by low buildings and surrounded by a double line of barbed wire fencing with observation posts at each corner. The bus slowed down, turned off the road, and entered through a strongly guarded gateway. They had arrived at the *Stalag* of Royal-Lieu-Compiègne.

The camp consisted of rows of wooden huts, with a large open space in the centre. Hundreds of prisoners were strolling about dressed in ordinary clothes, and as long as they kept away from the limit of the camp there seemed to be no constraint on their movements.

On descending from the bus the new arrivals were handed cards which they were told to hang from their necks. Each card bore a number. They were then conducted to their sleeping quarters: a long low shed standing on bare earth with a thin layer of straw for floor. A single window, permanently closed and covered with heavy wire netting, let in the only light.

After taking stock of his surroundings, Michel turned his attention to his room-mates; it was then to his joy that he recognised the man whose name he had heard pronounced during a roll call.

Jean Henri Daudemard was the informant who had put him on the track of the V.1 sites. A brilliant engineer employed by the French State Railways, he had only been working for the *réseau* for a short time when, thanks to a conversation overheard in a Rouen café, he had sent the report which led to the discovery of the first site. Shortly after, with Pierre Bouget, the station-master at Rouen, he had been betrayed to the Gestapo, arrested and imprisoned.

He and Michel had not met for five months, and their

reunion, even in such circumstances, was a happy occurrence for both of them. Daudemard knew nothing of the sequel to his action, and he was deeply interested to hear how much had followed from it.

For Michel, who had last met him in an imposing office surrounded by all the trappings of a responsible position, it was inspiring to meet a man who, in spite of degradation, remained calm, dignified and courageous.

Ever since his reprieve Michel had been obsessed by one idea: escape. There had been no chance on the drive from Paris; but now it seemed to him that there was an opportunity and he was determined not to lose it.

After inspecting it from as close as he dared approach, he decided that the enclosure was not an impassable barrier. The wire was not electrified, and the fence of metal spikes, which separated the inner and outer wires, could be crossed, he thought, with a plank. Doubtless sentries patrolled the perimeter, but by choosing the right moment he could probably slip through them. Anyhow it seemed worth trying.

After the evening meal of soup and a hunk of bread, the prisoners were locked in for the night. Few of them were in a mood to sleep, and talk and movement continued until the early hours, while Michel, lying awake on his bed of straw, waited impatiently for the inmates to settle down. When finally silence descended on the hut the first light was already filtering through. Michel got up quietly and stole to the window. To his satisfaction he saw that there was a thick mist outside.

After prising open the window with a spoon, he started to work on the wire mesh. Using a nail and the broken-off blade of a knife, which he had picked up earlier in the day, he was making satisfactory progress and had removed half the wire when he heard a low voice just behind him.

"You know, you are very foolish."

It was Daudemard.

Annoyed at being interrupted, Michel went on working.

"You have no hope of getting away," Daudemard continued. "You will only draw attention to yourself just at the moment when your case is being forgotten. It will remind the Germans that you are a dangerous enemy and they will probably decide to shoot you after all. And even if you succeed, what more can you do? Soon the Allies will be landing in France and your usefulness will have passed. I beg you, in your own interest, to give up the idea."

"It's my only chance," whispered Michel, without desisting from his labours. "Once they get us to Germany we're finished." Feverishly he tore at the wire.

"But the war will soon be over—perhaps even this year. Have a little patience and we may all survive yet."

The argument continued, their voices growing louder, until it awoke some of the other inmates. One or two got up and came over to the window. Soon the whole hut was aroused. Michel had no option but to abandon the attempt.

Replacing the wire as best he could and closing the window, he returned to his place and lay down. Although he realised that Daudemard had been actuated by the best motive, he could not suppress a feeling of bitter disappointment.

In the morning the door was opened and the inmates of the shed were let out and distributed among the other huts. Here they were provided with bunks and blankets and settled down not too uncomfortably to their new life.

Apart from keeping their quarters clean and tidying up the camp, the prisoners had nothing to do, and most of the day passed in idleness only interrupted by periodical roll calls and meals. The food was plain but sufficient, and could be supplemented by parcels sent by the prisoners' families. To his surprise, one came for Michel on the day after his arrival, brought by his sister, who had cycled the fifty miles from Paris.

The discovery of his whereabouts so quickly was the result of detective work by his family. On the previous day his daughter had called at Fresnes with the usual parcel, only to be told that the prisoner was no longer there. It was at first assumed he had been removed for execution; but inquiries at the cemetery of Ivry, where death sentences were carried out, showed a blank entry in the register of shootings for that day. The family then concluded correctly that he had been taken to the transit camp Royal-Lieu-Compiègne, prior to deportation.

To help pass the time the prisoners organised lectures and boxing matches. There were also religious services, held in a hut which was divided into a Catholic and a Protestant section. The latter was in charge of a Swiss pastor called Bornand, who had got into trouble with the Germans for being too friendly to the condemned men to whom he had been appointed as chaplain.

After Michel had volunteered to assist him, they shared the duty of hearing confessions. Some of the prisoners were tortured by problems of conscience. One man, at the moment of his arrest, had prayed that his daughter be spared, accompanying the prayer with a solemn promise that, if she was, he would never see her again. The girl had *not* been arrested and the question for the anguished father was whether God expected him to keep his promise until death.

Michel did his best to reassure him.

"We cannot judge," was his answer. "To assist your prayer you were ready to accept a heavy sacrifice. That is the important thing. But how do you know that God demands that particular sacrifice? Rather show Him your gratitude by the firmness and serenity of your faith. That will enable you to surmount any trial."

Whether the advice was acted on he never knew, but of one thing he was certain, that the recipient left him with courage and hope renewed.

Thus a week passed, not unpleasantly. The weather was magnificent and to those who had been living in a prison cell the effect of it, in the relative freedom of the camp, was almost dazzling. Michel, however, was in no mood to appreciate the weather. He continued to be haunted by the need to escape, and realised that with every day that passed the moment was drawing near when it would no longer be possible. The intense activity of the Allied Air Force, flying high above the camp, he read as a sign that great events were impending, heralding perhaps the end of the war. This only made him more desperate to regain his liberty.

By volunteering for some work in a neighbouring factory, he had succeeded in making and secreting two small saws, one for wood and the other for metal. He had no plans for using them, but felt sure they would be needed.

On the 1st June—a week before D Day—the prisoners were assembled and the names called of those designated for the next transportation to Germany. They numbered two thousand eight hundred. These were ordered to surrender all personal possessions and, after being warned that any concealment would be severely punished, were searched, wearing only their trousers. Michel had stuck the two saws to the inside of his thighs with adhesive tape, and though he was "frisked" by two soldiers, who ran their hands down his legs, one in front and one behind, neither of them discovered the thin strips of metal.

After being provided with a piece of sausage and a slice of bread for the journey, the deportees were herded for their last night into a different lot of huts without windows. Here Michel found himself among a party of youths, whom he had often noticed in the camp, usually accompanied by a priest. This was an abbé called Le Meur, who had been arrested with them and acted as shepherd of the flock. Michel decided to attach himself to it.

Later in the evening he was approached by another prisoner, and recognised him as a man he knew: a De Gaullist, Captain P——, whom he had met at Montélimar some months previously. P—— had pressed him to work for the Free French instead of the English and had offered dazzling inducements in the form of money, cigarettes and food, which he said he could obtain by parachute. Michel, on his guard against a trap, had replied that he would only change his arrangements if ordered to do so by the High Command, and there the matter had rested. His suspicions of P—— were now set at rest, and he was glad to renew their acquaintance.

In the hut with their leader were two members of his former band: Jim, an immense negro, the camp's champion boxer; and Jo, an ex-combatant with a wooden leg, in which were concealed, P—— told Michel, all the tools needed to break out of a sealed wagon.

"We mean to escape during the journey. It's all laid on."

"I had the same idea," said Michel.

"Then why not join us," P—— suggested, "and we'll make our get-away together?"

Feeling that this was a better bet than the abbé and his group of youths, Michel gladly accepted the invitation; and when next morning the deportees left the camp he marched in the same rank with P—— and his two companions.

Day was just breaking when the long column, five men to a

rank, wound its way to the station through the streets of Compiègne.On either side the route was lined with soldiers and behind them little groups of early risers watched the procession in silence. At certain points larger numbers of people, possibly relations of the exiles, had gathered to witness the scene. It struck Michel that they looked glummer than the prisoners themselves; perhaps because they knew what was in store for them, whereas the marchers only knew that they were going to Germany. After their relatively supportable sojourn at the transit camp, they did not envisage what lay ahead, and apart from home-sickness none of them yet felt any real anguish.

This mood soon changed when they reached the station. Here the atmosphere was very different from that of the transit camp. Uniformed members of the Security Police, carrying short leather whips and pistols in their belts, took charge of the column and halted it beside a long line of cattle wagons. Then one of them counted the leading twenty ranks, totalling one hundred men, and ordered these to enter the first wagon. By the time half the number had squeezed in, it was full. As the remainder stopped, seeing there was no room for them the German started lashing those standing in the opening. In a few seconds room was made and the rest crowded in. When the last had forced an entrance, encouraged by blows, the door of the wagon was bolted and secured with a padlock.

Michel was near the rear of the column and by the time his turn arrived everybody knew the drill. Under the menace of the whip, men who had been friends a moment before fought with each other so as not to be the last, and all sense of obligation to one's neighbour vanished.

The process of human degradation, deliberately planned and scientifically carried out, had already started to work.

When the door had closed the only light inside the wagon came from a small ventilation hole covered over with iron bars. At first Michel could see nothing, but as his eyes became accustomed to the darkness he dimly perceived the forms of his fellow travellers. The hundred men stood upright, pressed against each other, with just room for their feet without treading on a neighbour. In the centre, but inaccessible except to those nearest to it, was a metal barrel open at the top: their sole sanitary amenity.

Michel kept close to P——, whose bodyguard, the negro Jim, had obtained places for them both against the side of the wagon. After a time, however, Michel gave up his to an older man. In his immediate neighbourhood were prisoners of every class and profession: a civil servant, a mechanic, a railway-man, a bargee, a farmer, a tailor, an abbé in his cassock, and a young man wearing the uniform of an air force officer.

Few words were exchanged. The brutalising experience of being herded like cattle, the physical discomfort already felt, and the knowledge that it was only just beginning, had a dulling effect which deprived the prisoners of speech.

The abbé[1] was the first to break the silence. Raising his voice so that it could be heard by everybody in the wagon, he proposed that, as the journey was likely to last for several days, some attempt should be made at organisation. If, for example, each prisoner had a number, it would help in the fair distribution of food—always supposing that food was distributed.

There was a murmur of assent and the men at the end of the wagon started calling a number in turn. All went well for a time, then two people called the same number: after that there was confusion and the rest became discouraged.

The abbé next suggested that as numbering was too difficult they should divide themselves into sections: his own half of the wagon and Jim's. This two was agreed to, but before it could be acted on a series of violent shocks announced that the journey had begun.

With his thoughts still running on escape, Michel had care-fully noted, while waiting his turn to entrain, the constitution of the convoy. It consisted of about twenty cattle wagons, with passenger coaches in between which were occupied by soldiers. From these a constant watch was kept on the wagons by guards armed with rifles. A luggage van at the tail, with a machine-gun on its roof, served as an additional observation post. There was a rumour that it also carried a contraption

---

[1] The Abbé Carlotti. He survived deportation and is now a Canon of the Church and President of the *Fédération des Réseaux de la France Combattante*.

underneath, designed to kill any prisoner who dropped on the line. Nevertheless, it was known that men had escaped on their way to Germany and Michel did not despair of doing the same.

All day the journey continued with very few stops, and those only at larger stations. As the sun mounted and beat down on the roof the heat inside the wagon became insufferable. Soon the inmates were gasping for water. A few who were rash enough to eat their bit of sausage were driven almost mad by thirst.

Night brought a slight fall in temperature, but there was no relief for cramped limbs, immobilised by the congestion. One of Michel's legs was causing him acute pain, but he did not dare to ease it by lifting his foot, knowing that if he did so part of his standing space would be taken.

All his hopes were now centred in P—— and his team, and as the night wore on he waited, keyed up, for some sign that the plan of escape was maturing. After hours had passed with no news of it, he managed to get close enough to his companion to ask him what was happening. In the darkness he could not see the other two and had no idea what they were trying to do.

"We need a saw," P—— replied listlessly.

"For metal or wood?" Michel asked.

"Wood."

"Why didn't you tell me before? Here you are."

From inside his trousers he produced his hand-made saw and handed it over to P——.

"Will you be ready to-night?"

"I shouldn't think so. We'll probably have to wait till to-morrow."

Michel's heart sank. The farther they travelled and the nearer they approached to Germany, the less were the chances of success. In any case, the attempt was only possible at night, so the delay meant postponement for another twenty-four hours. In that time the train might have crossed the frontier.

The second day passed like the first, except that the prisoners were weaker. Tortured by thirst, panting for air, some collapsed, while others became feverish. Michel was carrying in his pocket two lemons which had come with his last parcel of food. By means of his saw he divided them into three slices, which he distributed among those he judged to be suffering most. The choice was not easy as nearly all were in desperate need.

Once or twice in the day, during a stop at some station, a bottle of water was passed in surreptitiously by some Good Samaritan in defiance of the guards.

On one such occasion the bottle was being passed towards a man who had fainted. As it reached him another prisoner, a young Marseillais, seized it and started to drink. At this Michel snatched the bottle and put it to the lips of the unconscious man. While he was still holding it, the bottle was snatched from him in turn. The next moment he saw the Marseillais, his face distorted with rage, raise it with the evident intention of smashing his skull. Just in time the madman was seized by some others and disarmed.

Another prisoner fell ill after drinking his own urine, and became delirious. At the next stop an appeal was made to the guards to remove him, but, like all such requests, it was simply ignored. Sometime during the night the man's cries ceased. In the morning he was found to be dead.

Such incidents were common, and few of the wagons arrived without their quotas of corpses.

This treatment was quite deliberate and, from a German point of view, entirely logical. Deportation had a double objective: to remove enemies of the Reich and to obtain slave labour. Hitler's Germany had no use for weaklings and one of the purposes of the journey was to kill them off. Those strong enough to survive it would also be good, it was calculated, for at least several months in a labour camp.

18

JOURNEY'S END

The second night arrived and again Michel waited for some sign that the plan of escape was maturing. After three hours he forced his way to the side of P——, only to be told that the preparations were held up for want of a saw to cut metal. Exasperated, Michel handed over his own.

Shortly after, the train slowed down and stopped. By pulling himself up with his arms, Michel was just able to look out through the ventilator. He read the name of the station: Avricourt. This was just inside Lorraine, therefore on German soil.[1] Avricourt was, in fact, the new frontier station.

During the long wait that ensued, the doors of the wagons were opened and a minute inspection carried out for any signs of an attempt to escape. Then, to the astonishment of the prisoners, there appeared on the platform an enormous container filled with steaming coffee. Mugs were produced and every man received a ladleful.

---

[1] Alsace and Lorraine, lost to France in the war of 1870 and reconquered in 1918, were re-annexed by Germany in 1940.

This was against all the rules and why it was allowed was a mystery. Many months later Michel learned that it was due to the charity of the French station-master, who had obtained permission by bribing the guards with a case of champagne. Undoubtedly his action saved many lives.

It was still pitch dark when the train started again. Although theoretically in Germany, they were still among a friendly population, who could be counted on to help a French prisoner; but once the eastern boundary of Lorraine was passed the last chance of escape would be gone. It was, therefore, now or never.

For the third time Michel sought out P———. He found him lying on the floor, supported by his bodyguard and taking up space at the expense of his immediate neighbours, who were deterred from protesting by fear of the negro.

On seeing him approach P——— muttered some lame excuse and in a flash Michel realised what a dupe he had been: the famous escape plan was an illusion and no preparations whatsoever had been made. He had put himself, and his precious saws, in the hands of a man of straw and in doing so had thrown away his last hope of freedom.

Too bitter even to utter a reproach, he turned his back in disgust, not only at his own deception, but at the selfish disregard for their fellows shown by P——— and his bully.

His disappointment would have been even greater had he known what he only learnt later: that during the same night, while the convoy was climbing a gradient near Bar-le-Duc, a group of forty-five prisoners escaped from another wagon and got clear away; and that this was none other than the party of youths, headed by the Abbé Le Meur, to whom Michel had originally attached himself. Had he remained with them instead of linking his fortunes with P———, he too would have escaped.

It was the abbé who organised and led the break-out. During their stay at Compiègne the party had procured four small saws and with the help of these they cut a hole in the side of the wagon. As the train slowed down they jumped in turn, using blankets—also brought from the transit camp—to lessen the shock of their fall. The escape was only discovered on arrival of the train at Avricourt.

With no further stop the convoy entered Germany. At the first light of day Michel hoisted himself up and took another look through the ventilator. All he could see was a forest of fir trees, but already he had the feeling of being in a foreign country, unfamiliar and hostile.

As the sun rose the atmosphere in the wagon again became suffocating. Two days and two nights its inmates had passed, standing bolt upright, their feet touching, with nothing to eat or drink, except one cup of coffee and a few drops of water. The need for fresh air, for space to move, and above all for liquid to quench their thirst, was ever more excruciating.

The train arrived at Cologne. Through the sides of the wagon they could hear the bustle of a large station. A loudspeaker announced: *Schnellzug nach Paris*. The thought that only a few feet away there were people occupying comfortable carriages, in a train bound for Paris, filled Michel with despair. A few minutes later a whistle blew, followed by a rumble of wheels. As the express gathered speed, the sound increased, then diminished, finally dying away like a last hope.

Soon the convoy moved off in the opposite direction. All the morning it pursued its interminable course through the pitiless heat of the summer day.

At one point Michel's neighbour, a young French policeman called Max, who shared with him a place near the ventilator, announced that he had seen the sea. Michel took a look but there was nothing in sight but a vast empty plain. The sea was an illusion, like the mirage of water seen by parched men in the desert.

Later there was a heavy shower of rain. The prisoners could hear it falling on the roof—and that was all the benefit they had from it. Max managed to catch a few drops, splattered through the bars of the ventilator, and sprinkled them on Michel's face. The effect was inconceivably refreshing; he felt revived as though by a cold shower.

At the next stop there was an unusual commotion outside. They could hear the soldiers shouting in German and the noise of people running.

Hoisting himself again, Michel looked out. The spectacle which met him was fantastic. The train had stopped in open country, and some thirty or forty prisoners, completely naked, were running up and down the track in front of a group of soldiers. Each time they passed the soldiers they turned their heads and saluted. Some of them were elderly, others emaciated; all were weak and moved with a shambling gait, stumbling on their bare feet and sometimes falling.

This was as much as Michel could see before his strength failed and he had to drop to the floor.

After a while there was more shouting, and the sounds of wagon doors being opened and closed. Finally the din died down and the train resumed its progress.

What Michel had witnessed, without realising it at the time, was the reprisal taken by the guards for the escape of the forty-five. They had waited for a convenient moment on German territory and then forced the remaining inmates of the wagon to strip and carry out the grotesque performance seen by Michel. After that, the prisoners, still naked, were distributed among the other wagons.

Hours later the train stopped again. Through the ventilator Michel read the name of the place: Bergedorf, a small junction east of Hamburg. A railway official with a gold-braided cap, presumably the station-master, was walking along the platform. Speaking in German, Michel inquired if their destination was Hamburg. Without stopping, the official shook his head, raising his eyes at the same time in a way that to Michel was only too significant.

The train started to move in the reverse direction, and after another ten minutes jolted to a stop. There were sounds of footsteps and the unlocking of doors. The infernal journey had come to an end.

A sky-light in the roof was opened from above. As daylight poured in—for the first time in sixty hours—the shocking scene inside the wagon, which had been felt rather than seen, was at last fully revealed.

About half the prisoners were still standing; the rest had either deliberately stretched themselves on the floor, selfishly taking up more than their share of space, or, after sticking it out as long as possible, had collapsed from weakness, and were lying inertly, in some cases on top of another body.

Their death's head expression, haggard eyes and foam-flecked lips, told of the ordeal which those who had withstood it had undergone. They looked more like living skeletons than men—but they were still standing!

One of them was the priest, the Abbé Carlotti, whose patience and fortitude had been outstanding. As the prisoners waited in a sort of daze for something to happen, he began to say a prayer of thanksgiving for their survival. Soon the words were being repeated by other voices.

There was the sound of padlocks being opened, and then a grinding noise as the door of the wagon slid sideways. Without waiting for orders the prisoners filed out. Dazzled by the daylight and crippled with stiffness, some of them missed the step and fell the three feet to the ground. Men of the S.S. in immaculate black uniforms were waiting to receive them with whips, and a lash across the shoulders was the reward for a tumble. From now on, the deportees were to learn, this was the only language they would hear from their guards.

For three days they had been treated as no animals would be in any civilised country. Henceforth they would be treated as slaves. It was something new in their situation, to which they were already adjusting themselves.

In their innocence of what they were going to, some of them agreed during the journey that at end of it they would lodge a protest, either with the officer in charge of the escort, or with the commandant of the camp. They could not imagine that any person in authority would have countenanced such conditions. So little had they understood the people they were dealing with. One look at the S.S. men was enough to open their eyes.

At Fresnes and other German prisons in France, and even at the transit camp of Royal-Lieu-Compiègne, the guards had been soldiers of the *Wehrmacht*. Consisting mostly of older men called up for the war, they were civilians in uniform with normal human feelings.

But the S.S. were a different race, almost a different species, educated and conditioned for one purpose: to assure the supremacy of the Nazi State. In the process they had been de-humanised and were no longer men but monsters: brutish, violent and pitiless. Michel noticed, for example, that even among themselves they never laughed or even smiled; their faces were masks set permanently in an expression which combined stubborn stupidity with callous indifference.

The prisoners were reformed in a column of fives. Their liberation from the wagons had a reviving effect on most, while those who found difficulty in getting up and walking were assisted by kicks and cracks of the whip, which acted like an electric shock. Even so, some of them had to be supported by their neighbours. A number were beyond any treatment and their unconscious forms or corpses were left where they lay.

The sky was grey but the rain had stopped. From the time which had passed since daybreak, Michel estimated that it was late afternoon. The place where they had arrived was in the middle of a sort of desert, with neither trees nor plants nor cultivation. Two hundred yards away he could see rows of low buildings, and, nearer, a high fence of barbed wire stretched between concrete posts. Porcelain insulators indicated that the fence was electrified. No other habitations were in sight.

The column moved off along a concrete road. In a few minutes the head of it turned right and penetrated the fence through double gates guarded by armed men. Other guards were stationed evey hundred yards all along the enclosure.

The column continued past the buildings until it arrived at a vast open space, where it was halted. From there the prisoners had a good view of their new surroundings.

Two groups of buildings, each consisting of forty units, were ranged on either side of the open ground. The buildings were long low sheds made of brick and painted a sickly green. At the end of the rows two new buildings, one storey higher than the others, were in process of construction. The men working on them were dressed in a variety of ill-fitting garments; their faces were emaciated and their eyes deep-sunk. Their heads had been partly shaved, leaving a bald strip, about two inches wide, which ran from the forehead to the nape of the neck. On the back of their jackets a large St. Andrew's cross was painted in bright yellow. They looked at the new arrivals with the indifference of people who have lost hope and interest.

Another prisoner, wearing a sailor's cap and rather better dressed, but whose coat was also marked with the cross, came running across the ground shouting orders. This was the *Lagerältester*, or camp leader, one of the privileged class who were given authority over the other prisoners. They were usually Germans serving a criminal sentence, but included Russians and Poles. The *Lagerältester* was their chief and responsible for the internal discipline of the camp.

Soon a small handcart appeared, drawn by two men. These were dressed like convicts in canvas suits covered with broad blue stripes. On the cart was a barrel containing a steaming liquid. Some shallow tin mugs were filled and handed to the men in the leading ranks. There were holes in the mugs where the handles had been removed which had to be blocked with the fingers to prevent the contents escaping. After the leading men had drunk, the mugs were refilled and passed to the next rank.

When Michel's turn came, he thought he could distinguish a faint flavour of lentils in the otherwise tasteless liquid. Others diagnosed chicory or acorns. But whatever it had been, the liquid would have tasted like champagne to a man who had drank practically nothing for three days, and Michel lapped it up greedily.

While this was going on an announcement was made in German that none of the water in the camp was drinkable. Michel acted as interpreter and took the opportunity of asking the *Lagerältester* where they were.

"For your great misfortune," was the reply, "you are, like us, in the concentration camp of Neuengamme."

An order was shouted and the column started to move. After advancing a short distance the head of it reached a building, where a steep staircase led to the cellars. Here the narrowness of the passage caused a block and brought the column to a standstill.

Suddenly there was a violent movement from the back. The Russian and Polish *Kapos* placed in charge of the new arrivals were beating the rear ranks with sticks. To escape the blows the men surged forward, pushing those in front, who in turn propelled the ranks ahead of them. The effect was like the succession of shocks which occur when a long goods train is being shunted. Under its stimulus the column was set in motion again and in no time disappeared down the staircase.

There followed a wait of several hours while the several

thousand men stood crushed together in semi-darkness. At intervals a hundred were taken out, marched to the bath-house and ordered to strip and wash. After this their heads and bodies were shaved by *Kapos*, their own clothes were removed and they were given their new apparel: a jacket and a pair of trousers handed out at random. Of every sort and shape, from a bus conductor's reefer to the full dress tunic of a dragoon, these ill-assorted garments were distributed with no regard to size. Though clean, they were old and usually in need of repair, with most of the buttons missing. For shoes each received a pair of oval-shaped boards with a strip of canvas nailed across. When they arrayed themselves, the prisoners looked like clowns in a circus.

Their first reaction was to laugh at their comic appearance. But the laughter sounded false; it was only the instinctive rejection of their own degradation. They were soon to discover how quickly a man who is made to look despicable loses first his pride, then his last illusions about himself, and finally his desire to live.

While they dressed in their ignoble attire, two men stood by with brushes and paint pot to implant the brand of slavery: two strokes on the back in the form of a cross, two vertical stripes on the front of the jacket, and two more on the legs of the trousers.

Finally, each was marked with a number. This was printed with a wooden type on pieces of canvas sewn to the jacket and the trousers. Michel's was F (for French) 33948.

When this last rite had been completed they were conducted to their quarters: four blocks of barracks set apart, where they were to spend the first ten days in quarantine.

The interior of the buildings was as bare as the outside: three tiers of wooden bunks and a long table were the only furniture. The bunks were two feet six inches wide and most of them were occupied by two, and sometimes by three men sleeping head to foot. A thin mattress and two horse blankets were provided for each.

At nine p.m. the lights were extinguished and all had to be in their bunks with their trousers removed. Anyone found wearing them after that was treated as an escaping prisoner and savagely punished.

Here at last, after three days and three nights on his feet, Michel was able to lie down. In his exhausted state neither discomfort nor hunger could keep him awake, and for a few hours at least found forgetfulness in sleep.

During the period of quarantine the new arrivals were kept apart and except for occasional chores were not made to work.

They spent most of their time lined up in front of their barracks, or standing about on the muddy patch of ground which separated one building from the next.

The interminable hours passed in a sort of numbed silence. Most of the prisoners were still suffering from the effects of the journey and the shock of their first experiences in the camp. Driven into themselves, they were cowed and listless, incapable of any effort that they were not forced to make.

During one of these long waits a Jesuit priest, Père Lavallard, delivered a lecture on the Books of the Old Testament. Speaking simply and clearly and quoting extensively from memory, he held the attention of an audience which, starting as a small group, eventually swelled to several hundred people.

At the end of it the speaker apologised for tackling a subject "which would have been better treated by a Protestant." Michel, who came from a family of Protestants and had many relations among the clergy, immediately protested against such modesty and expressed his warm appreciation of the talk.

Every evening, when the labour *Kommandos* returned from work, the whole population of the camp paraded on the place of assembly for the roll-call. This lasted for any time from one to two hours.

The new contingent took part in the ceremony for the first time on the day after their arrival. As the columns of prisoners marched in with military precision, they were deployed in two lines so as to form an immense square, leaving an empty space in the middle. At its centre, the twenty members of a brass band waited with their instruments ready. Facing them was a little man standing on a stool—the conductor.

When all were in position and the square had been completed, the conductor raised his baton and the band burst out in a well-known military march. At this moment, through a gap in one side of the square, four men appeared carrying a massive apparatus. As they advanced towards the centre of the square, it was seen that this consisted of two stout posts joined at the top by a cross-beam and resting on heavy wooden blocks secured by metal stays. From the centre of the beam a rope, ending in a noose, was dangling.

While the band continued to play the gallows was set up and a wooden stand placed underneath it. When everything was ready the music ceased. There was a moment of silence; then a young man dressed in the striped garments of a convict, with one arm in a sling and the other tied behind him, was seen to climb the stand. Painfully thin, with hollow features, and deathly pale, he looked no older than a youth in his teens.

The *Lagerältester*, a powerful man distinguished by the sailor's cap which he wore as a kind of badge of office, followed the condemned man up, and adjusted the rope round his neck.

Then turning to the assembled multitude and raising his voice to a shout he announced the reasons for the sentence: attempting to escape and stealing food.

"Does he not deserve to be hanged?" he demanded.

"Yes, he deserves to be hanged," someone answered.

This was greeted by shouts of approval from the nearest ranks. All round the square the cry was taken up and repeated by hundreds of obsequious voices. They were those of Russian and Polish prisoners seeking to ingratiate themselves with their masters. Of all the incidents witnessed by Michel in the camp, this servile demonstration was the most revolting.

For a moment longer the condemned man waited impassively, seeming on his stand to be disproportionately tall. Then the trap was released and he dropped. There was a jerk as the rope became taut, after a fall of less than three feet. The body revolved slowly, stopped, swung the other way, described several circles, and finally came to rest. After a while it was lowered to the ground, detached from the rope and dragged to one side. Two prisoners replaced the trap.

A second victim now appeared. A man of thirty-five, powerfully built, with a neck like a bull and square features full of energy, he did not wait to be pushed, but mounted the stand in two bounds, although his hands were tied behind him. The *Lagerältester* followed and placed the noose round his neck. Then he repeated his speech and once again hundreds of voices joined in the ignoble chorus of condemnation.

When the shouts had ceased the executioner pulled the lanyard, but the trap failed to function. Two more attempts were made unsuccessfully before the mechanism worked.

The condemned man dropped and hung by the rope, but he was very far from dead. Kicking and twisting he could be seen fighting for his life, his whole body convulsed with the violence of his movements.

The struggle continued a long time and was watched in silence by the thousands of onlookers. Gradually the movements of the dying man became weaker until at last he hung still, swinging gently.

Night was falling when the long columns moved off to their barracks. The evening meal of thin gruel was waiting, but, hungry as they were, few of the new arrivals could touch it.

The older inhabitants, hardened to such spectacles, were scarcely affected. Violence was something to which they had become accustomed. Moreover, they knew that a day never passed without someone in the camp dying; either in one of a row of cells, each of which was equipped with a rope fixed to a ring, and where executions were much more frequent than in public; or in the hospital as a result of a flogging; or at work or during the night simply from exhaustion and starvation. And every day they could see the yellow smoke pouring from the twin chimneys of the crematorium.

19

NEUENGAMME

With the termination of their period of quarantine the new arrivals were absorbed in the population of the camp and lost something more of their own identity.

A number of them had already been sent to other camps, and the remainder were now distributed among the eighty blocks. Each block contained between seven and eight hundred prisoners, of whom the vast majority were Germans, Russians, and Poles, and the French formed a minor minority.

The day started at four a.m., when the lights were switched on and the prisoners were aroused by the shouts of the *Blockältester*[1] and his two assistants. Each man leapt out, carrying his shoes and trousers (which he had used during the night as a pillow), and joined in the stampede to secure a place in the wash-house. Since the number of taps provided was quite inadequate, they were usually monopolised by the camp aristocracy—that is the Germans, Russians and Poles. The same people also occupied all the seats at the four dining

---

[1] Block-leader.

tables, while the rest ate standing, thinking themselves lucky if they found each a place to lean against.

Breakfast over and their bunks "made" in the regulation fashion, the prisoners converged on the parade ground, where they were allowed to stroll about and mix with one another until it was time to "fall in" for work. This was the hour of the day when they could meet their friends from other blocks, exchange news and enjoy some conversation. Because of the cold, everyone kept walking, either alone or with a companion, and for a short while the vast space with its human swarm, free from any restraint, was a scene of intense animation.

Then a bell rang and the *Kommandos* formed up behind their *Kapos*. The band started to play and in turn the columns marched off. In a few minutes the last had disappeared. The music stopped and the immense grey square was silent and deserted once again.

Michel's first day in a labour gang was spent shifting heavy plates of sheet iron. These, he gathered, were used in the construction of motor torpedo boats. After two hours of exhausting work there was a break of ten minutes, during which the Polish *vorarbeiter* in charge of the gang took Michel aside and inquired about his civilian occupation.

Michel replied that he had a business supplying gas engines. The Pole then disappeared, to return shortly afterwards with a *Meister*—one of the German foremen under whose direction the labour gangs worked. After questioning Michel to test his knowledge and receiving a satisfactory answer, the *Meister* made a note of his number and walked away.

Later Michel was informed by the Pole that he had been chosen as a technical assistant. This was considered a great privilege as he would work apart and directly under the orders of the *Meister*. The gas engines, burning wood, were being fitted to the new torpedo boats.

To the astonishment of the Pole, Michel showed no pleasure. He regretted that he had ever mentioned his qualifications. He had not risked imprisonment for refusing to supply gas engines to the Germans, only to assist them now with the benefit of his technical experience. Somehow or other he had to get out of it.

That afternoon, while the *Kommandos* paraded after lunch, a request was made for prisoners skilled in metallurgy. Seeing his opportunity, Michel stepped forward. With a number of others he was then enrolled in a special *Kommando* designated by the name *Metallwerke*.

The next morning, when the prisoners marched off for the day's work, Michel's new *Kommando* left the camp by a different gate. It was the first time he had been outside the wire enclosure. After passing the inner and outer fences and crossing a seven-foot moat, the column emerged into open country. To right and left a flat expanse of marshy land extended to the horizon without interruption. Not a tree nor a house was in sight, and the skyline was only broken by the M.T.B. workshops. Beyond could be seen the canal which connected the River Elbe with the camp.

Having penetrated another electrified barrier, the column arrived at the *Metallwerke* factory, a single-storey brick building in two long wings.

Here the prisoners dispersed to their various jobs, while the new recruits were interviewed by the civilian manager, before being handed over to the foremen and allocated work. Michel was put in charge of four machines which were turning out breech parts for machine-guns.

From his point of view, this was better than using his expert knowledge for the production of gas engines. All the same, and though he had no choice, it was still a form of collaboration which he was resolved to reduce to a minimum.

His quota was two hundred breech parts a day, and as a beginning he made sure that for various plausible reasons his actual production never exceeded one hundred. That, however, did not satisfy him and he therefore conceived of the plan of removing from the total four parts every day. These he concealed in the pockets of his trousers with a view to disposing of them on his return to camp.

No action could have been fraught with more danger. Sabotage by prisoners of the German war production was punished with the utmost severity. During Michel's first week at the factory a Belgian working near him was hanged before his eyes for having deliberately weakened a welding.

On its march back to the camp at the end of the day's work the column was halted by S.S. men, while a number of prisoners, chosen at random, were searched. Anything found on them which they could not have obtained in the camp was assumed to be stolen, even if it was only a toothbrush or a razor blade. It was confiscated and the possessor punished with a savage flogging.

Time and again men from the ranks just ahead or behind Michel were singled out for searching, but as luck would have it the guards always passed him by. Every evening when he took his place in the column he had to steel himself against a possible detection which could only lead to the gallows. On two hundred and sixty-one occasions he thus deliberately risked his head.

Of all Michel's exploits this was probably the bravest, as it was the most gratuitous, and, considering its negligible effect on the war, it might well be asked why he did it. After all that he achieved and suffered in the cause, he was surely entitled now to look to his own safety. The answer is that, being as he was, he conceived it his duty to go on fighting to the end, and this was the last weapon left to him. Had he flinched once from the risk—he would have considered himself almost as a deserter.

Running the gauntlet of the S.S. was not the only danger. When he had returned safely to the camp there was still the problem of getting rid of the four breech parts. Each of them measured twelve inches by one and a half inches by one and a quarter inches, and he had to conceal the bulge they made in his trouser pockets by pulling down the front of his cotton jacket and wrapping it across his thighs.

For a time he found it a fairly simple matter to drop the incriminating objects into one of the pits dug beneath the latrines at the end of each block. But as the pits filled up with discarded breech parts, the latter were no longer sufficiently covered, and the unloading of a new lot was liable to produce a dull clang as they fell on top of their predecessors. This would be heard by occupants of the neighbouring seats, for which there was usually a queue waiting, and since many of the prisoners, especially if they were Russians or Poles, were always ready to report another prisoner, the proceeding became highly dangerous.

In search of safer dumping grounds, he was forced to range
farther and farther afield—which itself was risky—and often
had to wait for an opportunity, while he hung about some
block with his pockets bulging, trying to appear unconcerned.
He nevertheless succeeded, without ever being detected, in
diverting from their proper use over a thousand breech cases,
and burying them in the bowels of the camp.

For the former chief of the *réseau "Agir"*, controlling over
a hundred agents and considered by Germans as a dangerous
enemy, this petty sabotage was a sad come-down; but it was
the best that he could do. More important, it kept alive his
spirit of resistance, helped to preserve his self-respect and
with it the will to survive.

Michel's first impression of Neuengamme was that of an
internment camp conducted as a convict settlement. (It must
be remembered that at this period nobody knew, except the
Germans, what was happening to their millions of prisoners,
and names such as Belsen and Ravensbrück which were later
to become all too familiar, were practically unheard of outside
Germany.) But as the relentless process of human destruction
proceeded, he became aware of the camp's true significance: it
was a place from which nobody was intended to return alive.

Such places, of which there were several and which subsequently became known as extermination camps, served a
dual purpose: firstly to liquidate Germany's enemies in the
most callous manner conceivable, after first subjecting them
to every brutality and humiliation; and secondly, not only to
remove all evidence of the crime by ensuring there were no
survivors to bear witness, but also to leave for posterity, in
the form of bricks and mortar, lasting proof that, in accordance
with civilised usage, proper accommodation was provided for
Germany's prisoners.

That the camp were conducted in the most inhuman way
possible, that the guards were specially selected for their cruelty,
that the object was to work and starve the inmates to death—
all this was a closely guarded secret which, had Germany won
the war, would never have been disclosed.

Of these camps, that of Neuengamme was as bad as any, if
not the worst. According to the official biographer of Count
Bernadotte—the heroic chief of the Swedish Red Cross and

the only foreigner ever permitted to visit the camp—out of its eighty thousand prisoners fifty thousand died or were exterminated between 3rd November, 1942, and 29th April, 1945, and "such was its reputation that even hardened prisoners from such notorious liquidation camps as Sachsenhausen and Dachau shuddered at its mention"[1] The Commandant, Thurmann—afterwards hanged as a war criminal—came from Auschwitz, where he had learnt his trade sending Jews to the gas chamber.

It was not only the physical hardship that made life unendurable—the twelve-hour day of exhausting work, sometimes in torrid heat, the interminable assemblies on the parade ground, the hurried and inadequate meals, the too short nights and frequent interruptions of sleep when air-raid warnings kept the prisoners herded for hours in the cellars; nor the ferocious punishments and the reign of terror under which they lived.

Their very surroundings contributed to their misery: the rows of ugly buildings; the arid terrain, with not a blade of grass or a shrub to relieve it; the hideous fence of wire and concrete; and, beyond, nothing in sight but the desolate featureless landscape stretching endlessly away.

Under the orders of the S.S. beds were dug at the end of some of the blocks and planted with flowers. To the prisoners this was a joke in bad taste, like making a condemned man put a coat of paint on his own gallows. The flowers, rapidly wilting under the blazing sun, seemed artificial and out of place, an insult to nature.

Even had there been one pleasant spot, a patch of greenery or the shadow of a tree, there was no possibility of enjoying it. Between "reveille" at four a.m. and "lights out" at nine p.m. there was not a moment the prisoner could call his own, when he could find some privacy in which to think or just relax.

For Michel this was perhaps the worst privation of all. He had always needed solitude in which to meditate and it was as

---

[1] See *Count Folke Bernadotte* by Ralph Hewins, p. 156. (Hutchinson, 1950).

necessary to him as smoking or drinking to an addict. So when the lights were extinguished he would slip out of his bunk and spend an hour communing with himself in the wash-house.

In doing so he risked punishment for two offences: being out of his bunk and wearing his trousers after dark. If he were caught he would be accused of attempying to escape and be punished with, at least, a flogging.

One night, while seated in the latrines, he was surprised by the *Blockältester*, who asked him what he was doing.

"I am praying," replied Michel calmly, and waited for the storm to burst.

Without a word the *Blockältester* returned to the block. A few moments later he reappeared carrying a stool, and placing his hand on Michel's shoulder in a friendly gesture signed him to make use of it. He then withdrew.

Too astonished even to thank him, Michel took the proffered seat. After that, his nocturnal meditations were never again interrupted.

In the middle of June, soon after Michel's arrival at the camp, the news reached it of the successful Allied landing in Normandy. This produced a tremendous sensation, particularly among the French prisoners. In a moment despair changed to hope, and even the most demoralised recovered their faith. For a few days there was an atmosphere almost of gaiety in the camp, as though any moment the liberators would appear and throw the gates wide open.

As the weeks passed, however, and then the months, and there was no sign of the war ending, pessimism descended again. If the Germans were still fighting in France, the prisoners argued, it would be months, perhaps years, before they were defeated. The prospect of freedom, which for a time seemed so close, receded indefinitely into the future.

The resultant disappointment made men more desperate than if their hopes had never been raised. For many it was the last straw. Convinced that now they could not last out, they gave up the struggle to survive, ceased to fight for their fair share of the miserable ration or to react when another prisoner grabbed their only blanket. Without the will to defend their right to live, they grew weaker every day and finally collapsed.

In this way many hundreds died in the summer and autumn of 1944.

In the German papers, which Michel sometimes saw while at work, the news of the landing was subordinated to that of the flying bomb offensive on London. This was depressing to Michel. He thought of Bois Carré, of André Comps, of his faithful team of cyclists risking their lives to track down the V.1 sites. Had all their efforts been in vain then? He could not know that, thanks largely to those efforts, the offensive was doomed to failure.

With the coming of winter cold was added to the other hardships. Naturally, the blocks were not heated, and the prisoners shivered inside them, or froze outside, dressed in the same wretched garments as they had worn all the summer. While they stood with chattering teeth on the parade ground, great flights of storks, on their way to warmer climes, passed high overhead, their legs towing behind.

Air-raid warnings were more and more frequent. Almost every night the prisoners were driven from their bunks to the cellars, while S.S. men stood outside with grenades ready to throw at the first sign of a riot. This was thought to be a precaution against any attempt at rescue by Allied parachutists.

As the conditions worsened and his fellow prisoners, weakened by exhaustion and hunger, were less and less able to support them, Michel realised that only a supreme effort of will would prevent his succumbing too. Accordingly he forced him-self to get up early and, whatever the weather, spend ten or fifteen minutes doing physical "jerks" in the open air. Besides keeping him fit—if the word could be applied to his debilitated body—this habit had the additional advantage of giving him the wash-house to himself every morning.

To occupy his mind he would recite poetry or make up verses which he then committed to memory. It was thus that he composed, entirely in his head—for, of course, he had no means of writing it down—a long poem entitled *Carnaval*. He had to wait nearly a year before he could put it on paper.

Since no religious services were permitted in the camp he decided to provide his own. Each week, again relying on memory, he would chose a text from the Bible and, taking it as his theme, prepare a sermon. On Sunday there was usually an hour or so when the prisoners were left to their own devices. Michel would find a quiet place, collect one or two friends and talk to them on his chosen theme.

The object of these talks was to assist his fellow victims in retaining some faith and some hope. Above all, he himself renewed his faith and his courage.

As time went on the audience grew larger and included, besides his own compatriots, Germans, Russians and Poles, who were usually hostile to the French. Since any gathering of prisoners was an infraction of the regulations, and a religious meeting more than any, Michel fully expected to be denounced. No one, however, was ever found to report him, and he continued to preach every Sunday for as long as he remained in the camp.

In Michel's block there was only one other Frenchman: Maurice Gacheny, an engineer from Monthéry, arrested and deported after the discovery in his house of a wireless transmitter used for communicating with London. Three others whom he met regularly at the *Metallwerke* factory were Albert Cinotti, a farmer from Normandy; Jacques Petitjean, owner of a bicycle shop in Toulouse; and Louis Pons, the youngest of the group.

These four, with Michel, formed a little French fraternity whose members forgathered daily. There was also a number of French speaking Swiss and Belgians with whom he occasionally had the chance to exchange a few words.

His circle of acquaintances was completed by a remarkable American named Jackson, formerly a doctor at the American Hospital at Neuilly. The latter arrived in the camp after Michel, accompanied by his fifteen-year-old son, Philip. Nobody knew why they had been deported and Jackson never talked about it. A man of sixty, very upright, with white hair, strong features, and a stern, almost hard, expression, he appeared as a person of great energy and forcible character. He was extremely reserved in manner and this and the dignity with which he supported the camp life immediately aroused the sympathy of Michel, with whom he soon established a tacit understanding. During their weekly meetings few words were exchanged and those only of a strictly practical use.

Jackson's main concern was to contrive that news of his

whereabouts and that of his child should reach his family in America. In this Michel was able to assist. Thanks to the presence of a sister in Switzerland, to whom he succeeded after many attempts in sending a postcard, the news eventually arrived in America, much to Jackson's relief.

Strolling on the parade ground one day, Michel ran into the Marseillais who had wanted to smash his skull in the cattle wagon. Shrunken in stature, looking half-starved and completely grotesque in his pitiable clothes, the young man was hardly recognisable as his former assailant. They shook hands warmly.

The season of Christmas arrived. A giant fir tree was erected on the side of the parade ground and hung with coloured lights. On Christmas Day, at the morning assembly, the S.S. appeared carrying enormous baskets, from which they handed out cigarettes: a packet to each prisoner. Then the order to dismiss was given, and the guards resumed their normal attitude, pursuing any dawdler with blows and kicks.

That evening, through the windows of one of the block-houses, there could be seen, seated at a long table, some forty or fifty prisoners. They were the German *Kapos*, the ruling class of prisoner. In front of each man the traditional Christmas candle was burning, which he watched in silence with his head inclined above it. The flickering lights, the motionless figures, and the brooding faces, produced on Michel, watching the scene from outside, an impression of utter despair.

From another block, where all nationalities were represented, but the Russians and Poles predominated, there suddenly poured forth the pure strains of a beautiful tenor voice. It was that of a young Frenchman singing a carol. As he sang he walked slowly up and down the block, his face lit up in ecstasy, while the prisoners, sprawling on their bunks, gazed and listened with a sort of wonder.

Sunday, in theory, was a holiday. The morning was spent cleaning and embellishing the blocks, and in the afternoon the prisoners were free inside the camp.

This was the time for the weekly black market, held between two of the blocks. Currency took the form of cigarettes and the unit of exchange was one "piece" or *stück*. Thus a shaving brush made from a paint brush stolen from some workshop would be offered at twenty *stück* and, after hard bargaining, sold for twelve or fifteen. The highest prices were paid for articles not to be found in the camp—and which it was therefore, unlawful to possess.

The main meeting place was the parade ground, which was always thronged on Sunday. Sometimes an attempt was made to play some game, but few of the prisoners had the energy to take part.

One Sunday, however, the place was deserted except for two prostrate human figures. They were the corpses of two prisoners, a Russian and a Yugoslav, who had been killed while attempting to escape. The torn and bloodstained garments and shockingly mutilated bodies showed that they had been torn to death by the ferocious police dogs which accompanied the night patrol.

At the beginning of the year there arrived at the camp several hundred Danish policemen, still wearing their smart dark uniform. After this had been exchanged for the camp dress they were distributed among the various blocks.

A few days later several lorries drove into the camp wearing the flag of the Swedish Red Cross. They contained parcels of food for the new arrivals, which the latter were allowed to receive, to the intense envy of other prisoners. Thus provided for, the Danes had no appetite for the camp food, which in any case was only edible by a starving man. However, instead of surrendering their portions to less fortunate neighbours, most of them refused to part with the smallest share except against payment in *stück*.

This was typical of the mentality which life in the camp produced. It was the philosophy of "survival of the fittest and devil take the hindmost"—a philosophy which the vast majority adopted. Under a system designed to eliminate human feeling, men became beasts, ferociously defending their own, and watching each other for the first sign of weakness by which to profit.

Soon after the arrival of the Danish policemen three hundred Norwegians made their appearance in the camp. On the insistence of Count Bernadotte, who was in process of negotiating their repatriation with Himmler, they were housed in a special block more comfortably furnished, and allowed to receive food supplied by the Red Cross.

Although separated from the other prisoners by a barbed wire fence, the Norwegians generously shared their parcels with them. Bread, biscuits, tinned meat and cigarettes were passed through the wire.

This charitable action probably saved many lives, since the miserable camp ration had recently been further reduced and was now down to one thin slice of bread a day and two cupfuls of a watery liquid.

Another group, of about a hundred, which arrived at the same period attracted attention for a different reason. Mostly in their thirties, speaking German, they looked harmless and pleasant people. However, they did not go out to work with the *Kommandos* and each wore on his sleeve an armlet bearing the words *TOR SPER* (exit forbidden).

At first the significance of this was not clear to the other prisoners. But after a time it was noticed that the latest arrivals, who spent the whole day on parade ground, were steadily reduced in number. Each day there was a further diminution until finally the last disappeared. Only then did it become known that they had all been "liquidated", in parcels of five or six, by hanging carried out in the death cells.

A second mass massacre occurred in February, when a number of boys of between nine and fourteen, who had only recently arrived, were seen to enter the *Revier*—that is the block used as an infirmary. None of them left it alive. It was afterwards learnt that they had all been lethally inoculated after being submitted to a series of biological experiments. Three French doctors who refused to take part in the experiments were executed in turn for trying to prevent them.[1]

It was rare in any case for anyone sent to the *Revier* to return. There was no proper nursing and people went there to die rather than to recover.

Although any approach to it by other prisoners was strictly forbidden, Michel gained admittance on several occasions for the purpose of visiting a sick neighbour. He achieved this either by bribing the prisoner in charge with a cigarette, or

[1] Dr. Quenouille of Villeneuve St. Georges and Drs. Florence and Thouert, both of the Faculty of Sciences at Lyons.

simply by climbing in. In the course of these visits he sometimes discovered other prisoners of his acquaintance who had been missing.

It was also in the *Revier* that he met for the first time one of the most remarkable men in the camp. Louis Martin-Chauffier, the French author and journalist, was known to him by reputation as a contributor to the *avant-garde* weekly, *Vendredi*, edited by André Chamson.[1] Before the war Michel had often read his articles, but never dreamed that the first opportunity to discuss them with the author would occur in the infirmary of a German concentration camp.

Martin-Chauffier was seriously ill, but his courage was undiminished, and while Michel sat on the edge of his camp bed, expecting at any moment to be discovered and dragged off, the two of them engaged in a purely intellectual conversation, as if they had just been introduced at some literary gathering in Paris.

Another distinguished compatriot whom he met in the *Revier* was the aged French General Bardy de Fourtou. After taking a leading part in the Resistance movement, this fine soldier had been deported and had already spent a year in the camp, where his courage and faith were an inspiration to the French colony. Now he was dying.

One day, as he was lying too ill to move, the Polish prisoner who acted as orderly, noticing that his bed was in disorder, shouted abuse at the invalid and called the other patients to witness his shameful untidiness.

The General's only reply was a faint movement of the hand. Thereupon the Pole rushed at his bed and started beating him about the head with his fists. When at last his fury abated, the dying man had ceased to breathe.

There was a silence and then a German voice was heard to exclaim: "*Keine Kultur!*" ("No education!")

It was assumed by the onlookers that this referred to the homicide.

But no, as appeared a moment later, it was not the Pole whom the German was criticising, but the General, for failing to make his bed.

[1] Now a member of the French Academy.

That, in the eyes of the German, was the scandal which showed such a lack of education.

One evening, when he was due to work on night shift, Michel stole a cabbage from the kitchen of the S.S. and smuggled it into the *Revier* for a Frenchman, who was there dying of starvation.[1]

As a result, when he arrived at the parade ground, the *Kommando* had left without him. Knowing that his absence would have been noted at the roll-call, he decided that the best course was to report to the guard-room and to plead that he had overlooked the time.

The excuse being rejected, he was ordered a beating of twenty-five strokes, to be administered on the spot.

For a time he bore punishment without flinching, but after the twentieth stroke he could no longer stand and fell full length on his face. At this the S.S. guard, who was wielding the stick, flew into a paroxysm of rage, and began kicking him frenziedly in the loins with his heavily studded boots.

Michel knew the S.S. He had seen how, once a man went down under punishment, they would lose control completely and go on hitting or kicking until there was nothing left but a corpse. Unless he could get to his feet he realised he was lost.

A few feet away from where he was lying there was a wall. He managed to squirm towards it, take hold with his hands, and pull himself up, first to his knees and then to his feet. Here he succeeded in maintaining himself upright, while the remaining five strokes were inflicted.

This had a calming effect on the S.S. man, who then conducted him peacefully to the *Metallwerke* factory.

Such incidents occurred daily. Prisoners were flogged because their clothes were in bad repair or the number sown on them was not sufficiently visible; or because their bunks were not "squared off", or they were in the wrong position at parade. The most commonly punished offence was failure to achieve the required quota of work.

Those who possessed no skills were employed carrying bricks, or pushing hand wagons filled with sand, their efforts being stimulated by overseers carrying sticks.

[1] The man survived and is now living in Blois.

Others, who had neither skill nor physical strength, were made to work in the cellar. Seated on the floor in a circle, surrounding a great pile of debris, they manufactured rope by plaiting together bits of rubbish: rags, threads, pieces of string, remnants of tyres. Each man had to produce a certain length in the day or accept the penalty of a beating.

This was the task usually given to clergy and intellectuals, who were the favourite target of the S.S. The higher the culture of the individual, the more satisfaction there was in reducing him to the level of a beast.

Soon after his arrival in the camp, a French speaking prisoner had said to Michel, "You know you've come here to die."

With his natural optimism Michel had not taken the remark seriously. But after six months he realised it was true. The end was inevitable, the only question being how long it could be postponed.

Meanwhile, there was one more duty: not to submit to the process of dehumanisation, and to go down fighting...still a man.

This was a much more difficult feat than keeping alive and only men of exceptional character were capable of rising to the level of heroism required.

Besides Michel himself, one of the few who did so was his camp comrade Louis Martin-Chauffier. Nobody has described more vividly than he the battle fought by those who, in spite of everything the enemy could do to crush their spirit and their manhood, remained, even in death, proud and undefeated.

The book he wrote on his return to France, under the title *L'Homme et la Bête*,[1] is not only one of the best accounts of the extermination camps; it is also a magnificent vindication of the power of the human spirit to resist the forces of evil.

A quotation from its pages may suitably end this chapter.

"The major crime of Hitlerism was to reduce human beings to such vileness that they no longer recognised their own degradation. Ninety-five out of a hundred of its victims succumbed; they lost their self-respect and ceased to resemble men.

"The miracle is that in such conditions—with every cruelty and humiliation that could be devised to break the spirit—

---

[1] Published by Gallimard, 1949.

with the Beast wielding absolute power and using both cunning and brute force—the miracle, I say, is that in one case out of twenty he could not prevail against the human soul, carried in a body which could hardly support it and which was its most insidious enemy.

"Yes, one man in twenty preserved his humanity intact, but grown in stature, stripped to the essentials and aware as never before of its origins and its destiny."

The first copy of the numbered edition of *L'Homme et le Bête* is dedicated to Michel. No higher tribute could be paid to him.

20

DE PROFUNDIS

By the spring of 1945 the population of the camp was much reduced. In the last months many had died, while large numbers had been evacuated to other extermination camps. The Danes and Norwegians, thanks to Count Bernadotte, had been repatriated.

The *Revier* was almost empty. The most seriously ill had been transferred to Belsen. Those who could walk were put on board a goods train, which left for an unknown destination. It was learnt later that after travelling for several days they arrived at Gardelegen, where they were shut inside a large barn. This was then set fire to by the S.S., when all the inmates perished, including the Swiss doctor, Morin, who had refused to leave his patients.

One day—it must have been about the 20th April—the sound of gunfire could be heard. It brought no joy to the prisoners. None of them expected to leave the camp alive, unless it was to be herded to their death elsewhere.

On the same day the twenty thousand still remaining were assembled on the parade ground and made to surrender their mattresses. The next morning the dispersal of the camp commenced, with the departure of the *Kommandos* to different destinations.

Michel, with his compatriot, Albert Cinotti, was to go with the kitchen *Kommando*, to which he had transferred on the closing down of the *Metallwerke* factory. At the last moment they tried to persuade their friend Gacheny to join them, but the latter was undecided; and since their group was already moving off they had to leave without him.

With the rest of the *Kommando* they were marched to the railway, where cattle wagons were waiting to receive them. These were similar to those which had brought them from Compiègne a year previously. This time, however, instead of a hundred, there were forty men to a wagon, and the top of the door was left open. Two soldiers kept guard in each wagon. Army reservists, they behaved without brutality.

The train started, and after passing the little junction at Bergedorf was soon approaching Hamburg. For mile after mile the landscape was covered with ramshackle huts, where the inhabitants had taken refuge from the bombing. As they stared at the train from the doorways of their temporary dwellings, with their children standing beside them, they looked more like gipsies than citizens of a great city.

The train continued across country, skirting Hamburg to the east, until it arrived at a stone quay overlooking a canal. Later Michel discovered that this led into the estuary of the River Trave, outside the port of Lübeck.

Two cargo ships were moored to the quay side by side. The prisoners descended from the wagons, crossed the first ship, which was called the *Elmenorst*, and entered the second, the *Thilbeck*, through narrow doors in its side. They then had to climb down several iron ladders to reach the lowest hold in the ship immediately above the keel.

By the time Michel reached the bottom of the last ladder the hold was already nearly filled with prisoners. It was pitch dark and he had to grope his way to find a vacant space on the sloping side of the ship's bottom. With Cinotti crouched beside him he took up a position at the extremity, next to one of the two iron ladders.

From now on this narrow perch of slippery metal, on

which he could neither stand or lie down, was to be his only resting place.

Michel never knew how long he spent in the hold of the *Thilbeck*—he soon lost count of time—but working backwards afterwards he calculated that it must have been eight or nine days at least. As the place was in permanent darkness, there was no means of telling night from day except when the manhole was opened to allow food to reach the prisoners.

Apart from an open tub in the centre, rapidly filling with excrement, every square inch of space that could be used was occupied by a human body. Only a proportion could find room on the flat bottom; the rest had to balance on the curved surface of the hull, which they occupied almost up to the level where it became vertical.

When the hatch was opened to admit food, or because some prisoner—always a Pole —was required for work, Michel would sneak up the ladder and spend a few second on deck. He was invariably driven below with curses and blows, but usually succeeded, before he was seen, in filling his lungs with fresh air, and sometimes even managed to find some water, in which to dip his hands and splash his face.

These moments of escape from the horror of the hold, which he achieved almost every day, albeit at the cost of several beatings-up, besides benefiting his physique helped to maintain his morale. The very fact that each time he defied authority, and took the risk of serious consequences, had a stimulating effect on his mind. Like his plans for escape at Fresnes, it was something to occupy his thoughts, kept him alert and prevented him from falling into the sort of fatalistic apathy which had overcome most of his companions in misery.

For none of them had any illusions as to their future. Obviously the Germans would not have hidden them in this living tomb if the intention was to release them on the arrival of the Allies. Otherwise they could simply have remained at the camp. Stories were already circulating among the Russians and Poles of shiploads of prisoners being taken to sea. . .and disappearing.

Michel's daily sorties on deck also gave him a chance of ex-amining his surroundings. The ship remained moored in the same place, outside the other. Standing on the quayside were two or three goods wagons, one of which appeared to be used as a sick bay. A short distance away the canal was crossed by a revolving bridge. Once, while Michel was watching, a tram passed over, filled with men and women on their way to work. The tram disappeared into a tree-lined avenue going in the direction of Lübeck. The spectacle of people still free, or relatively, filled him with inexpressible yearnings.

When the hatch was opened for the issue of food, a fatigue party descended carrying several containers of soup. The rush of starving men was such, however, that only those nearest had a chance, and even then, since no receptacle of any sort was provided, most of the liquid was spilt.

Fortunately there had been a distribution of food parcels, sent by the American Red Cross, shortly before the dispersal of the camp. The parcels had been shared by several hundred prisoners, some of whom, belonging to Michel's *Kommando*, had had the strength of mind to save a portion for their journey. They had existed on these for the first few days in the ship, and it was the empty tins which served as mugs for the soup.

One day there could be heard through the steel side of the ship the sounds of winches turning, followed by the hum of turbines. When Michel next succeeded in reaching the deck he saw that their companion ship, the *Elmenorst*, had gone, and that the *Thilbeck* was now attached directly to the quay.

Some time later the main hatch was opened wide, to permit the removal for emptying—long overdue—of the tub. Ropes were lowered and attached to the noisome receptable, which was then hoisted. As it reached the level of the upper deck, however, the thing tipped up, emptying its revolting contents on the heads of the prisoners who had gathered underneath for a glimpse of the open sky. Nobody attempted to clear up the mess—there was nothing to do it with anyhow—and thereafter they moved about ankle deep in human excrement. Nothing more was needed to complete their abject misery.

A few days later the sound of gunfire, which had not been heard since the departure from Neuengamme, penetrated faintly to the hold.

Shortly after there was again the noise of preparations, of winches turning and chains grinding, but this time too close to come from another ship. Soon the vibration of the hull, as the engines of the *Thilbeck* started up, confirmed that she was about to leave the quay.

While the prisoners listened in the darkness, an ominous silence fell on the hold and its fetid atmosphere grew heavy with a suffocating sense of doom. All had read the signs correctly and each knew instinctively what they portended. It was the beginning of the end of their journey.

At that moment a voice was raised. Speaking in French, very calmly, Michel addressed the darkness.

"My friends, our turn has come to set out for the unknown. We are all afraid, and I must admit that the prospect is far from reassuring. Is not this the moment to show what sort of men we are? Some of us are believers, or claim to be. This is the time to show it. We learn in our catechism what Christ said: 'Where two or three are gathered together in my name there shall I be and they shall not call upon me in vain.' Should we not remember His promise now, since we shall never have a better opportuniy of showing our faith in Him?"

He paused, but nobody spoke. Something in the quality of the silence, however, told him that his words had found an echo.

"We shall now make a chain with our hands and I will pray for God's help on behalf of us all."

There was a movement in the darkness as most of the French-speaking prisoners found their way towards the spot where Michel was standing. Hand groped for hand while a circle formed round him.

Michel lifted his voice again.

"O God, from the depth of our agony, we beseech you... to come to our aid and remove, if it please you, the danger that threatens the people in this ship. Remove it too from those it threatens in other ships...and whatever happens to us, protect, we implore you, our wives and our children and guard them against all evil...This, O God, is the prayer we address to you, and we beseech you humbly to grant it."

For a moment or two longer the hands remained joined.. Then the circle broke up as the men returned to their places.

But for many of them at least, as they told Michel later, the atmosphere was no longer so heavily charged with fear.

Michel had scarcely finished speaking when the noises on

deck, which had formed an accompaniment for his prayer, suddenly ceased. At the same time the vibration of the ship's engines died away.

For a few moments complete silence reigned in the hold, while the prisoners listened tensely for what was to come next.

Then the manhole was opened and a voice shouted in German: "All French-speaking prisoners on deck!"

There was no move—for nobody had taken it in. A few moments later the order was repeated, but in a sharper tone.

Michel, who was standing at the foot of the ladder, was the first to understand.

"They want us out," he shouted in French. "All who can speak French. Up on the deck. Quick."

He pushed his friend Cinotti towards the ladder. The rest followed, scrambling across the bodies of other prisoners. Some were too weak to climb and Michel had to assist them. When the last man had disappeared and he saw that the manhole was about to close, he followed quickly himself.

The ship was still at the quay. On the upper deck some two hundred prisoners—French, Belgian, Swiss and Dutch—were filing past a table, where a woman of the S.S. was entering their names and places of birth in a book.

None of them knew what this portended, but there could be read on every face a presentiment that it augured well. This was confirmed when a hose was turned on and they were allowed to wash the grime from their bodies.

It was a warm spring afternoon. Michel stripped off his filthy garments and let the cold water play on his body. He could not yet believe that they were really saved. So prompt an answer to his prayer bordered too close on the miraculous. But, whatever happened, a bath was at least something to be grateful for.

Shortly after, hopes were damped again when the two hundred were shut in another hold, nearer the bows of the ship, which was already occupied by Russians and Poles. Once more closed in total darkness, their future seemed as uncertain as ever.

There was, however, one encouraging sign. For a change the Russians and Poles showed no hostility to the other nationals, who seemed to have acquired a new prestige in their eyes. The French took this as a favourable omen: the instinctive mark of respect paid by the condemned to the reprieved.

The next morning the two hundred were called on deck again. This time there could be no doubt. They were leaving. A gangway was in position and the first prisoners were already filing across it.

On the quay there was now only one wagon left. Standing in its doorway was a tall white-haired man whom Michel recognised as a former camp-mate: the American doctor, Jackson.

He went and wrung the American's hand warmly.

"You must come with us," he urged.

Jackson made no answer but, raising his arm wearily, pointed to the prostrate figures covering the floor of the wagon. They were the bodies of his dying patients.

Michel could not wait; the column of prisoners was already moving off and he had to run to catch up with it. As he joined the last rank he looked round and saw the doctor gazing after him.

It was his last view of this devoted American.

It is necessary now to leave Michel for a time and follow the fortunes of the other prisoners.

A few hours after the departure of the French contingent, Dr. Jackson received the order to abandon his patients, most of whom by then were dead, and to embark on board the *Thilbeck*. There he was shut in a hold with some of the remaining prisoners. A few minutes later the ship cast off, and after navigating the canal headed for the open sea.

A mile outside the estuary a large steamship was lying at anchor in the bay. Except for an armament of A.A. guns, she had all the appearance of a luxury liner. Her name was the *Cap Arcona*.

The *Thilbeck* approached and secured alongside. Her three upper holds were opened and their occupants, including Dr. Jackson, were transferred to the other ship, which was already loaded with several thousand prisoners.

The *Thilbeck* with her lower holds still filled with prisoners, then cast off and dropped anchor a short distance away.

The next morning another prison ship, the *Athen*, came

alongside the *Cap Arcona*. This time the process was reversed, about two hundred prisoners leaving the *Cap Arcona* to be received on board the *Athen*.

As they were climbing over the rails, Dr. Jackson, watching from the deck of the *Cap Arcona*, spotted among them his son, Philip, from whom he had been separated since leaving the camp.

He shouted the boy's name and tried to push his way towards him. Philip, hearing the cry, turned and tried to return; but the S.S. guards pushed him brutally down the hold and out of his father's sight. Soon he was carried away as the *Athen* steamed off.

Among the group of Frenchmen in the same hold with Philip was Maurice Gacheny, the engineer, whom Michel had tried to persuade to join him just before leaving the camp.

Morale inside the hold was at the lowest ebb. From the other side of the bulkhead there was a sound of heavy hammering. Somehow this was sinister. Then the engines stopped. In the tense silence that followed nerves began to snap. Some of the prisoners, becoming hysterical, started shouting wildly and beating their fists against the hull.

Realising that something must be done to prevent the panic spreading, Gacheny decided to create a diversion. He started to talk on the first subject that came into his mind: the cutting power of metal tools. Being an engineer this had doubtless been suggested by the hammering noise next door.

He now discoursed on this theme in a loud voice, as if addressing a large lecture hall. The effect was so startling in the circumstances that it distracted his companions' attention from the other phenomena; and to such an extent that they scarcely noticed when the engines started again and the ship began moving *astern*.

By the time Gacheny had reached the end of his lecture the ship was stopped once more. There was a noise of footsteps on deck...then silence. One of the Frenchmen climbed the ladder. He found the hatch-cover loose, pushed it open and put his head out. The next moment the others heard him shout: "We're at the quay."

There was a rush to climb the ladder. When Gacheny reached the deck, prisoners from the other holds were swarming all over it. There was no sign either of the S.S. guards or the German crew; but standing on the quay was a little group of armed men. They wore khaki battle dress and shallow helmets and belonged to the advanced guard of Montgomery's army.

Meanwhile the last act of the drama had been enacted out at sea. At about the time when the *Athen* first stopped, and Gacheny was making his bid to quell the panic in her hold, some British fighter bombers appeared on the scene.

Seeing several German ships apparantly in flight, the R.A.F. commander signalled them to return to port. At the same time a warning bomb was dropped in the sea.

In reply the *Cap Arcona* opened fire, while the *Thilbeck*, and a fourth prison ship, the *Deutschland*, steamed away.

Only the *Athen* obeyed the order, and that because her skipper took charge. Ordering the engines to be put astern so as to avoid any misunderstanding, he steered the ship backwards towards the shore.

When the S.S. men realised what he was doing, they attempted to intervene, but were seized by the crew and disarmed; and on the arrival of the ship in harbour handed over to the British.

None of the four ships carried anything to indicate that they had prisoners on board, and the only people to be seen on their decks were their crews and the armed guards of the S.S.

Hence, when the order to return to port was ignored, the R.A.F. commander decided to attack. Direct hits were immediately scored on the *Thilbeck* and *Deutschland*, both of which sank immediately in a few minutes carrying all their prisoners with them.

The *Cap Arcona*, hit by an incendiary, caught fire, and with her highly inflammable upper works was soon blazing from end to end. Her crew and S.S. guards escaped in the boats, but most of the several thousand prisoners entombed inside her were either burnt alive, suffocated by flames, or drowned when the ship eventually turned over and sank.

Two or three hundred managed to reach the sea alive, where they were fired on by the S.S. from the lifeboats. Nearly all were killed either by gunshot or drowning.

A very few, kept afloat by wreckage, succeeded in floating ashore, but even there Germans were waiting to throw them back in to the sea.

In spite of this some twenty or thirty managed to make their way inland, where they appeared to the astonishment of the British soldiers like so many living skeletons thrown up by the deep.

Thus perished horribly the great majority of those who survived the horrors of Neuengamme.

The port to which the *Athen*, steaming astern, had put in, was Neustadt, on the north of Lübeck Bay.

As soon as the liberated prisoners set foot ashore, they were provided by the British with food and conducted to the German naval barracks, which had been turned over to them.

Since many were in the last stages of exhaustion or otherwise requiring immediate medical attention, Gacheny obtained permission to move them to the local hospital and was provided with transport for the purpose. A number of lives were saved in this way.

Gacheny then went down to the shore to look for more survivors from the wreck. After tramping the beach for several hours he took shelter late at night in a block-house.

He had scarcely fallen asleep when he was awakened by a voice calling his name. It was that of the young American, Philip Jackson, who had come from the town to find him.

With Jackson was a tall English officer, for whom he was acting as interpreter.

"This officer is inquiring for Michel Hollard," Jackson explained. "Some of the others said you might know what had become of him."

For a moment Gacheny could not find his voice. After his ten days; confinement in various ships' holds, with the expectation of death constantly with him, culminating in the appalling events of the previous twelve hours, his mind was confused and it required an effort to collect his wits.

"Do you know Michel Hollard?" the officer asked.

"Know him! I should think I do!" replied Gacheny. "I knew him better than anyone in the camp."

"But not as well as we do," said the officer.

"How can that be?"

"Because Michel Hollard is the man who saved London."

Knowing nothing of Michel's past except that he had been working with the British, Gacheny was completely mystified by this remark and therefore decided to let it go.

"We are very anxious to find him," the officer continued, "and I hoped you could help us."

"He was my best friend in the camp, but I lost sight of him when we dispersed. I've no idea where he is, and I very much fear the worst."

"If you are right it is tragic news," said the officer. He then took his departure with Jackson, after thanking Gacheny and apologising for disturbing him.

They had not gone far when Gacheny ran after them to request that he should be informed if there was any news of Michel. The officer promised and they said good night again.

A few days later, while Gacheny was visiting patients at the hospital, the officer reappeared.

"I've come to give you news of Hollard," he announced. "We have just heard that he is safe and has landed in Sweden."

We can now return to Michel—last seen, it will be remembered, marching away from the doomed *Thilbeck* with the other French-speaking prisoners.

They still did not know where they were going, or what their fate was to be, but the mere fact of being removed from the ship, which none of them expected to leave alive, had an exhilarating effect; and the general impression was that their fortunes had at last taken a turn for the better. As for Michel, it was the first time since his arrest, fifteen months before, that he allowed himself to indulge in hope.

At the end of the quay a number of lorries were waiting. The men in charge were not members of the S.S. and did not even look like soldiers. They wore leather belts but carried no weapons.

The prisoners mounted the lorries, which then drove off. They did not go very far, however, and in a very short time arrived at another quay, where two fine merchant ships were lying.

Each was flying a blue flag with a golden cross, and her

name could be read on the counter. One was called the *Magdalena*, and the other *Lily Mathessen*.

The prisoners filed on board the *Magdalena*, and after descending a couple of decks found themselves in a well-lit, clean, and relatively spacious compartment. When they had all arrived a tall young man with fair hair handed to each a large ship's biscuit. It was the first solid food any of them had eaten for a week.

The impression of favourable developments became stronger. There was, however, one disturbing factor: the gangway to the ship was guarded by a German N.C.O., while an officer of the S.S. supervised the embarkation.

Several hours passed during which the other ship also received a contingent of prisoners. These were all women.

At last the engines of the *Magdalena* started up. Through the portholes the prisoners could see the widening gap as she moved slowly away from the quay. But they could also see, following in the wake of the ship, a German naval vessel, and the S.S. officer was still on board.

Soon the *Magdalena* had passed the estuary and was heading for the open sea. Rapidly the land was left behind. When it was nearly out of sight the ship was stopped and a ladder lowered over the side. The S.S officer climbed down it and stepped on to the escorting craft, which then turned and headed for the shore.

Only at that moment did the last doubt vanish. They were no longer prisoners but free men. Someone started to sing, and with one accord Frenchmen, Belgians and Swiss burst into the *Marseillaise*.

For Michel, however, a shadow hung over the jubilation. Mixed with immense relief and thankfulness for his own safety was the thought of those who remained in the holds of the *Thilbeck*. What had happened to them? Haunted by a foreboding of the terrible evil which he could not know was being consummated almost at that moment, just over the horizon, he found he had no heart for celebrations.

Nor was he in a state to inquire into the cause of his deliverance, which was only revealed some weeks later. It then transpired that he and his companions owed their survival to the action of one of their number, a Frenchman. This man, during the performance of a fatigue duty which necessitated his landing from the *Thilbeck* and walking some distance allong the quay, had passed some sailors wearing a uniform which did not appear to be German. Thinking they might be foreigners from some neutral ship, he contrived, when he was next allowed ashore, to scratch on a piece of stone an SOS message and leave it in the path where he had seen them. It seems probable that this was read by the Swedes and resulted in the release of a small part of the *Thilbeck's* prisoners.

If so, it must have been a purely local arrangement, made between the S.S. commander and the captain of the Swedish ship, possibly in exchange for food or medical necessities in which the Germans were lacking. Had it been the result of higher orders, presumably all the French-speaking prisoners would have been released, whereas in fact only one of the *Thilbeck's* holds was opened and that in which Maurice Gacheny and many others were held remained battened down and its inmates did not even know of their more fortunate compatriots' escape.[1]

It is true that for many weeks Count Bernadotte had been conducting active negotiations with Himmler and his chief of staff, Schellenburg, for the release of all political prisoners, but up to the moment of the German collapse, although he had succeeded—in perhaps the greatest single-handed rescue operation in history—in saving nearly all the Scandinavians and some twenty-five thousand others, mostly women prisoners from Ravensbrück, the fate of the rest was still in the balance.

It is also true that Bernadotte's main effort, apart from Ravensbrück, was directed at Neuengamme, where he had persuaded Himmler to assemble all the Scandinavian prisoners as a first step towards their repatriation (these included the Danes and Norwegians mentioned in the previous chapter). He was still working to obtain the release of the remaining twenty thousand survivors of all nationalities—of which Michel was one—when the abrupt evacuation of the camp on 18th April, 1945, dashed his hopes. All he ever knew of their fate was that they had been removed in cattle wagons for an

---

[1] Later Gacheny was transferred first to the *Cap Arcona* and then to the *Athen.*

unknown destination and repeated inquiries addressed to
Thurmann, the camp commandant, always met with the reply
that there was "still no news" of them. Thus it can safely be
assumed that Michel's escape was due to a lucky chance, and
not to any deliberate decision by the high German authorities.

One question remains. If the intentions of the Germans
towards the twenty thousand were that they should disappear—
and of this there can be little doubt—what was their motive?
The war was lost, the Third Reich collapsing hourly, what
was to be gained by adding yet another to its crimes?

The answer can only be found in the German mentality and
in the determination of the Nazi chiefs, if they were to fall, to
drag the whole world down with them. To these maniacs,
apart from the natural desire to remove evidence of their
crimes, the twenty thousand, up to the last moment, represented
an asset, something they still controlled; and except in exchange
for some advantage, such as an amnesty for themselves from
Allied retribution, they were not going to surrender it. When
it became obvious that the prisoners could not be used as a
bargaining counter, the logical course, from the Nazi point of
view, was to destroy them—as the only form of scorched
earth policy still practicable. They had lost the rubber but
could still take a trick. And after all, it was so many fewer
enemies of the Fourth Reich which must surely arise from the
ruins of the Third.

Zigzagging to avoid minefields and anchoring at night, the
Magdalena took three days to reach the Swedish coast. On
the way she passed many German warships, coming from the
east with their flags at half-mast. It was rumoured that Hitler
had perished, but nobody believed this.

Many of the prisoners stayed in their bunks, having collapsed
as the result of their experiences. Most of the others remained
on deck, unable, in spite of the cold, to tear themselves away
from the sight of the sea. Michel employed his time removing
several hundred lice from his body.

Late on the third day the ship entered a small port and
secured alongside a jetty. The two hundred survivors, less two
who died on the voyage, disembarked. Many had to be supported, while those who could not walk were carried ashore

on stretchers. Women of the Swedish Red Cross were waiting to receive them with cigarettes.

The fittest were taken to a public bath and, after their clothes had been removed for burning, were energetically scrubbed by hospital nurses wearing protective overalls, rubber gloves and masks. They were then provided with a new suit, linen and shaving gear. The fact that the suits actually fitted was almost unbelievable. Men who had long since ceased to think of themselves as such, seeing in their reflection decently clothed people, suddenly recovered their self-respect. It was as though with their grotesque and hideous garments they had thrown off all the shame and degradation they had suffered.

Next, postcards were distributed by the French Embassy, and, after each had written a message to his family, were collected for official dispatch to France.

Michel duly filled in his card, but, having little faith in official channels, obtained another and dispatched it to his wife by the simple method of throwing it out of the window — for fear of infection the survivors were confined indoors — and signalling to a passer-by to post it.

This precaution was fully justified by the result. The unofficial card reached Paris in five days; the other, sent through the embassy, arrived ten days later.

However, it was not by a postcard that Mme. Hollard heard the news of her huband's escape. The day after his arrival in Sweden she received a visit from a high British official who informed her of the fact that Michel was safe and would soon be joining her in Paris. He added that His Majesty the King had been informed, had expressed great pleasure in the news, and desired to mark the occasion by graciously conferring on her husband the highest military decoration for which a foreigner was eligible, namely the Distinguished Service Order. Moreover, the visitor stated, he was charged by His Majesty's Government to inquire in what further way they could show their gratitude for the great services rendered by Captain Hollard.

Mme. Hollard warmly thanked her visitor, said she was extremely touched by His Majesty's interest and the Government's offer but could not, on behalf of herself or her husband, accept any material reward.

Although Michel had stood up better to the ordeal than most, it was six weeks before he was considered fit to travel.

On the 18th June, an R.A.F. plane landed in Sweden with orders to fly him back to France via London, where a special reception was being arranged for him.

Unfortunately it arrived too late. Michel had already left—though only a few hours earlier—being one of the party of ten ex-prisoners, the first to be repatriated by the Swedish Red Cross. This privilege, which he had not sought, was accorded him by the unanimous vote of his own compatriots.

To conform with military requirements the D.C.4 flew over the sea, following the coast line of Denmark, Holland, Belgium, and France. During the whole of the flight, which lasted five hours, Michel remained glued to a porthole, so as not to lose an instant of the marvellous journey.

"Marvellous" is perhaps not sufficiently expressive. That he should not only be returning from an exile, which until the eleventh hour of the last day there appeared no hope of surviving, but doing so as a free man to a free country, seemed more like a dream than reality.

Over Dieppe the plane crossed the coast and, turning south, followed the direction of the main road to Rouen. Leaving Auffay on the left, it passed close enough to the V.1 site at Bonnetot le Faubourg for Michel to see the effect of the R.A.F. bombing eighteen months earlier. The place was still a mass of rubble and twisted girders.

This was the climax of the dream. To be able to look down in perfect security on the ruins of the diabolical device, which he himself had helped to defeat and which was intended to destroy the freedom he had just recovered—that for Michel was the supreme experience, the miracle; and it was still as one dazed by a miracle that, half an hour later, he stepped out of the plane to be welcomed in the arms of his family.